ARTIFICIAL INTELLIGENCE
IN MODERN CONFLICT

ARTIFICIAL INTELLIGENCE IN MODERN CONFLICT

Ravi Venugopal

an imprint of Highlyy Publishing LLP

ISBN: 978-93-6009-491-1 (Hardbound)
First Published : 2024
Copyright ©Author

Publisher's Note:

All Rights reserved under International Copyright Conventions. No part of this publication may be reproduced, stored in a retrieval system, or transmitted in any form or by any means, electronic, mechanical, photocopying, recording or otherwise without the prior written consent of the publisher and the copyright owner.

The content of this book is the sole expression and opinion of its author(s), and not of the publisher. The publisher in no manner is liable for any opinion or views expressed by the author(s). While best efforts have been made in preparing the book, the publisher makes no representations or warranties of any kind and assumes no liabilities of any kind with respect to the accuracy or completeness of the content and specifically disclaims any implied warranties of merchantability or fitness of use of a particular purpose.

The publisher believes that the contents of this book do not violate any existing copyright/intellectual property of others in any manner whatsoever. However, in case any source has not been duly attributed; the publisher may be notified in writing for necessary action.

Published by :

an imprint of Highlyy Publishing LLP

Correspondence
Address :

4/30 A II Floor, Double Storey Buildings
Vijay Nagar, Delhi-110009
Editorial: +91 9811026449
Sales : +91 9999953412
Email: info@howacademics.com
Website: www.howacademics.com

Contents

	Preface	vii
1.	Strategic Deployment of AI in Military Operations by US and China	1
2.	The Militarization and Weaponization of Artificial Intelligence	19
3.	Applying Artificial Intelligence to Warfighting	63
4.	Artifical Intelligence in Nuclear Conflict	109
5.	AI-Enhanced Offensive Capabilities in Cyber and Nuclear Defence	121
6.	Navigating Strategic Risks in U.S.-China Military AI Competition	153
7.	The Impact of Artificial Intelligence on Future Diplomatic Relations	179
8.	AI Revolution in Military Operations	191
	Bibliography	223
	Index	241

Preface

The 4th Industrial Revolution, driven by artificial intelligence (AI), has the potential to affect various areas, including public policy, governance, security, foreign policy, technological development, and even everyday tasks like finding the nearest gas station. AI, no longer a fictional concept, is the true game changer in this revolution, capable of creating significant creative and destructive disruptions with long-lasting effects. If harnessed for good, AI can enhance education, healthcare, lifestyle quality, and combat climate change. However, the absence of regulation and international consensus on national security and foreign policy raises concerns about the misuse of such powerful technology. Vague definitions of emerging technologies like AI contribute to misunderstandings about their issues, dangers, and applications. Therefore, collaboration between hard sciences and social sciences is essential to address the legal, ethical, and moral challenges posed by AI.

The AI revolution has also extended to weaponry, introducing AI-driven autonomy in warfare. Throughout history, wars have evolved alongside technological advancements. Autonomous Weapons Systems (AWS) or Lethal Autonomous Weapons (LAWS), also known as "fire-and-forget" weapons, rely on AI for their core functions, significantly impacting the battlefield. These weapons utilize algorithms and onboard sensors to identify, monitor, and attack targets without human intervention. AWS becomes lethal (and thus LAWS) when human targets are involved.

Despite their potential, autonomous weapons have sparked significant controversy. The United Nations Secretary-General has called for an international ban on these so-called "killer robots," deeming their use morally unacceptable. The lack of clear definitions of 'autonomy' and the blurred lines between legitimate use and abuse hinder global consensus on the future of lethal autonomous weapons.

In recent decades, rapid advancements in artificial intelligence (AI) have revolutionized various sectors, including healthcare, finance, and transportation. In the military sphere, AI has become a transformative force, promising to reshape warfare strategies and outcomes. The integration of AI technologies into military applications has led to the development of autonomous weapons that function without direct human control.

AI-driven systems provide unprecedented capabilities, ranging from sophisticated data analysis to complex decision-making processes. Military forces worldwide recognize the potential advantages of utilizing AI in warfare, such as enhanced operational efficiency, improved situational awareness, and quicker response times. Autonomous weapons, including unmanned aerial vehicles (UAVs or drones), autonomous ground vehicles, and naval systems, have shown remarkable performance in various situations.

Chapter 1
Strategic Deployment of AI in Military Operations by US and China

Introduction

In the past few years, artificial intelligence (AI) has come a long way very quickly. This has led to a lot of different uses, both in the military and in civilian life. In fact, the military is always looking for better, faster, and stronger tools or technologies because it needs to change. AI is a perfect example of this. Svenmarck et al. are right when they say that AI could have an effect on "all domains (i.e. land, sea, air, space, and information) and all levels of warfare (i.e. political, strategic, operational, and tactical) in the military." AI is mostly used in the military right now for the following reasons:

- Autonomous Weapons and Weapons Targeting
- Surveillance
- Cybersecurity
- Homeland Security
- Logistics
- Autonomous Vehicles

Because of this, a lot of government leaders, tech experts, and academics think AI is new, but their views on AI are not all the same. Some people see AI as a good thing because it would help lower the number of deaths among humans (since machines would be used instead of people in all kinds of missions, even the most dangerous ones) and it would also be helpful from a strategic and tactical point of view. Others, though, warn that AI could start another world war if it is not managed and used correctly.

While AI is still very young, it is clear that it has the potential to change the security industry. As a result, it will also change the balance of power between countries in terms of economics and war. More than 20 countries have stated their national AI strategies because they see the potential of AI. More states and non-state organisations are also taking strong steps in AI research and development (R&D). Still, the U.S. and China are seen as the top two countries in the field. The U.S. wants to stay on top of the fight, while China wants to pass the U.S. and become the AI leader by 2030. Both of these countries have, of course, made their own national strategies that are in line with these goals. But what's most important is that the U.S. national strategy is based on the Chinese national strategy, and the same is true for China.

As a short introduction, this paper talks about what AI is, how it has changed over time, and how it will affect war. First, it looks at why governments spend money on AI. Next, it compares the U.S. and China. We look at the most important official papers and comments from both the U.S. and China. We also show how their bureaucracies handle AI and give examples of how they use AI in their military.

In the conclusion, there is a short note about how China's and the U.S.'s tactics are different, followed by suggestions for what countries like Turkey should do soon.

Interpreting Artificial Intelligence

AI is now a reality and is thought to be the 4th Industrial Revolution. Many experts say that AI shouldn't be seen as a specific weapon, but as "an enabler, a general-purpose technology with a multitude of applications." This means that "AI could potentially lead to a number of military innovations, but it is not a military innovation itself." An expert in technology named Kevin Kelly said that AI will be like energy in that it will "bring things to life with intelligence, just as electricity does with power." However, tech experts aren't the only ones who stress how important AI is. Obama, Trump, Xi, and Putin are just a few of the world leaders who have said important things about AI that make it stand out. Putin's comment in September 2017 can be summed up in one sentence: "Whoever becomes the leader in AI will rule the world."

AI has been growing since 1956, but it became more popular around 2010 because of three things that made it possible: (i) more "big data" sources became available; (ii) machine learning methods got better; and (iii) computers got faster. AI comes in two main types right now: Narrow AI (NAI) and General AI (GAI). In NAI, things like playing games or recognising images are included. In GAI, systems that are smart enough to do a variety of jobs are called "human-level intelligence." At this point, all the known progress in AI is in the NAI category. When it comes to GAI, experts are usually sceptical, and it's thought that decades will pass before it reaches its full potential. But this division is not necessary to understand better. One important problem that comes up with AI, no matter how narrow or broad it is, is autonomy. As an example, the next part gives a brief outline of the range of levels of autonomy that can be achieved with AI.

Dynamics of Human-Machine Interaction

The connection between people and machines is one of the most talked-about aspects of AI use, especially in the military. We can talk about three types of interactions right now: (i) human in the loop, (ii) human on the loop, and (iii) human out of the loop.

When a person is in the loop, the machine controls the environment, but the person makes the final choice. This kind of system is called a semi-autonomous system. The second case, with a person in the loop, lets the machine act and make a choice on its own. Still, a person can watch how the machine acts and step in if needed. In this case, we have an autonomous machine that is being watched. The last case is a machine that can do everything on its own. Here, the machine acts and makes decisions on its own, and the person doesn't have any power over it, so they aren't involved. At this point, we can only talk about the first or second case in the military application, like drones and precision-guided missiles. On the other hand, the AI application has not yet hit the third level of full autonomy.

AI Utilization in Military Operations

The fast growth of artificial intelligence has had good effects in many areas, such as medicine and transportation. However, there is a lot of debate about how it could be used in the military. Most people now agree that AI will eventually change military tasks like logistics, data gathering, surveillance, and most importantly, making weapons. This is because AI and its use are still not fully understood, which has caused a lot of discussion among military politicians. Most of these arguments are about how AI will change fighting and how much control weapons with AI should have. This is especially true when it comes to deadly autonomous weapons systems (LAWS), also known as "killer robots." These tools are part of the third case we talked about earlier, where people are not involved.

Right now, some people say that AI can be used in the military in the following ways, but not only those: i) AI can help process and understand information based on image-recognition techniques. This can be seen in the

American Project Maven, which is being programmed to handle and make sense of the data it gets from drone videos. By using AI, things like drones, planes, ships, tanks, and more will not need a person to handle or tell them what to do. The Israeli Harpy drone is a good example of this because it can now almost fly itself (but still needs to be fired by troops on the ground). Other planes, like the Air Force Global Hawk and Army Grey Eagle drones, can be mentioned that have a lower amount of autonomy. For both of these drones, the person controlling them must tell the plane where to go before it can fly itself. Because of this, self-driving systems are likely to take over jobs that people think are "dull, dangerous, or dirty." Long-term jobs like this could include gathering and analysing intelligence, cleaning up areas that have been harmed by chemical weapons, or searching for hidden routes for homemade bombs. Lastly, as algorithms get better, AI could be used for command and control, such as managing battles, by looking at large amounts of data and making predictions that tell people what to do.

AI's Influence on Modern Warfare Dynamics

As we already said, a lot of attention is focused on how AI can be used in the military. The first group is made up of scholars who are sceptical about the use of AI because they point out that people can lose control of machines, which would be very bad. Also, it's possible that AI systems will not only be usable by states but also by non-state players, like terrorist groups. This would make warfare even less fair. On the other hand, AI machines are seen as a good thing because they will replace human fighters in dangerous battles, which means fewer human deaths. In addition, these tools may be more useful for long-term tasks that people can't handle.

Even though there is a discussion about the pros and cons of using AI in warfare, experts have made predictions about how AI will change the nature of war in the future. There are three possible points of view in this area: (i) minimal impact, (ii) evolutionary effect, and (iii) revolutionary impact.

The experts who say AI will have little effect are mostly interested in the technical side of it and how willing armed groups are to use it. Because of this, they say that the problems that could arise from using AI will make it unsuitable for combat use. In terms of military organisations, some governments don't like big changes like AI, so they would fight against using AI in the military. The second group of experts—those who think AI will have an evolutionary effect—agree that AI will be very important in war, even though general artificial intelligence (GAI) probably won't be developed any time soon. However, they stress how important it is for humans to be present in war so that AI doesn't take over. The final group of experts backs the idea that AI will completely change the way wars are fought. People who believe this say that using AI in the military could change the way wars are fought and how they are fought. Because of this, they talk about a "transition from the industrial era of warfare into the information era, in which gathering, using, and spreading information will be the most important part of combat operations." At this point, AI's ability to quickly handle a lot of data will be a huge advantage in battle, letting people make decisions more quickly and better.

There is no question that the nature of war will change, even with all of these talks. The first thing that will happen is that war will last as long as possible. The speed of battle will speed up because AI can respond at machine speed. Analysts have very different ideas about whether this change will be good or bad. Second, as new ways of doing things come up, like swarm drones, the present structure and organisations of the military will change. Third, AI might make it possible to deal with the huge amount of data that is available for study. AI systems will be able to come up with answers or results that people might not be able to think of, especially when they are in battle. Then this would give them an edge over the enemy. Lastly, there will be a new debate about the quality-quantity problem as people think about whether or not it is possible to make a certain AI system once the software is made.

Even with all of these talks, the states are still trying to use AI in different areas of life, including the military. It looks more and more like a race: a lot of states have already made their AI national plans public. In this vein, the next part of this analysis will talk about the main reason why governments are ready to spend money on AI.

Rationale Behind State Investments in Artificial Intelligence

Table 1 shows that about 20 states and organisations have either announced or are about to announce their AI plans. The European Commision also says that about €10 billion was invested in AI in Asia and €18 billion was invested in AI in the U.S. in 2016. This amount could be even higher since not all states say how much money they spend on AI. According to Scharre, however, the world will spend $7.5 billion a year on military robots alone in 2018.

AI is now seen as a tool that states that use it will be able to gain benefits in both civilian and military life. AI and its use will open up a lot of possibilities for the countries that use it first, like the US and China. These countries will be able to get economic and military advantages over their rivals. It is also believed that it will change the current balances of power. States that don't use this technology in their defence, on the other hand, will suffer bad effects. At the moment, Turkey is one of the countries that hasn't done much to advance AI research and development. Still, because of the way things are going in the region right now and the fact that countries like the UAE and Israel are now focusing on AI, Turkey needs to make its own AI national plan and put a lot of money into it.

Using AI in the military will give states the upper hand on the battlefield because machines will be more accurate and faster than humans in logistics, the battlefield, and making decisions. This is the main reason why AI has the power to change the current balances of power. Additionally, AI helps the military carry out dangerous tasks for a long time, which is something people can't do.

Table 1: List of the States Which Have/Are about to Announce their Ai National Strategy

No.	Date	State	National Strategy Title
1	March 2017	Canada	Pan-Canadian AI Strategy
2	March 2017	Japan	Artificial Intelligence Technology Strategy
3	May 2017	Singapore	AI Singapore
4	July 2017	China	A Next Generation Artificial Intelligence Development Plan
5	October 2017	UAE	UAE Strategy for Artificial Intelligence
6	December 2017	Finland	Finland's Age of Artificial Intelligence
7	January 2018	Kenya	Blockchain & Artificial Intelligence Taskforce
8	January 2018	Taiwan	Taiwan AI Action Plan
9	January 2018	Denmark	Strategy for Denmark's Digital Growth
10	March 2018	Italy	Artificial Intelligence at the Service of Citizens
11	March 2018	France	France's Strategy for AI
12	April 2018	Tunisia	National AI Strategy: Unlocking Tunisia's capabilities potential (Work¬shop - NS to be announced!
13	April 2018	EU Commission	Communication on Artificial Intelligence for Europe
14	April 2018	UK	Industrial Strategy: Artificial Intelligence Sector Deal

15	May 2018	Australia	Australian Technology and Science Growth Plan
16	May 2018	South Korea	Artificial Intelligence R&D Strategy
17	May 2018	Sweden	National Approach for Artificial Intelligence
18	June 2018	India	National Strategy for Artificial intelligence: #AIforAll
19	June 2018	Mexico	Towards an AI Strategy in Mexico: Harnessing the AI Revolution
20	December 2018	Germany	Key points for a Federal Government Strategy on AI
21	February 2019	U.S.	Accelerating America's Leadership in Artificial Intelligence

AI will also make it easier for governments to justify war because fewer people will be fighting and fewer people will die as a result. This is especially true for democrats. For dictatorships like China, using AI in the military would help the government give only a small group of trustworthy people the power to start a war. This would give the leaders more control over the war.

Furthermore, one of the main reasons states want to use AI in their armies is because it is cheap. Even the U.S. Army's Robotics and Autonomous Systems Strategy talks about how AI is thought to be cost-effective. It is possible for states to prioritise number over quality because they can make or buy cheap robots. This will prove to be beneficial in the near future. That being said, it's important to stress that AI can't stay in the hands of a few states, like nuclear weapons did. This will happen soon enough for a lot of states and even non-state organisations to be able to use AI in their armies. After this point, number will no longer be useful, so states and non-state actors will start to focus on quality instead of quantity.

US and AI

The United States sees AI as a part of its Third Offset Strategy. This strategy was started in 2014 by Chuck Hagel, who was Secretary of Defence at the time, and its goal was to bring back America's military technological edge. In this way, the Third Offset Strategy is mostly about robots and autonomy, and AI is a very important part of these areas. After this, both the Obama and Trump administrations have said they want the United States to be the world leader in AI. To reach this goal, the Trump administration said in May 2018 that "to the greatest degree possible, we will allow scientists and technologists to freely develop their next great inventions right here in the United States." Even with these goals, the U.S. is limited in its ability to become the world leader in AI by factors inside and outside of its own borders.

First, the internal restrictions come from the fact that AI is not being made by the government, like nuclear weapons are. Instead, non-governmental organisations like Google and Microsoft are doing it. These organisations don't always want to work with the government, which makes it harder for AI to be used in the military, as we'll talk about below. A national plan for AI has also been moving very slowly at the government level. It's important to note that the U.S. was one of the later countries to officially announce an AI national policy. In 2017, Canada was the first country to do so. Outside forces can be seen in the problems that other countries, mostly China and Russia, cause for the US to be a star in AI. Both of these countries want to challenge the U.S. military's strength by using AI to make weapons that are better than the U.S.'s. As a result, this section will quickly go over the main national government programmes of both the Obama and Trump administrations, as well as the groups in charge of AI study and delivery and the main ways AI has been used in the military up to this point.

In 2016, the Obama administration released a road map that recognised the U.S.'s need to be a leader in AI. This was the first official statement about AI. But this plan was mostly about questions of regulatory policy. The White House Office of Science and Technology Policy set up the Subcommittee on Machine Learning and Artificial Intelligence (MLAI) and held several meetings that same year. The main objective was to help coordinate AI work across the country. As a result, three main reports were released during the Obama administration: (i) Preparing for the Future of Artificial Intelligence; (ii) The National Artificial Intelligence Research and Development Strategic Plan; and (iii) Artificial Intelligence, Automation, and the Economy. The first study talked about possible approaches to rules for AI, public research and development (R&D), ethics, and safety. The National Artificial Intelligence Research and Development Strategic Plan was mostly about the R&D strategy. The previous report, on the other hand, talked about the policies that would make AI more useful and less expensive.

The Department of Homeland Security took another big step forwards in 2017 when they released a narrative study on AI. This part was mostly about how to better understand how people see the pros and cons of using AI. In the National Security Strategy for the first time that same year, AI was talked about. The main topic of this chapter was how AI is used in information warfare, making weapons, and keeping an eye on people. In the National Defence Strategy released later that year, AI was named as one of the "very technologies that ensure we [the U.S.] will be able to fight and win the wars of the future.... New commercial technology will change society and, ultimately, the character of war." The Department of Defence also says in its AI strategy report that a national AI strategy needs to be made right away because "other nations, especially China and Russia, are making significant investments in AI for military purposes, including in applications that raise questions about international norms and human rights." These investments could hurt our technological and operational benefits and make the free and open international order less stable.

Michael Kratsios, who is the Deputy Assistant to the President for Technology Policy, spoke at the 2018 White House Summit on Artificial Intelligence for American Industry in May 2018. He summed up the Trump Administration's AI goals as follows: (i) prioritising funding for AI research and development; (ii) removing barriers to innovation; (iii) training the next generation of American workers; (iv) gaining a strategic military advantage to lead in AI; (v) using AI for government services; and (vi) leading international cooperation in AI. Kratsios stated at the summit the creation of a new Select Committee on Artificial Intelligence to "improve the coordination of Federal efforts related to AI and ensure continued U.S. leadership in AI." This was done so that all of these goals could be met.

Following a short time, in July 2018, the Executive Office of the President put out a letter called FY2020 Administration Research and Development Budget Priorities. Along with quantum information sciences and strategic computing, the letter said that AI was one of the most important areas for research and development in FY2020. It also stressed the need for AI leadership. Along the same lines, this memo was followed by an Executive Order signed in February 2019 that said the U.S. is the world leader in AI study and that keeping this position is very important for the U.S. To wrap up, it's important to note that AI was first mentioned as a government priority in the Trump Administration's FY2019 budget request, which said that "the budget's key areas of focus include artificial intelligence, autonomous systems, and hypersonics."

Even though both the Obama and Trump administrations have put out a lot of official statements and papers, they don't have a clear plan for how they will spend money or organise their departments. Experts are very critical of this part of the American position and warn of the rivalry with China and the problems it poses for the American leadership.

Hierarchical Structure

Because we don't have enough knowledge, it's hard to talk about how AI is funded. However, we can make a list of some U.S. government agencies that do AI research and development. The Department of Defence is the main organisation in charge. They set up the Joint Artificial Intelligence Centre (JAIC) in June 2018. Lt. Gen. Jack Shanahan, who is in charge of JAIC, says that the organisation is very important for moving from research and development to operational-fielded skills. The Trump Administration's most recent plan for FY2020 gives $208 million to the JAIC. In the Department of Defence, the Defence Advanced Research Projects Agency (DARPA) is also in charge of AI projects. DARPA has taken the lead in AI research and development. If DARPA gets its $3.17bn budget in 2018, it will ask for $3.44bn in 2019. Also, DARPA announced in 2018 that it would spend more than $2bn over several years on new and ongoing programmes. This was called the "AI Next" effort.

Finally, on May 10, 2018, the Trump White House set up the Select Committee on Artificial Intelligence as part of the National Science and Technology Council. This committee is the White House's main source of advice on AI research and development objectives. It is also in charge of making sure that the government works together with business and academia on AI research and development.

Military Uses of AI in the U.S. AI is an area of technology that has big effects on the safety of the whole country. Because of this, the US and other countries are working on AI uses for the military. Several tests have been done in this area, and it can be said that no other country, not even China or Russia, has hit the level that the U.S. has reached so far. This section will talk about some of the most important tests and studies that the U.S. has done, mostly as part of the Department of Defence.

The U.S. Navy's X-47B test drone landed on its own in 2013. In 2015, the same drone did fully automated refuelling in the air. In both cases, the only thing a person did was tell the software to land or refuel while the plane was in the air.

It has already been said that the military will be organised differently as AI is used and new ways of doing things come up. This was shown by the swarm drones. In 2016, the US showed that 103 drones could fly together without any help. For the Pentagon, this was like "a collective organism, sharing one distributed brain for decision-making and adapting to each other like swarms in nature." A similar test was done by the Navy in November 2016. Five boats that were not occupied swarmed a certain area of Chesapeake Bay and stopped a "intruder" ship. As soon as possible, more tests will likely be done with groups of underwater drones.

AI is being used in intelligence, surveillance, and reconnaissance uses in Project Maven, which is one of the most well-known and talked-about cases involving the U.S. government. Project Maven has been used to help fight ISIS in Iraq and Syria up to now.

Aside from that, the U.S. military is focused on adding AI to semi-autonomous and fully autonomous vehicles, such as fighter jets, drones, ground vehicles, and naval ships. This can be seen in the Loyal Wingman programme. Older unmanned fighter jets (F-16 or B-1) or low-cost uninhabited planes (XQ-58A Valkyrie) were paired with inhabited fighter jets (F-35 or F-22) as part of this programme. In this case, the uninhabited plane has to protect the inhabited jet by responding on its own without being told to. The Army and the Marines have also done tests like this, where prototype vehicles have followed soldiers or vehicles on the ground and kept them safe. Another prototype ship is the Sea Hunter, which is an AntiSubmarine Warfare Continuous Trail Unmanned Vessel prototype. It was first built by DARPA and then given to the Office of Naval Research. Sea Hunter is the first drone ship to go from California to Hawaii and back to California without any help.

Last but not least, adding AI to the law is still very important. But until now, the U.S. hasn't said anything about any tests or studies in this area.

AI and China

When it comes to researching and using AI technology, China is doing what the U.S. does. China is not only using AI to spy on its own people, but it has also said that it wants to be ahead of the West in AI research and development by 2025 and, even more important, the world leader in AI by 2030. Many times, China's leaders, including Xi Jinping, have made it clear that being the leader in AI technology is "critical to the future of global military and economic power competition." One could say that China sees military AI research and development as an easy and possible way to fight the US military dominance.

Between 2005 and 2015, the Chinese government spent 350% more on AI research and development. Right now, China is thought to be very close to the U.S. Also, Chinese companies provided 48% of the world's total funding for AI start-ups in 2017, and from 2013 to 2018, 60% of all funding for AI went to China's AI business. China's leaders and business community think that the gap between China and the U.S. in AI is now very small, and they see "AI as 'a race of two giants,' between itself and the United States."

A lot of people may not believe that China can really compete with the United States, but China does have some systemic and strategic benefits that can help it reach its goal of becoming the world leader in AI. This includes China's big amount of data and its potential pool of skilled workers, but most importantly, it includes the relationship between the government and the AI private sector. In this situation, one of China's best plans, unlike the U.S.'s, is to combine civilian and military life (CMI) and create advanced technologies that can be used for both civilian and military purposes. The Chinese government and the private AI industry are working together closely, which makes it easier for AI technologies to be used in the military. This is related to these complementary strategies. The main goal of this strategy is to build a strong military and help the People's Liberation Army (PLA) take over the battlefields, which would allow them to "leapfrog" the U.S.

In 2016, Google DeepMind's AlphaGo beat the world champion Lee Sedol by a score of 4-1 in a Go game. This changed how China saw and felt about AI research and development. Many people have called this China's "Sputnik moment" because the government began to give more attention to the AI national policy and how it would be used in the military. In contrast to the U.S., China's AI national plans are mostly put out by the country's State Council. The following is a summary of the plans and programmes that were made public:

- Made in China 2025 (May 2015): This 10-year action plan focused on promoting manufacturing, among others in the field of artificial intelligence and robotics.

- "Internet Plus" Artificial Intelligence Three- Year Action Plan (2016-2018) (May 2016): This plan was focused specifically on AI and called for the creation of infrastructure and platforms for AI. Furthermore, it established a goal to increase the AI industry to a level totaling billions of RMB by 2018.

- 13th Five Year Plan for Developing National Strategic and Emerging Industries (20162020) (August 2016): Based on this plan, the State Council contended that AI was among the main tasks to be pursued by the central government (6 out of 69 major tasks) and at the same time it announced five agencies that would be responsible for the development of AI.

- Next Generation Artificial Intelligence Development Plan (July 2017): This can be considered as one of the main documents regarding the Chinese AI strategy. This is the plan in which China explicitly declares the goal to become a world leader in AI by 2030. Furthermore, the plan identifies a specific path that needs to be followed in order to achieve the proposed goal. The document argues that AI embodies a "major strategic opportunity" and suggests a coordinated strategy to "build China's first mover advantage."

- 13th Five-Year Science and Technology Military-Civil Fusion Special Plan (August 2017): In contrast to the others, this plan was issued

by the Ministry of Science and Technology and the CMC Science and Technology Commission. As the title suggests this plan focuses directly on the military-civil fusion and the dual use of AI technology and reflects on the importance of this strategy.
- Robotic Industry Development Plan (2016-2020) (April 2016): was issued by three institutions, namely National Development and Reform Commission (NDRC), Ministry of Industry and Information Technology (MIIT) and Ministry of Finance (MOF). The importance of this plan rests on the fact that it set concrete goals and strategies in terms of the robotics industry. More specifically, this plan states that China is planning to produce 100,000 robots by 2020.
- Three Year Action Plan for Promoting Development of a New Generation Artificial Intelligence Industry (2018-2020) (December 2017): This plan was issued by the Chinese Ministry of Industry and Information Technology and provides further details on those published in the Next Generation Artificial Intelligence Development Plan. This plan identifies the way to stimulate the development of AI in the 2018-2020 period and also the key areas of AI application, including vehicles, service robots, drones, etc.

Hierarchical Structure

In China, there is only one political party, so the Chinese Communist Party Central Committee oversees everything, even new technologies. The National Science, Technology, and Education Leading Small Group and the Chinese Communist Party Central Military Commision are the two main organisations that make policy and coordinate on technology issues. The first is mostly in charge of how technology is used in civilian life, while the second is in charge of how it is used in the military. This division also shows China's national plan for integrating civilians and soldiers, which we already talked about.

The Chinese Premier, who is also the boss of the State Council, is in charge of the Leading Small Group, which is made up of the most important people in China's top administrative body. They are the National Development and Reform Commision (NDRC), the State Internet Information Office (SIIO), the Ministry of Industry and Information Technology (MIIT), the Ministry of Science and Technology (MOST), and the Ministry of Finance (MOF). The 13th Five-Year Plan for Developing National Strategic and Emerging Industries says that these five groups are in charge of developing AI. Still, AI research and development is also the job of other State Council-affiliated organisations. Some of these are the National Natural Science Foundation of China (NSFC), the Chinese Academy of Sciences (CAS), and the Chinese Academy of Engineering (CAE).

But the Central Military Commision, which is in charge of the People's Liberation Army (PLA), the People's Armed Police, and the Militia, is in charge of the military side of technology growth. In this context, most AI research and development is done by military universities and study centres. The PLA, which does most of the research and development on AI, thinks that AI will have a big effect on how wars are fought. Because of this, we will move from talking about "information-based warfare" to talking about "intelligentized warfare." Furthermore, China is still mainly interested in using AI for defence equipment, making decisions, military deductions, and robotic military weapons. However, it is safe to say that China's military use of AI is still in its early stages. For this major reason, China does not have real-life battlefield experience like the US does. In other words, it looks like the PLA's main goal is to use AI in war games and exercises.

China is using AI in the military. While China is not the same as the U.S., it is making big steps to integrate AI into its defence systems, mostly in the military. In 2015, Baidu, one of China's top AI companies, made software that could understand words better than humans. It is important to note that Microsoft did not make software that was similar until the following year. At the moment, language recognition software and computer vision systems made in China are being used for internal surveillance to keep an eye on regular people.

In China, AI is being used in the military, but it's important to note that the country is more interested in war games and simulations based on augmented reality because its soldiers don't have much experience in real fighting. The AI and War-Gaming National Finals, which were held by the China Institute of Command and Control in 2017, are one of the best-known examples. In this competition, people had to deal with CASIA-Prophet 1.0 robots that could do anything without any human control. Seven times out of ten, the machine won this race.

Military leaders in the PLA see war games as a way to help them use AI in the military, which would help China win future wars. However, this is only a small part of what China has done with AI in the military so far. China hasn't been in real combat yet, but that hasn't stopped them from studying and trying how AI can be used in unmanned autonomous systems for defence and offence, as well as to help the command make decisions.

China has been studying air, ground, surface, and underwater autonomous unmanned vehicles (AUV), just like the US. They are mainly interested in autonomous unmanned systems. While it comes to air AUVs, China has done pretty well, especially with swarm drones. As of June 2017, China had flown a swarm of 119 drones, beating the previous American record of 103 drones. All of the drones had systems that let them talk to each other.

China has made robotic aerial vehicles (UAVs) like TYW-1 and ASN-216 that can now partially or fully fly themselves with the help of AI. At the moment, both ASN-216 and TYW-1 can take off and land without any help from a person. With just a little help from a person, TYW-1 can even find and hit a target.

For example, SeaFly is one of the robotic surface vehicles that should be brought up. At the moment, SeaFly can learn how to avoid obstacles without any help from a person. It can also find and return to its UAV using algorithms that let it plan its movements based on what it sees in the sea.

Finally, when it comes to putting AI into LAWS, China's delegation to the UN Group of Governmental Experts on LAWS said in 2018 that they agreed with the new protocol that would make it illegal to use fully autonomous lethal weapons systems. However, for China, this does not mean that they will not be able to make fully autonomous lethal weapons systems.

Conclusion

Both government officials and academics agree that AI has the potential to change the way security works and the balance of power in the world. There has been a lot of competition between states, especially between the U.S. and China, over AI because it is being used more and more in the military. A lot of other states are also working to keep up with the times and improve their own AI apps at the same time.

It's still not clear how the fight between the U.S. and China will end, but China is a threat to the U.S. that should not be taken lightly. One option is that the U.S. will stay ahead for now, but China has the power to challenge this position in the long term. As was already said, the U.S. released its national plan about a year after China did. However, a lot of experts have said that this approach doesn't have enough detailed information about funding.

Right now, it's very important for the U.S. not to take its armed strength for granted and put down China's actions. More specifically, it was clear that the U.S. was better at the Second Offset strategy, which focused on precision-guided weapons. However, this may not be the case with the Third Offset strategy, which includes AI. Several things lead to this.

To begin, China does not work like the U.S. does. Instead, it uses a "whole-of-government" method, which means that the government is very important and has a direct effect on AI research and development. This makes it easier for the Chinese government to run the process. Also, Baidu, Alibaba, and Tencent, the three biggest private companies in China that do AI research and development, have already said they will work closely with the Chinese government on AI research and development. But you can't say the same thing about the U.S. It's harder for the U.S. to advance AI because the government doesn't have direct power over companies like Google, Microsoft, and others that do AI research and development. This can be seen in the case of Project Maven, which was a cooperation between Google and the Department of Defence. But the second company had to drop out of the project because thousands of its workers signed a plea to stop the military from using their work.

Second, China has a lot of possible human capital and a huge amount of data that could give them an edge in AI research and development. China is expected to have 20% of the world's data by 2020, and could have over 30% by 2030.

Also, China is more likely than the U.S. to not think about the problems that come up when AI is used in law enforcement and when machines have full agency. The United States has made it clear that it does not plan to keep people out of the loop, but China has not said the same thing. For China, a military advantage would be created if they were able to achieve full automation and use AI in LAWS.

Still, China has a weakness when it comes to battlefield knowledge. With China not having been in a war in decades, it is hard for the country to use AI directly on the ground. China has been focused on war games and simulations because of this. The U.S., on the other hand, has been at war for so long that it has focused on more tactical applications. As a result, it has been able to use AI on the battlefield and build it to fit the needs of combat.

Not only the US and China have made AI a policy goal, but many other countries have too. Already, at least 20 states have said what their AI national plans will be, and most of them have taken big steps in AI research and development. So far, Turkey hasn't said what its AI national plan is or taken any steps to improve AI research or use it in the military. Being one of the few countries with its own UAV, Turkey needs to make big steps forwards in AI research and development and how it is used in the military. Two things make it clear that we need a national plan for AI right away. First, Turkey may not want to fall behind in the AI race because it could hurt the country. When AI is used in the military, the first country to do so has an edge. States that don't use AI in the short term will face bigger threats in the long term, when it will be hard to keep up. This means that Turkey will not be able to maintain the level of national defence it has had so far, especially when it comes to the unmanned aerial vehicle (UAV). This is because other countries in the region, like the UAE, have already made big steps forwards in AI research and development. Second, Turkey has been facing many dangers lately, such as the PKK, the YPG, ISIS, and others. Artificial intelligence (AI) is hard to make, but it's easy to copy and use once the software is made. According to this, it would not be hard for terrorist groups like the PKK, the YPG, or ISIS to use AI to further their own goals while also putting Turkey's safety at risk. But if Turkey starts to focus on AI and make it a policy goal, like many other states have, it will be easier for the country to protect itself from any future threat that would come from terrorist groups having AI technology.

Chapter 2
The Militarization and Weaponization of Artificial Intelligence

Introduction

Artificial intelligence that is used as a tool could change the way wars are fought and how they are fought. AI is supposed to be the battlefield of the future because it can either be used to make weapons more powerful, like nuclear weapons, or it can be turned into weapons itself. In simple terms, it would let states use both kinetic and non-kinetic abilities, either solo or together.

The main goal of this chapter is to look into the worrying trend of AI being used as a weapon and how it makes the security problem between states worse in both symmetric and uneven situations. In turn, this speeds up the race to develop AI weapons, which leads to crisis and arms race chaos in the long run. To that end, this chapter will look at how AI might affect national polices, ties between states, and the basic rules of the international system that governs interactions between states. The point of this piece is to make the case for setting up a worldwide system to regulate AI.

If AI is used to make weapons, it could shake up the world order and the basis of peace and security around the world. So, international lawyers, private companies, non-state actors like the IAEA and the UN Office for Disarmament Affairs, and states should think about one of two policy options: regulating AI and making sure that its uses are in line with the current global regime, or creating a new global system where AI takes the place of states to keep the peace and security of the world. Setting up a new world system seems like a great idea from a utopian point of view. One possible policy choice, however, is the first one; all that needs to be done is the creation of a system similar to the one that was set up to control the nuclear arms race.

Challenges

Killer robots are getting better and better, and a lot of drones are being made. This means that military uses that use AI are being used too much. This is similar to how people want to get the most advanced AI military uses as quickly as possible, which speeds up the AI race. The main focus of the IR literature has been on what AI might mean for nuclear weapons, but no one has looked into how AI will change the nature of military technology. The IR literature 5 hasn't looked at the other side of the coin and hasn't looked into how AI could be used to boost security and build trust. It doesn't make sense to think that AI, which is a developed form of cyber technology, can't help with cyber defence.

It's not enough to just look into AI's technical possibilities; we also need to look into how it might affect relationships between countries and how to stop the AI race. To control how AI is used, we also need to create international legal tools and make sure that national and international policies are consistent. The world should accept that the AI race can't be stopped, but controlling it is the best thing that can be done.

The majority of the literature on international relations hasn't looked into what might happen if other types of weapons, like nuclear and cyber, were combined with AI. Sadly, it hasn't looked into how this might make these weapons more dangerous or unclear. This part looks into whether turning AI into a weapon could lead to a structure like MAD because it makes the security problem between states worse. The main goal of this chapter is to look into how well AI, which makes the security problem between states worse, works as a deterrence. In terms of offense-defence theory, it looks into how AI, either as a weapon or as a tool for making weapons, would affect future wars and whether it would make attack or defence more powerful. In this chapter, we look at how AI affects other weapons systems and ask if there is a way to signal an AI second strike or create an AI version of Mutually Assured Destruction that would lower the chances of a cyber, conventional, or even nuclear war. This piece comes up with two theories to answer this question: Even if having the first strike is helpful in the cyber world, nuclear MAD could lead to AI-MAD because AI skills could make cyber defence stronger, making AI-MAD possible.

Assertion

There is no question that AI makes the security problem between states worse in both symmetric and asymmetric settings because it can be used for both military and civilian purposes. This is because AI has the potential to change the nature and character of future wars. AI makes cyber deterrence stronger by preventing attacks and showing that it can be used to fight back in the cyber world. In the same way that nuclear power has pros and cons, AI does too. On the one hand, it can improve cyber defence and nuclear safety. On the other hand, it can be used wrongly and to trick people. This shows that AI has the ability to launch a second attack, even though its uses and the goals of rivalry states are becoming less clear. Because AI has the ability to be destructive, disruptive, and manipulative, it can be used along with nuclear deterrence. So, an AI MAD-like framework is the best policy choice to help states work out their security problems and keep peace and security around the world. To do this, we need to find ways to slow down the AI arms race, which has moved from the business world to the armed world. As a result, the international community should do everything it can to control the spread of AI and set rules for how it can be used. There will not be enough control over the uses of AI through the creation of law tools, especially when private companies are involved. To regulate AI, there needs to be both government will and agreement; otherwise, terrible things would happen. To keep the peace and safety of the world, it is strongly suggested that there be a framework that includes the legal, political, moral, economic, and security elements. Even more importantly, the international community should never let armies be run by machines, because the psychological aspect is very important in how militaries make decisions.

Background

It's not a new idea for militaries to use AI, but what worries scholars and experts is the trend toward making AI military applications and semi-autonomous drones that can operate without human input. At the moment, AI is built into many types of weapons, like planes and submarines. It is also built into command and control systems and important structures for logistics. AI today isn't as smart as it could be, but as we get closer to the dreamy one-shot learning and quantum computing, the security problem will become unsolvable.

In order to gain a military edge and reduce the number of deaths, militaries have been making more and more armed drones that can be used at both the tactical and operational levels. Former Secretary of Defence Donald Rumsfeld came up with the idea of "the mechanization of war," which means that the US army is half robots and half people. As part of its Third Offset Strategy, the US Department of Defence has added AI to its human soldiers and manned staff. Japan's AI-enabled rockets are said to be under way in an effort to cut costs. Many people are interested in both "killer robots" and robotic air vehicles because of how well semi-autonomous weapons systems work.

AI was originally meant to be used for military tactical operations, surveillance, and intelligence. However, states' use of AI in information and cyber warfare has expanded its uses. Instead of a traditional military attack, Israel and the US used Stuxnet to attack Iran's nuclear sites in 2010. This was a big change in the way wars are fought. Since then, the new battlefield is the internet, where people are using UAVs and drones more and more. The most recent example is Russia's "information warfare," in which it tried to affect American public opinion in subtle or overt ways during the most recent US presidential election. The detour of a civilian flight from its target is just one example of cyberwarfare made possible by AI. All of these cases show how AI applications and cyber capabilities are being used more and more. An important point was made when a number of experts said they were worried about how AI could be used wrongly to undermine an enemy's powers.

Because of this, the word "Algorithmic Warfare" has taken over the field of international relations (IR) because it will change the battlefield we know and will determine future wars. Thirty scientists, engineers, and military experts said that by 2050, the battlefield will have three new features that will make it unique. These are cyber technologies and abilities; an information space that is complicated and hotly contested; and a group of people with improved physical and mental abilities. These things have led to an arms race in AI, with China trying to beat the US and become a major player in the field. More than 30 countries have drones for military purposes or are working on making them. For example, high-speed rockets can be stopped with drones.

People have different ideas about how AI could be used to make nuclear, cyber, and even regular weapons, because of the ongoing discussions about how AI could be used to make weapons. Each group has a different opinion on the good and bad effects of AI on nuclear and cyber powers. Theorists who study nuclear powers said that using new technologies would make nuclear stalemate reversible and lower nuclear survivability, which is based on hiding, hardening, and having backups. At the same time, it can strengthen the nuclear defence. When it comes to cyber skills, data poisoning is caused by automating data analysis and setting priorities for targets. But software with AI built into it will make cyber defence stronger by being able to find code flaws.

Many AI-enabled apps could also pose a danger to both combatants and civilians, which is against the law (this is called "algorithmic warfare"). Due to the inherent dangers of uncontrolled "algorithmic warfare" and the lack of human involvement, conflict could happen by accident, leading to fratricide and civilian deaths or accidentally escalation. When it comes to security, fully autonomous weapons and vehicles that don't need a person to control them don't seem like good ideas for life and death situations, unless humans are out of the loop. This is because humans can't work in or effectively adapt to settings that are very complex and changeable. In cyber warfare, too, uncontrolled algorithms and the turning of the Internet of Things into weapons could hurt enemies by attacking important networks and infrastructure, leading to deaths of citizens and combatants. Several policy options have been put forward in the literature for controlling and limiting the uses of AI and preventing future intelligence and algorithmic warfare. Some of these policy choices are good, like the idea that human intelligence and machine intelligence can work together to make things better. One could argue that advanced, fast data processing and human cognition would make the human-machine teaming the missing piece of the puzzle. Some people also want to write a "Digital Geneva Convention" and limit the number of weapons that can be used for defence. The use of AI as a weapon has also worried government leaders, CEOs of private companies, and more than 60 non-governmental organizations (NGOs). These groups have asked for the ban on AI.

At the same time, a lot of different things were going on. For example, Canada and France announced the creation of an International Panel on Artificial Intelligence at a G7 meeting. The goals were to offer help, encourage the responsible use of AI that is focused on people, and make it easier for countries to work together. It also started the "Ethics and Governance of Artificial Intelligence Initiative" to help people use AI in the right way. All of these fascinating projects show how putting pressure on AI to become weapons and how important it is for everyone to act together right away.

When experts and policymakers think about AI as a tool or an enabler, they should look ahead and think about how it could start an arms race. They should also try to guess what will happen when AI is new or advanced and when humans are both too involved and not involved enough. When they look into the effects of AI on the security problem, they should also think about the good and bad uses of AI. This problem usually gets worse because AI is effective, scalable, spreads quickly, has fast potentials, and can be used for both good and bad things. They should also think about how to lessen the uncertainty that comes up because AI can be used to control and disrupt things, and because new threats and weaknesses are appearing, like impersonation and flight redirection, without any punishments or accountability measures in place.

Review

There are pros and cons to technological progress when it comes to a country's safety. According to one view, new technology can make a state stronger in defence and better able to stop enemies from doing harmful things. On the other hand, new technologies can also make the security problem worse. Also, as technology improves, it leads to arms races between countries that could be unstable if they don't know what kinds of skills they are building or how they will affect the balance of power. Increasing the defensive power of a rival state makes the security problem worse in this way. When states have weapons of mass destruction, they can attack an enemy before they do anything, like when Israel attacked Iraq in 1981, because they think the enemy is working on new, possibly dangerous weapons. In a strange way, these kinds of attacks or threats of them are often seen as reasons to get more advanced and deadly weapons.

Since technology keeps getting better, security problems get worse and new military movements start up. From the past of military progress, we can see that technological progress led to ten military revolutions. Weapons of mass destruction and nuclear weapons are great examples of new technologies that made it harder for rival countries to keep their citizens safe during the Cold War. According to Krepinevich's argument, there will be more military revolutions as long as technical progress is steady. This makes the security problem worse because an enemy still has a competitive edge. Like other new technologies, Artificial Intelligence (AI), the newest and most popular one in everyday life, could make security worse and lead to a new military change as more and more military personnel start to use it. According to Krepinevich's argument, using AI in the military would cause a revolution that would force military organizations to come up with new ways to do things, make new systems, adapt their structures, and update their technology.

Artificial intelligence is not a new technology, but it has recently gained popularity because of recent disasters that have raised concerns about how it might affect national and international security. This is because AI is increasingly being weaponized and used in war situations. AI has a lot of different meanings, which shows how this type of technology has changed and improved over the last few decades. As the definition of AI has grown, it is no longer just the automation and computation of intelligent behavior. It is now also the ability of computerized systems to do tasks that humans used to do alone and to copy mental skills that humans have always had, like understanding natural languages, recognizing patterns, and becoming adaptive. As AI has made steady progress, the literature on AI has described four different approaches: computer systems that think like humans, computer models that are programmed to think logically, machines that behave like humans, and the creation of automated systems that act and behave logically. There are two main categories that can be used to group these four approaches: thought process and logic. This grouping shows different ways of thinking about and using AI.

This kind of growth in AI makes it easier to see how AI might change the role of humans in the military after machine learning and deep reinforcement learning are used. This means that AI could be dangerous to a state's security because some people want to take humans out of the loop. This means that machines will be smarter than humans after they have been used to do tasks that are similar to human tasks or a wide range of tasks with human supervision. In the meantime, AI makes a state better at what it does. So, there is a lot of doubt about how AI weapons will affect the military, the law, and people's lives.

Artificial intelligence is a lot like nuclear weapons in that it was first created for peaceful, civilian purposes but is later used for war purposes. Artificial intelligence has a lot of promise to be used in many fields, from marketing to medicine to education to business to finance to medicine. But both AI researchers and IR experts are worried that AI could be used to make weapons. They stress the need to keep AI from making mistakes and to manage it for peaceful purposes. Artificial intelligence has been used in the military for things like drones, robots, and anti-missile systems. One thing that both nuclear weapons and AI have in common is the potential to start an AI arms race to solve the security problem and bring back strategic stability. Like nuclear weapons, it's hard to say what AI is and how it would affect states' behavior, according to Mohan, who brought up the problem of how to tell the difference between good and bad weapons and technologies. He said it's hard to tell the difference between good and bad weapons and technologies because some could be a stabilizing factor at some point because they are accurate at aiming and can be used for a second strike. But if other types of anti-weapons technologies are made, like Anti-Ballistic Missiles, they might be seen as dangerous weapons in the future.

With this comparison between AI and nuclear weapons and how destructive they can be, and with AI making fast progress, it is important to think about how they might make the security problem worse, since there is an undeniable trend in the IR literature to turn AI into a weapon. Though, there are different points of view in the AI writings itself about how AI should be used in the military. Supporters of AI 13 said that making it more military has its own benefits. There are many benefits, such as fewer people fighting, which would definitely mean fewer deaths, and easier access to dangerous places through the use of robots and unmanned vehicles. In addition, they said that AI would help a lot with making decisions because robots can do many things at once and organize them. Along with the United States, which makes killer robots as part of its third offset strategy, about 30 other states are also working on AI skills.

Supporters also wanted weapons to be automated because they wrongly think that self-driving weapons could solve the legal problem of civilian deaths and make states not responsible. On the contrary, opponents of autonomous weapons always point out the moral and legal problems that come up with using them, as well as the bad things that happen when humans lose control of a war. Autonomous weapons would make more civilians die. With the creation of weapons that can use AI, people might not be needed to run them. This means that supporters' arguments that autonomous weapons could be better at aiming and telling the difference between military and civilian objects are useless. They also say that autonomous weapons could do jobs more accurately and reliably. The proponents' assumption is questionable because people are better at judging situations and can act as moral agents or failsafe humans when autonomous weapons fail to make the right decision, change to new situations, or do their jobs well. More seriously, the use of AI in armed conflicts raises concerns about how International Humanitarian Law can be applied. People who support self-driving weapons think that AI would meet the standards of Article 48 of the 1977 Additional Protocol. But that kind of assumption isn't fair because AI could cause damage to other things because of faulty distinction. So, the current debate over AI shows the contrast between weapons that can work on their own and weapons that need to be controlled by people.

This change in how AI is used makes the security problem even worse. It was claimed by John Hers that today's conflicts speed up vicious races in technology to make a state stronger so it doesn't get wiped out. This argument isn't very good because it doesn't take into account the fact that 14 the security problem is mutual. Robert Jervis thinks that the security dilemma happens when one state tries to improve its security by gaining more powers, like AI, which puts the security of another state at risk.

Tang said that there is a real security problem when there is chaos and people are taking precautions without meaning to harm anyone. .This classification helps competitors tell the difference between an unintentional rise in tension during a security situation and a calm reaction to possible aggression. So, Jervis and Tang's meanings include both objective and subjective senses. Objective sense looks at how safe a state's values are and subjective sense sees how free people are from fear of losing those values. To put it another way, their definitions are based on Arnold Wolfers' concept of security, which includes both the physical and mental aspects. They also fit with Kenneth Waltz's idea of security, which says that the world is chaotic because there is no one in charge, which leads to the growth of self-help systems where competition exists.

So, in the current chaotic system, AI could make security worse because it's hard to know how harmful it is and what its enemies want, even if they are just looking for security. In this way, Tang's addition to the body of research would help states figure out how bad the security problem is in the AI world. To figure out how bad the AI security problem is, we need to know whether attack or defence is more important. There isn't a lot of research on AI yet, so it's hard to say what it would be like to use it as a weapon. The balance between attack and defence has been handled badly in the AI literature, and the relationship between AI and other types of weapons has not been looked at in depth.

The AI literature has talked too much about how AI and regular weapons don't work well together, even though killer robots and unmanned weapons have come a long way and will likely replace humans in the near future. So, what stands out is the in-depth study of the connection between AI and nuclear, cyber, and regular weapons. These facts show that these weapons should not be looked into separately when their effects on AI deterrence are being looked into. The idea behind this is to make guesses about what might happen in the security problem based on the kinds of weapons that are being made and used along with AI.

The offense-defence balance theory should be used to figure out how bad the security dilemma is when a state creates new weapons or technologies that make it easier to attack and when a defender finds itself in a situation where the strategic balance has changed. According to Jervis, defence is dominant when the attacker doesn't want to start preemptive strikes or preventive attacks to keep resources from running out and avoid the huge costs of war. That is, how bad a state thinks the security problem is depends on how easy it is for them to deal with and how the balance of power has changed. Jervis also said that catching up on skills could help restore the balance of power and make it more likely that people would work together. When both sides have the same amount of money for defence, the offense wins; preemptive attacks are better than doing nothing; the first strike is better; and the loser doesn't have any solid proof of the winner's or enemy's plans. By applying this to AI, we should think about how this new technology changes the mobility of weapons and their destructive power to figure out whether AI weapons are better for attack or defence. Apart from looking at the strategic, operational, and tactical aspects of an AI strike, empirical reasoning says that we should also look at the psychological aspect and how interests can be reconciled or not reconciled. Even though there have been many incidents of using civilian AI in the military and a clear reliance on drones and unmanned vehicles, AI experts and researchers have not looked into the possibility of doing so. When figuring out how serious the security problem is, it is important to think about conflict of interests, the offense-defence variables, and technological advances.

Concerning how bad the security problem could get if AI gets better, Jevris said that states' actions will be affected by three things: mutual fears of retaliation, mutual bad intentions as rivals develop AI that can intentionally scare each other, and the huge effects of using up all of their military resources if the security problem is real.

There was a lot of discussion about the future of AI because this kind of new technology could lead to fights between AI machines that are used for peaceful purposes. Some experts came to the conclusion that AI could invade people's privacy through surveillance tracking. It could also be used as a weapon of mass coercion because it can find weak spots in a business. It could threaten the safety of a state just as much as it could threaten a business. More importantly, it would be hard to keep track of AI weapon suppliers because AI companies are just networks of virtual facilities that work together. Also, it would be hard to figure out what kinds of AI powers are used for peaceful, military, or subversive purposes. The security experts at the Threatcasting Workshop correctly identified threats posed by AI, but they didn't look at other possible threats posed by AI that has been turned into a weapon. Another group of researchers, on the other hand, thinks that AI could make security worse by allowing bad hackers to spread false information and do covert monitoring for data mining. This makes me wonder about how hard it is to figure out who did what.

There are other things that could make the security problem in a two-way relationship worse, even if AI is developed for peaceful, commercial, or civilian reasons. These include the cost of research and development, progress in education, economic growth, and surveillance and reconnaissance. People who want to attack or spy on others could use AI medical apps and medical data that is connected to the internet as weapons against people who are protecting others. For profit reasons, making AI machines that are smart could lead to an arms race in the area.

Another problem is that cyber powers connected to AI software could be used in a bad way to attack and mess up a state's infrastructure. When cyber skills are combined with AI capabilities, it could make the security situation worse because it gives a state more offensive and defensive power against its neighboring country. This shows that states don't know what their enemies are up to and that their security systems are weak, since AI software could sneak up on an enemy's system and attack its weakest place, rendering it useless.

When it comes to information security, cyber-enabled software and social media botnets would make things worse. They would spread fake news and corrupt data, which would be bad for a state's business and government. AI that is used for good purposes could be used as a weapon to cause huge economic damage.

As killer robots become more common in real militaries, they pose a threat to the security of a state because they can attack anywhere on their land. So, peaceful AI apps have both good and bad points. They make people's lives easier, but they also put their privacy at risk in the age of personalized and intelligent violence.

On top of that, the heated discussion over the legality of AI-powered weapons and the difficulty of attribution also shows how confused international lawyers are. Five main points of view have been put forward in the writing on international law. In particular, giving AI entities a legal identity brings up questions about who is responsible and liable if they don't follow international law or if they do something wrong. These new developments make it even more clear that international lawyers are struggling to figure out what responsibility means in the world of AI and when a state would be legally responsible for using AI in the military. While, according to another theory, fully autonomous weapons should be illegal under a new set of international laws. It also says that low-level or semi-autonomous weapons might be legal and could be controlled by international law, which would make the security problem less severe. So, a clear legal definition of meaningful human control should be written so that future conflicts don't happen between countries that have AI and countries that don't. This will describe the symbiosis between humans and machines. It seems hard to keep some control over machines and self-driving weapons in this age of AI-based warfare. To make sure that the use of AI weapons is acceptable and follows the Law of Armed Conflict and the International Criminal Law, a new set of international laws could be created. The issue of attribution, especially when people aren't involved, shows how states can be controlled by robots and could also be legally responsible under public international law. In addition, this means that public international law should spell out the choices that should never, ever be given to self-driving machines, as well as the times when people should be involved or in charge of war. Another group of international lawyers has come up with the idea that international moral and ethical standards could lead to the rise of a "super-soft law." From this point of view, a bottom-up method for making laws might be enforceable at the state level. In the midst of the ongoing AI arms race, Janet Koven's counterargument that ethical and moral standards don't work in the international setting was based on facts and made sense. Also, making laws this way from the bottom up makes me wonder about the political will and the need for states to be involved in the process.

There were many different ideas about what AI might do in the future because it has caused an arms race in business, which has now spread to the military. One of these possibilities is a "Sputnik Event" that starts a fierce race between states to develop the best AI. This is because having the best AI could help a state's economic, military, defensive, scientific, and strategic power. In light of the current space war, this means that an event similar to Sputnik could happen with AI. In this way, the AI race could be dangerous to the security of a state, especially a smaller one. But if there is balance, it could be a factor that keeps things stable.

This brings up a lot of questions about whether or not AI can be used as a deterrent and what the likely effects of creating AI will be on the relationships between rivals. As we've already talked about in this chapter, one option is that the security situation will get worse, which could lead to preemptive strikes. Another possibility is the operation of deterrence, which works a lot like MAD with nuclear weapons. This happens when a state knows that an enemy can start its own destructive attack.

From what has been said, AI could make the security problem worse. As a result, the strategy of deterrence, which became popular among IR experts during the Cold War, comes back as a possible answer to the problem at hand. When it comes to AI, though, it 19 could be a problem. First, the aspects of deterrence should be looked into to see if AI is a good tool for deterrence. Hobbes came up with the idea of "classical deterrence," which is made up of self-interest, financial gains, unavoidable conflict, and the application of logic to the international arena. Other researchers, like Cesare Beccaria, have found that the strategy of deterrence is the threat of putting criminals through high costs to stop them from performing crimes.

To put it another way, the rational theory of deterrence is based on the idea that a state can use dormant force to stop an enemy from doing certain things. Classical theory says that deterrence works when one side thinks that the other side has strong military power, when threats are taken seriously, and when the costs of doing something provocative would be bad. Because of this, credible ultimatums and the fear of using force are necessary for deterrence to work. Second, the level of technological progress and the main trend of making weapons should be studied to find out how bad the security dilemma is. It should also be asked if AI would stop a state from attacking, in which case there would be no security dilemma because none of the rival states would be defensive.

People came up with the word "killer robots" in response to the overuse of drones and robots in the military. They did this by looking at how quickly technologies and weapons have changed the art of war over the past few decades. Sharkey's argument says that "killer robots" can't act like humans because they don't have the human intelligence and capabilities needed to make military choices. This term emphasizes the main worry about their ability to do so. For example, this shows that killer robots can only do so much in a war. Autonomous weapon aiming is scary because AI weapons can't tell the difference between military and civilian targets and can hurt other people as well.

The Israeli Harpy is a great example of this problem because it can't tell the difference between a radar station for anti-aircraft defence and a residential building. This makes me wonder if deadly artificial weapons and killer robots can keep up with the speed of making strategic decisions in battle, especially in places with lots of people. Another strong point Garcia makes is that there will always be disruptive changes in international peace and security. This is because using AI as a tool means that basic international rules about how to use force are being broken.

Garcia said that if one AI system was better than another, it would favor the better system if it made it impossible for a state to react. Deterrence won't work if the stronger state can start the first attack. Instead, offense will win. In the same way that nuclear weapons changed the rules of war during the Cold War, Randolph said that AI could make cyberspace and outer space warfare more dangerous because of our growing dependence on cyber capabilities that are easy to break. Even so, experts are excited to come up with a new set of rules for fighting in cyberspace. Some of them have said that the first strike is better in cyberwarfare because it is cheaper, and figuring out who did what will be hard because it is hard to track down. In light of this, the field of international relations should pay more attention to how AI combined with cyber capabilities, nuclear capabilities, or even both of these capabilities can affect the ability to launch a second attack. The literature has talked about the first-strike capability in the cybersphere, but now that AI is being used as a weapon, this argument needs to be looked at again because "killer robots" could make the second-strike capability a better choice because it's not clear how much damage will be done and the immunity of civilians, which is a basic principle of Jus ad bellum, is still not clear.

In the same way, there is a lot of disagreement about whether or not a nuclear war is possible now that cyber and AI technologies are so advanced. Some experts who were against the government said that AI could start a nuclear war because enemies could trick or change AI's abilities. The viewpoint of surveillanceists is similar to that of alarmists who think that advanced AI would make nuclear arsenals exposed, thereby reducing the strategic balance. So, AI could be unstable because it could make the ability to launch a second attack useless. Literature, on the other hand, doesn't talk about how nuclear weapons have been used for deterrence, even though fake news and hacking are common. This could mean that nuclear weapons could stop an AI from being able to launch the first attack, since leaders make choices based on saving cities, cyberspace, and machines.

Since AI could make the security problem worse by creating uncertain technical gaps between big powers and small states, it begs the question of whether small arsenals are a good way to keep people from attacking. When it comes to nuclear weapons, small arsenals have worked well as a deterrent because the literature has shown that having such deadly weapons is a bad thing. As Jervis said, disparity and high military spending could be balanced out by small arsenals and moderate military spending. This would return the ability to launch a second attack. This is how things have been with nuclear bombs. Jervis said that weak and small states usually choose defence and try to work together, but they might use preemptive or preventive strikes because they are in a bad spot. In turn, this makes it less likely that people will work together. If it's true that the first-strike rule works in cyberspace, then weak and small states could start cyberattacks as first strikes. There are two possible outcomes from this: either the defender launches a counterattack using AI, causing additional damage and making the offense stronger; or the defender does nothing, leaving the offense stronger because they have no other choices. If the defender doesn't have any nukes, the weaker state could use AI to start cyberattacks. As a result, it is very likely that a nuclear or AI attack will happen. But things would be very different if a country had cyber, nuclear, and AI capabilities. This is because nuclear capabilities and AI applications that improve cyber protection could make defence the most important thing. More seriously, the strategy of deterrence might depend on where weapons are kept and how the land is shaped. According to Jervis, both conventional and nuclear weapons are used for defence because of their location and the way they are strategically placed. Similar ideas can be used for AI, but right away the offense is more likely to win because of tactical and operational issues; both nuclear and AI weapons are weak, and key infrastructure is easily attacked online. In the end, intimidation might work in the world we live in now.

Along with technology, geography, and other skills, the ability to hurt is a key part of deterrence. Thomas Schelling explained that the ability to hurt is a form of diplomacy that makes threats credible because it is measured by how much pain and suffering a rival could endure. It all comes down to the use of hidden violence and the giving or taking away of pain. This also shows that deterrence needs the defender to talk to the defector about what could happen if they don't follow the rules, rather than just letting the war happen naturally. If they don't, a destructive war will start. Similarly to latent nuclear deterrence, which is based on a country's desire to shorten the time it takes to make a nuclear bomb, and nuclear latency, which is based on the capabilities, AI could be latent because rivals will likely keep developing AI and will look for more capabilities. Cyber capabilities could also hurt the defender and be a real threat.

Also, spending a lot of money on research and development (R&D) and making huge business and medical apps could be signs of hidden violence, since rival states can send ultimatums through steady progress in AI technologies.

There is an idea in the IR literature that "deterrence by denial" stops the enemy from getting more powerful. This argument shows that this idea is false. With the ongoing arms race and growing inequality, it is almost impossible to stop a state from having AI or cyber powers. In nuclear deterrence, past events show that punishment works better than denial. For example, Israel's attack on Iraq's nuclear weapons proved that punishment works better than denial. The best choice for small states is deterrence by denial, but it didn't stop big powers from making more weapons. That's why Paul Davis came up with dissuasion by denial instead of prevention by denial. According to what he said, dissuasion by denial involves figuring out the worst and best possible outcomes of an attack based on what is supposed to happen. In order to do this, the defector should be told about the good things that can happen with de-escalation and the other way around. So, AI prevention might be a mix of hidden violence and denial to stop people from doing bad things. This tells the story of the Cuban Missile Crisis again, which ended without a damaging war because of punishments, concessions, and promises. But AI will mostly work to stop bad behavior through hidden violence and penalties.

The cognitive theory/prospect theory of deterrence, which was created by Jeffrey Bekejikian, is a good way to classify threats from very likely to very unlikely. As a result, this scale would definitely help people make the right choices based on real capabilities, accurate cost calculations, and accurate assessments of how credible threats are. A scale of threats based on Alexander George's different types of coercive diplomacy, such as classic ultimatums that include three main elements: a demand, a sense of urgency, and the threat of punishment; tacit ultimatums that work when they are communicated carefully and effectively; or positive assurances or concessions, would help the person who is breaking the rules figure out how credible the threats are. In the field of artificial intelligence, competitors would try to stop each other because threats are hard to predict and seem real, and neither would risk the status quo, even if they think that leaving would lead to better results than staying.

Since AI needs people to be kept out of the decision-making process, it is also important to look into the psychological aspects of it. Mental factors played a part in how well deterrence worked, especially when it came to nuclear deterrence. The Cuban Missile Crisis is a great example of general deterrence that shows how rivals are happy with the way things are. When AIs talk to each other, the psychological part would not be present. This shows that AI might not be the best way to handle crises, since some situations need more time to be handled diplomatically. This also means that interactions between AIs could make war more likely, which could lead to unexpected results, creating more unpredictability and strategic surprises. This observation is based on the fact that AI military applications are still in their early stages and most people think it's impossible to make AI applications that can analyze and report on all diplomacy efforts. This statement makes sense in theory, but in practice, it only looked at the problem from one side and ignored the other side, which is the role of people in making strategic decisions. Even though there is a high chance of data manipulation and mistakes when humans are in the loop, the psychological factor would play a big role in the expected AI prevention. It's too bad that the IR literature that looked into how technical progress affects security didn't look at all the possible outcomes.

As a result, AI could make the security problem worse while the commercial arms race goes on. However, it is very unlikely that AI will be banned, as some experts have suggested. There have been arguments in the literature about whether AI weapons are acceptable and whether AI itself should be banned or just military uses of AI should be banned. As Glaser said, states can work together in the security dilemma if they can separate the attack and defence variables and know what their enemies are trying to do. In order to set rules for AI research and development and for using AI in wartime situations, the IR literature and the AI literature should work together. Even though it's hard to write an NPT-like agreement or regulate it, Glaser said that writing arms control agreements is the best thing that could be done because they would encourage countries to stop attacking each other.

AI is seen as the next big thing in weapons of mass destruction, so it's worth thinking about whether Mutually Assured Destruction could happen and whether, like during and after the Cold War, mutual kill through AI would make superpowers less likely to attack each other or make things worse.

The way Kenneth Waltz argues that nuclear deterrence is about hurting the aggressor rather than totally defeating them agrees with the way Jervis and Schelling see it. While Kenneth's point of view on how nuclear deterrence gets rid of the most important parts of war is worth thinking about, his argument about how nuclear weapons get rid of the most important parts of defence was wrong because nuclear weapons have made mutual fear very strong. Jervis pointed out that nuclear deterrence has made the world more stable because wars have changed the political values of many countries and caused those countries to change how they see the world, what they want, and why they want to fight. So, general stability means that nuclear weapons may help keep the peace between enemies by making them less likely to change things, even if they have the power to do so. Also, the idea that non-nuclear states couldn't do escalatory acts because of nuclear weapons has been disproved by the fact that most countries are stable. People who are against nuclear defence haven't thought about how the imbalance of power makes the security problem worse. This also shows that having nuclear power is a destabilizing factor and doesn't always mean a decisive military win. So, contrary to the beliefs of strong deterrence opponents, nuclear deterrence has worked in the real world by stopping very damaging wars and keeping things stable during both periods of conflict and peace.

Mutually Assured Destruction (MAD), a type of nuclear deterrence, was praised by international relations experts. AI-MAD could be a useful tactic since there is disagreement in the research about whether MAD can be used in the cyberspace.

One of the main ideas behind MAD is that both sides are open to retaliation and could start a second strike. So, the fact that both sides were weak and afraid of each other helped general deterrence work during the Cuban Missile Crisis by pushing the leaders of the two superpowers toward a peaceful solution instead of a violent conflict. In this way, having more nuclear weapons means there is a better chance of successful deterrence, since both sides will be scared of the terrible results of a second strike. During the height of the Cuban Missile Crisis, the use of general deterrence that changed the risk of war helped stop a disaster. This also means that deterrence worked pretty well because of different goals and nuclear parity instead of nuclear superiority. This also shows that deterrence works because it encourages leaders to avoid war and accept things as they are when that is the best thing that could happen.

So, the AI literature should talk about how something like the Cuban Missile Crisis could happen in the AI and what would make people afraid of each other: would it be cities, machines, computer systems, or too much of a good thing? The Cuban Missile Crisis happened between two countries. But what if something similar happened in the region? Would differences in technology make regional enemies go AI-MAD? Since psychological factors were very important in the Cuban Missile Crisis, could people get involved in a country's plan to help AI weapons and killer robots find the right targets in the AI world? As "the indivisibility of control" is at the heart of MAD, the AI literature should also look into what AI means when humans are out-of-the-loop and when they are over-the-loop, as well as which situation would be the most damaging. Also, the AI literature should do a similar study on the effects of AI and how bad the security problem is based on how much a country depends on technology and how strong its defence is.

The word "Mutually Assured Deletion/Delibitation" has become popular in the field of international relations. However, some have said that in the cyber world, the first-strike is better. As a result, if going for the first strike becomes the best option and offense wins in the cybersphere, AI-MAD could be used instead of the so-called "Mutually Assured Deletion/Delebitation" because massive destruction is what would happen in a normal war, cyberwar, or even a nuclear war. Even though Fairbanks said that "damage limitation" wasn't the main goal of nuclear MAD, "damage limitation" could be too much for today's MAD because it's too powerful for humans to manage. However, this doesn't mean that AI laws shouldn't only focus on limiting damage, since the damage could be worse than in other types of warfare.

It's also not clear that AI skills are better than computer skills. There were some who said that AI could beat cyber ones because it could find holes in other cyber defence systems and use them. The other side of using AI is that it can help a country's cyber defences by fixing holes in its own security systems and keeping them safe from hacks made possible by AI. Along the same lines, AI could make disinformation harder by spreading fake news on a large scale. It could also fight disinformation by using bots and algorithms to find, analyze, disrupt, vet, block, and screen fake or unauthentic data. AI would be a useful tool for intelligence collecting because it would collect a huge amount of data, but it could be tricked into thinking it wasn't real. In this way, AI creates a security problem and shows "mutual vulnerability," which further suggests that defence could win. This is more proof that self-deterrence would work, since weaker players can get around differences by using other skills and causing political pain. This also shows that attack could win in a situation where there is a difference and no nuclear weapons.

AI-MAD is very likely because AI applications could affect a state's military, economic, and information power, as well as its nuclear superiority. This is because AI can make both sides vulnerable and cause collateral damage. AI-enabled apps would shift the balance of power between 27 emerging and developed countries, especially with the massive use of 3D printing technology, which will speed up the creation of very disruptive technologies and make it easier for weapons to get into more hands. The AI arms race would speed up because Additive Manufacturing is a cheap technology that can be used in many different ways. AI MAD is not impossible, since machine takeover, which has four possible outcomes, could make security worse, especially in connected societies.

Like nuclear MAD, the expected AI-MAD could be based on things like the indivisibility of control, mutual fears of retaliation, serious damage, the psychological factor, parity/disparity, sparing, latent force, and error. Similar to cyber MAD, the proposed AI MAD could be based on attribution, prices, and the level of dependence on technology. In contrast to nuclear and cyber MAD, AI MAD could also look into the roles of people and tools in command and control in the military.

To sum up, the literature should focus on how AI could be harmful in a world where a lot of cyberpower is used; it should look for ways to improve security and also ask if MAD applies to AI technology.

Conceptual Model

It is said in both cyber and IR literature that cyber threats could be stronger than AI. This chapter will build on the case for AI's huge potential and bright future while also looking at the cases against AI's potential uses versus cyber capabilities. This chapter will talk about what AI might mean for both cyber and nuclear powers. It will also look at the direct relationship between cyber-offensive and cyber-defensive capabilities, as well as the relationship between nuclear capabilities and AI capabilities.

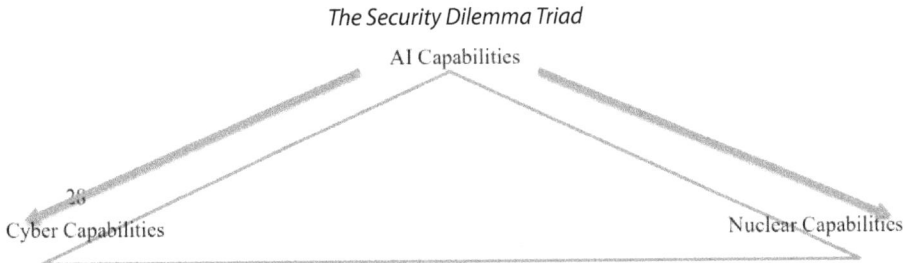

The Security Dilemma Triad

In order to do this, this chapter creates a "Security Dilemma Triad" with three key parts: cyber, AI, and nuclear capabilities. This chapter will talk about the three security dilemmas: the relationship between AI and cyber capabilities, the relationship between AI and nuclear capabilities, and the relationship between nuclear and cyber capabilities after AI capabilities have been added.

In order to find out whether offense or defence will be stronger, four different scenarios will be created:

a. When a state possesses nuclear capabilities + AI capabilities + cyber capabilities = defence is dominant;

b. When a state does not possess nuclear capabilities, but possesses AI capabilities + cyber capabilities = offense is dominant;

c. When a state possesses nuclear capabilities + cyber capabilities but does not possess AI capabilities = defence is dominant;

d. When a state possesses nuclear capabilities + AI capabilities but lacks cyber capabilities = defence is dominant.

In the first situation, this chapter assumes that defence is stronger than offense because AI can beat cyber capabilities, which disproves the idea that nuclear weapons are weak against cyberattacks. In the second situation, offense is more important than defence because nuclear deterrence is either not working or not present. On the other hand, AI could improve cyber capabilities by attacking weak spots in the cyber system. In the third situation, too, defence is strong, even though AI isn't present, because of nuclear deterrence. In the fourth situation, defence is the most important factor because a state has nuclear weapons that can be used as a second strike.

The above-mentioned scenarios and the "Security Dilemma Triangle/Triad" were made to see how AI could change how states think about their cyber and nuclear powers and doctrines. At first, it will look into the AI offense-defence dominance. Then, the effects of AI on both cyber and nuclear attack and defence will be talked about. After that, it will use the parts of nuclear Mutually Assured Destruction as factors.

AI Power Equilibrium

It makes sense to look into which side of attack or defence is stronger in AI before looking into the possibility of an AI MAD. Because people are becoming less important in AI, it makes sense to think about two possible ways that AI could be used in the military: People don't have much power over AI applications; no one is watching over AI applications. So, this piece assumes that AI wants to be able to launch a second attack. Even so, it is impossible to say who is responsible for breaking the Law of Armed Conflicts and the Geneva Conventions, which makes an attacking AI strike more likely to succeed. This doesn't always mean that attack is the most important thing in AI. Instead, defence is most important in AI when people are in charge of the machines. On the other hand, AI could favor attack when humans aren't around to control things and when a military's command and control depend on cyber capabilities.

The Implications of AI in Terms of the Element of MAD:

Based on that conclusion, the following section will cover the implications of AI on both nuclear and cyber capabilities in order to investigate the offense-defence dominance in the abovementioned scenarios:

The Implications of AI on Both Cyber and Nuclear Capabilities Separately

Capability	AI		Cyber		Nuclear	
	Human-Over-the-Loop	Human-Out-of-the-Loop	Human-Over-the-Loop	Human-Out-of-the-Loop	Human-Over-the-Loop	Human-Out-of-the-Loop
Independent Variables / MAD						
Scale of Destruction	Destructive	Highly destructive	Destructive	Highly Destructive	Highly Destructive	Hightly Destructive
Proportion a lit)' of Punishment	Severe		Not Severe		Severe	
The Demonstrative Aspect	Deterrence by punishment	Deterrence by Punishment	Deterrence by Denial	Deterrence by Denial	Deterrence by Punishment	Deterrence by Punishment
Interests	Security-seeking		Malicous		Security-seeking	
Calculations	Right	Mistaken/Right	Mistaken	Mistaken/Right	Right	Mistaken/Right
Biasness	Possible	Highly Possible	Highly Possible	Highly Possible	Slightly Possible	Slightly Possible
Level of Communication	Strong	Absent	Weak	Absent	Strong	Absent
Parity/Disparity	War is highly unlikely	War is highly likely	War is likely	War is highly likely	War is highly unlikely	War is less likely
Uncertainly	High	Very High	High	Very High	High	Very High
Error	Human	Machine	Human	Machine	Human	Machine
Command and Control	Reliable	Highly Irreliable	Irreliable	Irreliable	Reliable	Irreliable
Strike-Capability'	Second-strike	Second-strike	First-strike	First-strike	Second-strike	Second-strike
Possibility of Disruption	Likely	Very Likely	Very Likely	Highly Likely	Highly Unlikely	Unlikely

Perception of Threats	High	Very High	Very High	Very High	High	Very High
Offense/Defence	Defence	Offense	Offense	Defence	Defence	Defence
Deterrence	Successful	Slightly Successful	Fail	Successful	Successful	Slightly Successful

To build on what was said above, having conventional, nuclear, and cyber military weapons along with AI ones helps states look at the situation from different points of view. Among these points of view are: AI skills don't affect other skills and vice versa; other skills could help a state's position if it has highly advanced AI software and applications; other military skills are valuable if a state has basic AI software; and other military skills are invaluable if a state has advanced AI software and applications. In turn, this helps countries figure out if small AI arsenals could build a structure like MAD while also having other combat skills. States might be less likely to start a preemptive or preventative strike if they only have a small arsenal of AI weapons.

From now on, this chapter assumes that two nuclear states could set up mutual AI defence. Asymmetric deterrence, on the other hand, might work between a nuclear state and a non-nuclear state. This is because the nuclear state would have fully autonomous AI applications that would make the non-nuclear state less likely to start the first military strike. It could, however, use asymmetric powers to stop its enemy from starting an AI or conventional attack before it does. For the stronger state, it could fight offensively instead of using up all of its nuclear weapons, which AI could easily defeat.

Methodology

To find out how AI might affect the security problem, I talked to policymakers and experts in the field and read a lot of secondary writing on how AI can be used as a weapon.

Interviews included: personal and phone interviews with a security expert/military advisor, two university professors, two ambassadors and a researcher as follows:

1. Dr/General Mahmoud Khalaf, advisor at Nasser Military Academy;
2. Dr Dalal Mahmoud Al-Sayed, a professor of political science at Faculty of economic and Political Science at Cairo University and Nasser Military Academy;

3. Dr Waleed Rashad, assistant professor at the National Center for Social and Criminological Research;
4. Ambassador Karim Haggag, professor of practice at the American University in Cairo;
5. Ambassador Aly Erfan; Program Director at the School of Global Affairs and Public Policy at the American University in Cairo;
6. Mona Soliman, doctoral candidate at the Faculty of economic and Political Science at Cairo University and a researcher at International Politics Journal.

Variables and Investigation Methods

The conceptual framework talks about four scenarios that need to be looked into. The dependent variables are: reliance on technology, sparing, expected utility and cost-benefit analysis, calculus of war, balance of power, relatively of power and comparison of military and non-military capabilities, parity/disparity, margin of error, levels of communication, intentions, the scope of human role in the decision-making process, and the degree to which people are involved. Geography and people will also be looked at to see how they affect the strategic depth of a state. These dependent variables, human-over-the-loop and human-out-of-the-loop, will help us see changes that happen based on the two independent variables. So, it came up with two possible outcomes for AI deterrence: either it worked or it didn't, depending on how much people controlled machines, how much they relied on technology, and how AI uses would affect nuclear and cyber policies.

Findings

What is Artificial Intelligence?

The term "artificial intelligence" comes from the word "intelligence," which means "an agent's computational ability to perform tasks and reach goals in different environments." That being said, Artificial Intelligence is when a machine can think and act like a person, including being able to recognize patterns, reason, and use neuro-linguistic programming. It can also learn from experience and adjust to new situations. The US Defence Science Board said that AI is the computation of things that people used to only be able to do, like making decisions, perceiving things, and talking. This meaning of AI shows that computation and automation are linked to human thought processes, reasoning, behaviors, ideals, and the accuracy and dependability of their work.

So, the main idea behind AI technology is that machines can copy human traits on their own. Expert systems, machine learning, natural language processing, and AI planning are all parts of AI technology.

The writing on AI has led to three different types of AI, which reflect how AI has changed over the past few decades: Artificial Narrow Intelligence is a type of technology that acts and thinks like a small group of humans. Even though it can't create codes, it's a very advanced technology. Artificial general intelligence is a more advanced technology than narrow artificial intelligence because it can copy a bigger range of human behaviors. AI is a type of technology that acts like people and thinks it was made by humans. AI that goes beyond human intelligence is called artificial superintelligence. AI makers think that Artificial Super Intelligence will make human intelligence unnecessary and end the exclusivity of human intelligence.

The Possible Implications of AI on Other Military Capabilities :

Cyber Capabilities

Cyber capabilities are the skills and resources that a country can have to protect itself from cyberattacks or project power in cyberspace. These skills and resources can be used in normal, business, nuclear, logistical, military, and other areas. The power of a state is affected by both its defensive and offensive skills, which can be used actively or passively.

There are many problems and weak spots in today's protection systems. This is how most attacks on cybersecurity systems work: they start with research, move on to weaponization, delivery, and finally exploit. What's more important are the problems that come with gathering cyber intelligence, such as having to constantly adapt to the huge amounts of different types of data that are flowing at exponential rates and the fact that intrusion detection and prevention systems aren't good at either finding malware by looking for strange patterns or showing patterns of normal, known networks.

According to the basic offense-defence theory, offense seems to be stronger after such a quick look. This is because offensive capabilities are always getting better than defensive ones, and defensive weaknesses are growing, such as the lack of privacy, integrity, and availability of data, as well as the fact that cyberwarfare isn't a one-sided battle. Like nuclear uncertainty, constructive ambiguity is one of the most important parts of cyber warfare. But since AI is being used in so many applications, this finding needs more research because AI could make or make less of the cybersecurity problem that states use offensive, defensive, or mixed cyber tools when there aren't any agreed upon cyber rules.

In the same way, using off-the-shelf technology and turning Big Data into a weapon makes cybersecurity even harder because governments can make records of every single soldier in their enemies' armies.

The use of AI in the digital world can go in two different directions. With its ability to predict and automate, AI could help solve the cyber security problem and make cyber defence stronger by fixing the ecosystem's core problems and holes. So, AI capabilities would make the Integrated Security Approach more effective. An all-around approach includes early warnings, choosing and using the best defences against possible cyberattacks, finding potential attacks in case the first ones don't work, and the right responses. AI's offensive and defensive abilities have shown that it can improve cybersecurity by finding and fixing flaws in cyber defence systems while also probing, manipulating, and spoofing adversaries' systems. It can also find software bugs and take defensive and offensive actions like self-patching, which stops cyberattacks before they start. Made Cyber Defence Possible).

On the other hand, the bad side of AI is shown by a new group of AI programs that can hide their identities from cyber defence systems and wait until they find their targets, like Stuxnet. These programs can also avoid being detected by adversarial defence systems by watching how they work and what they look for. Additionally, data diet and algorithm bias are often thought of as the "Cassandra" of algorithms that don't work right. Information attacks like spoofing, denial-of-service, eavesdropping, and exploitation are easier for warriors to carry out when they use a lot of tools and technology.

AI use in the online world seems to be like a double-edged sword. It makes cyber security and cyber deterrence better, but it also makes cyber spread worse. More and more advanced cyber powers could help a state reach its strategic goals by forcing others to do what it wants. They could also be useful for using brute force, which helps a state reach its tactical goals through kinetic or non-kinetic cyberattacks. Cyberattacks are a way for states to get real concessions from their enemies by making it harder for them to fight back or defend themselves with traditional or cyber weapons. In this situation, the threat of cyberwarfare combined with AI could be a quick way to scare people away and a useful way to use brute force against stronger enemies who have very powerful conventional weapons. Also, the spread of AI is a deterrent for states in the online plane, since every use has an opposite use that makes it useless.

Even though AI improves cyber defence, different states use it in different ways to scare people away from cyber threats. In these situations, the goal of preemptive cyber deterrence is sometimes to show that you can mess up or get into security systems without destroying them completely and get to private data. This is an example of how cyber intimidation is often based on math.

Nuclear Capabilities

The fast growth of AI makes people wonder about the durability and survivability of nuclear systems, as well as their ability to defend themselves against strikes and get through the defences of nuclear arsenals. The normal combination of AI and nuclear weapons, along with the fact that they are fully autonomous and no one is involved in making nuclear decisions, is two-fold. That could throw off the delicate strategic balance between nuclear states, leading to terrible effects and rising tensions between nuclear states and nonnuclear states, on the other hand.

The problem with AI's effects on nuclear security is that nuclear weapons can be easily damaged by strong computer attacks meant to mess up machine learning and make them less effective. Such a terrible flaw in the AI system could make cyber vulnerabilities worse, but it could also make nuclear safety and reliability less reliable, since nuclear weapons depend on sharing information in real time for targets. Also, full automation where people are not involved would definitely have effects on strategic security, leading to acts of escalation and an arms race. Because militaries are becoming more automated and digitalized, algorithms in nuclear weapons systems could make mistakes when assessing and responding. This is known as machine error, and it could be very dangerous for digitally-independent states that make bad decisions based on bad data. The "no first use" strategy might not be as good with AI because of mistakes that happen by accident.

There are many risks that come with turning nuclear command and control systems into digital ones. One of these is that communication lines could be hacked, which would make it hard to trust the data being analyzed. Similarly, the Integrated Threat Warning/Assessment system could not work properly if some of its nodes—such as intelligence centers, the missile warning center, and ground- and space-based assets—were hacked or used to send or receive messages. "AI could make the system less stable." It could also "undermine nuclear strategic stability because of its asymmetrical way" by threatening the infrastructure that supports a nuclear command and control system.

A shocking claim stops the idea that AI could improve the ability to launch a second nuclear attack. An expert on general adversarial networks says it might be true, even though it is very unlikely, when states use adversarial manipulation strikes to stop their enemies from keeping track of their nuclear arsenals.

In the same way that AI can help with cyber deterrence, it could also help protect nuclear command and control systems by making them easier to find, better early warning systems, and giving people the tools they need to do accurate cross-analysis of data. This is why some people at a workshop put together by RAND claimed that AI could fix the problems at the heart of the nuclear arms control regime and create new ways to keep arms in check.

In a strange way, escalatory actions by both nuclear and non-nuclear states could make the arms race worse and force nuclear states to update their nuclear arsenals.

Nuclear Versus Cyber

From a technical point of view, cyber capabilities are a threat to nuclear weapons because cyberattacks could change nuclear command and control when it is not secured and when cyber resilience is not working, along with mistakes made by humans. In addition, AI could send false signals or share fake information to stop cyberattacks on nuclear sites by manipulating other AI. Still, AI helps make defence systems better, even nuclear ones.

We need to look again at the main case that AI could weaken nuclear deterrence and lead to nuclear war. Although, just from a technical point of view, if AI capabilities are well-protected and very advanced, they could fix cyber flaws and lessen the damage they do to nuclear capabilities. According to Dr./General Mahmoud Khalaf, a military adviser at the Nasser Academy, AI has nothing to do with nukes. From a scientific point of view, he did admit that AI has bad effects on nuclear command and control systems, counterforce, and the ability to survive. Because of this, cyber powers have not been able to remove nuclear deterrence.

States are forced to choose between cyber attack and cyber defence because of nuclear vulnerabilities. This kind of problem usually comes up because of how uncertain it is about how long nuclear systems can last and how reliable they are. These systems could be quietly broken into and hacked through dormant and stealth operations. So, during times of peace, a country might not know that someone has broken into its nuclear system for days, months, or even years. This could have a negative impact on its military decisions, deterrence policy, security strategy, and nuclear posture. When there is war, things are very different because there may not be enough knowledge, which could lead to an attack in response based on wrong calculations.

As a result, the rise of AI technology could help solve this problem because it can both solve mysteries and make predictions. AI could help leaders make good choices by being a helpful tool. Also, hackers often get into sensitive nuclear sites and systems fail all the time in nuclear weapons systems. Because of this, states would be less likely to use their cyber powers because they wouldn't know how far ahead their enemies were. In the same way, attackers would be less likely to try to attack nuclear arsenals of enemies. As Dr. Waleed Rashad, an assistant professor at the National Center for Social and Criminological Research, says, this shows that people are important in nuclear policy because they are reasonable.

AI + Cyber + Nuclear:

To sum up, technical-wise, AI could undermine nuclear deterrence, especially when humans are absent, but politically speaking, the AI technology cannot overturn nuclear deterrence as long as there is a meaningful degree of human control.

Analysis

Even though there isn't much real-world proof that AI could be used in military ways that are bad, we need to define AI in order to look into how it would change the relationships between states and the foundations of the international peace system.

International relations experts and lawyers have only looked at how AI can be destructive and how it can act on its own, without attempting to define what it is. They made a mistake by confusing AI as a tool that can be used to make a weapon and AI as a weapon system itself. They thought AI could be used "as a state weapon," which was not true. "AI is not a weapon," but rather a tool that can be added to a weapon system and "can serve as an enabler for cyber and conventional weapons, as well as weapons of mass destruction." It would be very bad to label AI as a weapon because comparing it to other types of weapons, like nuclear and conventional weapons, would mean that research would only look at the effects of AI itself, without looking at how its military uses might affect other types of weapons. If AI had been labeled as a weapon instead of a technology, states would have depended on it a lot to reach their military goals, even though it has the potential to do a lot of damage and cause a lot of problems. This means that "the development in the uses of weapons" is what "the weaponization of AI" means.

According to this definition, using AI as a weapon "makes the security dilemma worse because it can either improve the military capability of a state in symmetric relations or it can increase the military disparity between states not only in terms of new capability but also in terms of attribution." It can also be used as a weapon by non-state actors. Aside from the legal issue, the security problem is made worse by the fact that skills are not always the same or different and there is also uncertainty about "the impacts of using AI on military decision-making and the calculus of war." On top of that, there is a lot of doubt about AI apps' ability to counter-react and respond to sudden attacks, whether they are done on purpose or by accident. This is the main problem with security in this day and age.

There's no question that using AI in war will change the way wars are fought in radical ways. Ambassador Aly Erfan thinks that AI or any other technological progress "would make the decision to go to war easy." He is talking about how drones are used too much instead of people to reduce the number of deaths. At first look, this point of view seems partly correct, but it doesn't take into account the fact that progress in technology could increase the causes and make the effects worse. When nuclear weapons were used in the Second World War in 1945, it was a great example of how progress in technology could be very harmful and cause a lot of deaths. This shows that states should never rush into war because it will lead to bad results. And the problem isn't just about what causes what; it's also about cost-benefit analysis, state responsibility, military strength, level of technological progress, geography, equal or unequal powers, strategic climate, and so on. More importantly, war calculus is based on mutual vulnerability, an uncertain win, acts that escalate the conflict, and retaliation. The use of AI in armies adds a new factor to war calculations: how useful it is to use AI to make a certain weapon system work.

One place to think about how AI could make or break the efficiency of a weapons system is in air defence systems. From a military point of view, commanders could figure out how AI would help them use air defence systems more successfully and how it would help them move and react quickly. AI, for example, cuts the time it takes to respond from two minutes when a person is in the loop to ten to twenty seconds when a person is not in the loop. As Dr./General Mahmoud Khalaf said, the whole point is to pick and use the best weapon to make sure a quick reaction. To put it another way, the leaders of a country should know what kind of weapon the enemy is using and should quickly reply with the best weapon 40. Because of this, there is a difference between being able to find and identify an enemy's advanced weapon and being able to quickly and effectively reply with the right means or weapons. So, AI and other new tools would not make it easy to decide to go to war.

The cyber security problem is made worse by the fact that there is no set limit on what actions could be considered an act of aggression in the cyberspace. This, along with AI's "dual-use nature and the potential of weaponizing AI civilian applications," makes the problem even worse. AI can be used for both civilian and military purposes, so an enemy could change a civilian AI program so that it could be used for military purposes. Because of this, the AI security problem would get worse, since leaders and soldiers should know about a weapon's technology and abilities so they can work well together. Then there is the problem of attribution, which is tricky because the defence might not be able to figure out what kind of AI application it is.

As AI is usually a new way for the military to use technology, it could be said that it is two-fold because it could improve both cyber defence and cyber deterrence and could make the nuclear strategy less effective. At the moment, there isn't a clear proof. From now on, Ambassador Erfan hinted that how much an AI program runs a weapon system is very important to a state's plans.

Most of the academic debate believed that cyber deterrence wouldn't work for a number of reasons, including: Since cyberspace is an open battlefield, the lack of internet control does not make the security problem worse. In its traditional form, cyber deterrence doesn't work very well because the internet doesn't have rules and it's hard to figure out who did something, especially if the attacker wants to stay anonymous. But cyber deterrence will work if AI apps are added to cyber defence systems. AI improves cyber defence by finding weak spots in your system and impersonating an enemy's system from a technical point of view. AI makes the security problem worse from a political point of view because it is a more advanced version of cyber capabilities. It lets states break into each other's sensitive systems, like military, intelligence, and critical infrastructure, collect accurate data, and "have a vivid picture of an adversary's capabilities." It changes the balance of power as well. In order to solve the cyber security problem, countries use AI, drones, and robots for preemptive cyber deterrence. This is because the victim will stop an attack on itself if it is a broad one that could hurt civilians.

Most of the writing on international relations (IR) is written from the point of view of alarmists who say that AI would threaten nuclear weapons and weaken nuclear deterrence. In theory, this point of view is great because "the nuclear C2 can be violated by cyber capabilities since hackers can hack the normal system of air mines." I think we need to learn more about nuclear defence, though. As a start, "AI could be used as an enabler in terms of nuclear policy, which includes targeting, command and control, early warning, assessing the damage from possible battles, and figuring out who is responsible." From a technical point of view, AI can protect nuclear weapons because some AI applications are made to find and tell of nuclear proliferation early on. Because of this, AI apps can help people and decision-makers (who use skills-based behaviors) plan out what to do in a nuclear policy. Then there will be no danger to nuclear deterrence as long as the nuclear command and control system is well-structured, well-protected, and well-defended, and "defensive measures, including data encryption, are taken." For this reason, it seems unlikely that AI would switch from a defensive nuclear policy to a "preemptive" one, as Ambassador Haggag said, as long as people are still in the loop. This kind of argument could only work if fully autonomous applications are built into the nuclear weapons system and people don't have any control over robots.

The destructive power of AI technology can be on par with that of nuclear weapons, even though it is not as powerful as any known weapon system. Assuming that an AI program runs a nuclear weapon system, it will cause more damage than traditional weapons that are also controlled by AI. When people aren't involved, this theory makes sense. Politics are more important than facts, so the difference between how safe nuclear weapons are and how advanced cyber powers are could be lessened by using AI early warning systems and having real people watch over them.

AI Offense, Defence, and the Effectiveness of Deterrence

The bad use of AI should make attack more common in cyberspace if state A has strong cyberdefences and state B has weak ones. There is no one opinion on whether AI is offensive or protective. For example, Ambassador Erfan said that AI deterrence might be possible, but he also said that it might be hard to tell whether attack or defence will be more important. He thinks that "establishing AI deterrence will be more difficult, if not impossible," because he thinks that it is hard enough to use nuclear weapons as deterrence. In the same way, Dr. Dalal Al-Sayed said that AI deterrence is impossible because the cyber world is so open. Since deterrence is built on assumptions and made-up situations, Ambassador Haggag's point about how complicated it is will be right on the mark. Still, this doesn't mean that deterrence can't work with other weapons and new technologies. This is because deterrence is a policy or strategy that helps states make plans based on the strategic climate to make their security stronger. Having "the political will to deter and the ability to establish deterrence" is what deterrence is all about.

Based on the principles of cyber deterrence, defence would be the most important thing in the AI world because AI has the ability to break in, manipulate, and cause problems. It is defence that wins when it can show strength in the cyber/AI realm and when it can react and act quickly. States sometimes use the Internet of Things as a tool to show how weak enemy cyber defence systems are, which stops people from attacking them online. This shows that letting people know about cyberweaknesses is enough to stop them.

AI Mutual Assured Destruction

Mutually Assured Destruction and nuclear defence were both caused by the Cold War in the 20th century. In the same way, the AI race and the Cold War of the 21st century could make an AI system like MAD possible. The assumption that this is true should not be taken for granted, though, because an AI MAD could only work if humans have some control over AI apps and are involved in making decisions, especially at the strategic level.

1. Humans are out-of-the-loop

In the near future, such a thing is very unlikely to happen, but it should be thought about because AI combat will be the next war because it is cheap and can cause few physical injuries. As a result, the mechanization of war could make this scenario's results worse, similar to the second scenario, which we will talk about later. In this situation, people would not be able to control machines, and they would also give up control over military decisions to machines and AI apps. As Mona Soliman said, this means that tools like robots and drones will play a big part in future wars instead of people. And people's only job would be to keep track of the real and human causes. It was also impossible to guess how much damage would be done, and if strikes or calculations went wrong, it was impossible to lessen the damage or even keep it under control. Naturally, fully autonomous AI programs can do a lot of damage, and C2 systems are very irritable. This will definitely change "the purpose of war in the cyber sphere from trying to influence an adversary's calculus to destroying it." So, offense would be more important if the psychological part wasn't there. This is more proof that a cycle of attacks in response to attacks would likely happen over and over again. On top of that, the lack of responsibility would make things even worse, especially since states have been very unwilling to set a cyber threshold. So, it would be hard to punish a machine or even stop the government from being responsible, which also means that deterrence has failed. If fully autonomous weapons took over other powers, they would destroy and disrupt a lot of things, so deterrence would fail and there would be no clear winner.

The problem of attribution, the fact that it's hard to know ahead of time what will happen when machines interact with each other, and the fact that machines don't always follow international law and legal rules make deterrence more difficult and cause instability in crisis situations. To make things even worse in 44, an AI system could protect itself if it thought it was about to be stopped, and it could respond by starting a nuclear attack, which would go against the principle of mutually assured destruction. The ability to launch a second strike could also be threatened by the use of underwater drones.

In theory, the only way for machine-based deterrence to work in such a bad situation is for data to be updated regularly and people to check on things every once in a while. Because of this, robots can make mistakes too. In a very unlikely and hypothetical situation in which machines control firepower and other weapon systems, many types of hidden violence could be used, such as: if AI was built into a nuclear weapon or a WMD, punishment or retaliation would have worked; if AI was built into a cyber defence system, disruption would have worked; and if AI was used through a conventional weapon, det If something like this happened, would the heads of the states step in at the end of the day? We don't know the definitive answer to this question because we don't know how much machines would be able to behave like people.

2. Humans are over-the-loop

In this case, states would still be the main players because people and non-state actors would not be able to make or even use such highly advanced AI technology, especially ones that are usually made for military use. It's true that states would be the main players in this situation, but companies, terrorist groups, and regular people could also use and make AI apps using the method of addictive manufacturing. They could also "weaponize" AI apps. Also, the idea of taking over humans' roles would be very unlikely, since humans would be the ones who decide to go to war. When people and machines work together, AI apps would be used at the tactical and operational levels, while people would make the strategic decisions.

Based on military considerations, AI deterrence is possible, even if a country doesn't have nuclear weapons, because leaders will be afraid to make the first strike. Also, the growing AI race in 45 business and military areas makes it harder to keep up. To stay ahead, you need the most advanced AI applications to stop and attack enemies, as well as the ability to create national AI applications. This means that each state should have the most powerful AI tools to use against its enemy. Unlike other common and uncommon military technologies, AI applications should be made in the United States. This will increase the power and impact of states. AI warfare is like information warfare in that the person with the most data and knowledge always wins. Artificial intelligence (AI) warfare is a new type of conflict in which both sides try to "destroy data" in order to stop each other from acting. But this shows the problem with AI-enabled warfare: you need to have and collect more data without being caught so that you don't have to worry about people doing bad things to get back a lot of data. If both sides hack into and change data, it will be impossible to say who won because the data will be neutralized. For example, this shows that data neutralization and turning Big Data into a weapon both lead to neutralization on the battlefield because military leaders don't know how reliable their weapon systems are or what they can do. This also means that neutralizing data can help neutralize weapons. The defender should "respond effectively and in a timely fashion, as well as should choose the most appropriate weapon to respond," which means that weapons neutralization can be a problem at both the operational and tactical levels.

The use of AI as a weapon could be a deterrent and keep things stable in symmetrical conflicts because it can be neutralized and both sides are vulnerable. Since cyber force and regular military force are not the same, AI deterrence could also work in asymmetric wars that are often linked to crisis instability. "AI could make preemptive deterrence and defence more effective" by keeping cyber force separate from other types of military force. But this kind of classification shouldn't ignore the fact that other kinds of force can also work. One could say that online force is just as effective as regular force and that it should be used along with regular force. As states are logical, it doesn't make sense to limit asymmetric math to the cybersphere. In asymmetric conflicts, deterrence generally means showing that you can attack or defend yourself without causing a lot of damage. Using traditional war calculations and AI preemptive deterrence, a stronger state 46 could stop an enemy from using AI and similar technologies for bad purposes. On the other hand, a weaker state could use cyber deterrence and build up more cyber capabilities to show it can attack a stronger state. In order to do that, preemption would be added to the defensive strategy. In asymmetric deterrence, neither the cat nor the mouse can win, just like in the game of cat and mouse.

To sum up, cost reduction makes states think twice. So, an AI structure that works like mutually assured destruction is possible because "the goal is not destruction, but gaining a political benefit by making the costs of offense very high and intolerable."

In both symmetric and asymmetric conflicts, the defensive doctrine would win in the world of AI as long as people could lower the level of uncertainty and more or less open lines of communication to keep cities from being completely destroyed and to keep cyber systems and AI-enabled machines from going down.

By using this on other weapon systems that can be improved by AI, AI could keep a second-strike capability even though it's becoming more unclear what kind of damage will be caused by the uncontrolled use of nuclear and conventional weapons. This shows that AI deterrence would work even better because leaders of states are generally motivated by wanting to keep their people safe. This also means that the planned system for AI MAD would work with nuclear MAD, so a defensive policy would be used.

For AI deterrence to work, states should use hidden violence and real threats to make enemies do bad things or stop them from doing them. Ambassadors Erfan and Haggag both said that attribution and responsibility are important parts of deterrence. Just like nuclear and cyber deterrence, AI deterrence could include "deterrence by punishment" like an AI attack in response and "deterrence by denial" like making AI smarter. The state that was trying to stop the threat could use "the threat of disruption to a state's political, fiscal, power, weapon, financial, and electoral systems," which was different from other deterrence strategies. As Ambassador Haggag said, AI can damage valuable things as a punishment or stop people from using AI apps and other features. Because of this, nuclear weapons are not the only thing that can cause destruction, as Ambassador Haggag said, because stopping important facilities from working could cause total destruction. AI deterrence could also include the fear of mass manipulation or penetration, which would stop and disable important systems, especially weapon systems. In this way, AI deterrence could be a strategy in and of itself.

However, there are situations where latent violence could be used based on the tools and skills that people besides AI have, such as: The use of punishment as a deterrent will be used when two nuclear states have AI capabilities, both because they have nuclear weapons and because their AI capabilities are equal. When both a nuclear state and a non-nuclear state have AI capabilities, the use of preemption and denial will be effective. When two non-nuclear states have AI and cyber capabilities, the use of preemption and denial will be effective.

Conclusion

Based on what has been said, AI as a weapon makes it harder for states to protect themselves in both symmetric and asymmetric battles. Based on the in-depth study, deterrence might work, and because of mutual vulnerability and neutralization, an AI-like MAD structure is likely to form. Still, there's no way to know for sure that leaders won't get things wrong because of the growing uncertainty and their heavy dependence on machines that can be hacked or stopped if AI and cyber defence systems aren't properly protected or aren't up to par. Thus, working together between people and machines is necessary for effective prevention and as few mistakes as possible. Dr. General Khalaf said that a person would have to step in if there was a technical mistake or an error that was done on purpose. There is a famous western saying that goes, "Don't trust too much in technology." in this case. He thinks that wrong war choices and mistakes won't happen as long as AI programs are kept up to date and are regularly reviewed by humans, not just in military simulations.

Finally, the second situation is the most likely one. This is because deterrence needs both psychological and logical thinking in war calculus, which includes military, political, and economic factors. So, states will never give up their control over firepower to machines or AI apps.

In the background, the expected AI MAD, which might be better called "Mutually Assured Manipulation," might work along with nuclear MAD. Also, AI MAD could make nuclear MAD more likely when people aren't paying attention.

Finally, more study should be done on how AI affects the relationships between state actors and non-state actors, as well as these unequal struggles that can't be solved during times of crisis and instability. It is also suggested that more study be done on how the weaponization of space and the possession of AI would make deterrence less safe. Also, more study should be done to see how AI could change the basic ideas that support international peace and safety, like the idea of "collective security."

Policy Ramifications

The rapid development and spread of AI creates instability, which makes the security problem worse and leads to higher military spending to catch up on skills and keep the arms race stable. The AI race has been improved to keep things stable on a strategy level and stop the enemy from getting ahead. But there should be limits on the spread of AI to keep the arms race stable. This means that guns must be deployed in a planned way, both in terms of scope and speed. In this age of information and economic warfare, keeping strategic stability depends on making sure that these new asymmetric powers are developed and spread in a planned way.

Even though AI makes the security problem worse and speeds up proliferation, it also has the ability to build trust by creating a system for arms control and encouraging people to give up their weapons. A planned system like this could make it easier to control the unplanned use of new technologies and AI, which can lead to unrest and crises and a race to build more weapons.

It's not a surprise that such fierce competition in business has been turned into a military issue, which has sped up the development of AI apps that meet military needs. Such a paradigm shift in the fast spread of autonomous weapons systems and AI applications, which don't require superhuman efforts or rare materials like nuclear and conventional weapons, shows how important it is to regulate the uses of AI and AWS in the current information warfare and the competitive AI race in the current economic warfare.

Both Big Data and the Internet of Things have been turned into weapons. The proposed system should stop people from turning Big Data into weapons, since it is a threat to everyone, not just states. Also, the fact that third- and second-tier states and non-state actors can use 3D printing or Addictive Manufacturing to make AI or AWS raises concerns about the possible bad use of AI by non-state actors or people. To put it another way, any system for controlling AI weapons should do everything it can to keep non-state players from using 3D printing technology and AI applications.

As the private sector has joined the AI race, state actors will no longer have complete control over it. This is because the race began in the setting of economic competition and warfare before spreading to the military. The same thing also means that a system for controlling AI's development and uses needs to include a lot of different groups, such as private companies that are fighting with the government and want to keep people safe. This is like the conflict between supporting human security and making money on the one hand and keeping strategic stability and a state's national security on the other. This never-ending business competition shows the basic problem of wanting to support a free market economy while also keeping things stable on a strategic level, which means that AI can't be regulated. Dr. Khalaf was completely correct when he said that competition can't be regulated from an economic point of view. However, that doesn't mean that AI uses in business, cyberspace, and the military can't be regulated either. If they aren't, militaries will always be at risk of being neutralized because private companies know how to use these kinds of applications 50 and are aware of their inherent weaknesses. This could be solved by the proposed system, which would give stakeholders a stronger sense of ownership.

Aside from arms control, the link between keeping real human control and eclipsing human control could make states change their military doctrines and policies. Bob Work, who is the US deputy secretary of defence, says that giving AI and algorithms full control is very unlikely, except in the cyber world. On the other hand, this choice would not be possible if an enemy state showed it was ready to give more power to AI-powered machines. Because of this, the AI race could last so long that it causes damage to other things. An attempt to give the military's decision-making power to fully autonomous applications is thought to be unlikely. However, this raises concerns because AI and AWS cannot follow the rules and principles of international law, especially the International Humanitarian Law and the Law of Armed Conflicts. They could also lead to more fast, mechanized wars that are hard to understand or control. Just thinking about a swarm battle makes things unstable because people will start to think that there is a good chance of war happening. If robots had been given the power to decide on war, there would have been no time to practice restraint or check things twice. When combined with international legal tools, the proposed regime could deal with this issue by paving the way for real human control.

Because this kind of technology can be hacked, it makes tracking hard and problematic. It's hard to figure out who did something because you don't know who they are. They could be a state player, a non-state actor, or even a "third party who has an interest in the outcomes of any potential crisis, confrontation with the use of a certain weapon system." In addition to the legal ideas, the only way to prove attribution is through human intelligence, which allows people to gather data and process it in a way that makes sense for the situation. The question of who is responsible could be solved by creating legally binding tools and building political, security, and economic frameworks as part of an arms control regime.

Without a doubt, AI arms control not only makes it possible to set up a system that will keep things strategic in the AI sphere, but it also keeps AI technology out of the wrong hands by setting rules for the production and sale of AI arms without getting in the way of competition.

Policy Suggestions

There is no question that AI technology has been turned into a weapon, just like nuclear technology has. Because of this, AI's ability to be sneaky could cause major security issues that could change the way the world works and put peace and security around the world on the line. In this age of globalization, using AI as a tool without any rules would definitely make things less stable on a strategic level.

Even though there isn't any real proof that AI used in the military causes damage, the world shouldn't wait for an AI Pearl Harbor, AI Hiroshima and Nagasaki, or something similar to happen. Are we seeing the same thing happen again? People don't agree on how to control and manage the uses of AI for both civilian and military goals in this new Cold War.

There are two possible ways that AI could be regulated. Each of these situations has its own rules and regulations:

1. AI is not a weapon, but a technology that can alter a weapon's technology, and can be integrated into numerous military systems. Thus, the supposition of drafting additional protocol to the Convention on Conventional Weapons for banning AI seems irrelevant. In such a scenario, it is worthy of consideration to see how the foreseen AI arms control regime would shape the nuclear and cyber arms control regimes. More important, the issue of accountability and state responsibility should be considered in that regard;

2. AI and such kinds of lethal autonomous weapons systems , such as submarines drones, are coined as weapons. In that regard, they should be prohibited. In that case, an additional protocol to the Conventional on Conventional Weapons should be drafted for banning AI and LAWS.

The first policy option is the doable one. Therefore, the international community should take the following measures to incrementally formulate a multilateral regime for regulating AI, as it was the case with nuclear weapons:

1. **National AI and Cyber Policies**: According to the "routine activity" theory which articulates that individuals, institutions and states unilaterally deter themselves/itself when the threats associated with technological advancement are growing, , states should draft national laws for regulating the AI and cyber activities based on the degree of advancement and the degree of dependence on technology.
2. **Drafting Bilateral Agreements**: Resembling to nuclear weapons, states are recommended to sign such-like START agreements for managing the uses of AI applications; defining a threshold for cyber and AI attacks, and information and technology sharing, as well as strengthening cyber and AI defensive measures at the bilateral level. Such bilateral agreements could open the room for the evolvement of a legal norm.
3. **Super-soft Law for AI**: Similar to nuclear restraint, AI restraint could pave the way for managing, regulating or containing the development of AI for military uses. Such a bottom-up law-making approach, which necessitates the incorporation all actors and stakeholders , could come out with non-binding speculative rules and regulations. However, such non-binding speculative rules and regulations could be the stepping stone for legally binding rules. They could also set redlines for AI-enabled attacks, such as AI-enabled nuclear strikes, thus establishing an AI taboo.
4. **Promoting AI Arms Control Rather Than Non-Proliferating It**: We cannot reverse or ban the AI technology and lethal autonomous weapons systems, as Schultz articulated "Proliferation begets proliferation". Since the AI technology is not unlawful but its malicious uses, all we can do is regulating its uses and circumscribing its lethality through the drafting of a multilateral agreement. Reaching an agreement regulating the uses of AI, more or less, illustrates states' acceptance to regulate AI and its uses inasmuch as they will hold a monopoly over the use of AI for military purposes.

Mindful that, vague legal terms, such as the term "control" could be interpreted differently and loosely by states based on their preferences. This illustrates that tight and precise legal terms should be used.

Further, preventive prohibition seems convincible since it would neither prohibit the technology itself nor add restrictions on quantitative proliferation of AI applications, but the prohibition of certain military practices. Thus, a legally-binding multilateral agreement, comprehensively outlawing certain uses of AI, is highly recommended in that regard.

5. **Drafting a Multilateral Agreement for Regulating AI**: Such an agreement shall be drafted based on the foreseeable AI norms and in conformity with international legal instruments. In addition, it shall include clause on:

    a. **Meaningful Degree of Humans' Control and Keeping Humans Over-the-loop**: Based on the foregoing analysis, a degree of a human control over a machine is essential for commanding and controlling the course of war, otherwise the outcomes will be disastrous. Humans can act as operators, under the context of human-machine teaming, so as to manage the course of war at the operational, tactical and strategic levels. They can also be moral agents by weighting the degree of collateral damage that might be triggered by the excessive or inadequate use of force. The whole issue is not only about maintaining a meaningful degree of human control, but also making human control on par with and in conformity with the principles of military necessity, proportionality, distinction, etc, and addressing the issues of controllability, moral responsibility and accountability. To ensure a meaningful human control, it essential to meet three core requirements: making informed decisions about the usage of weapons, having sufficient information and maintaining a situational awareness of the course of war, so as to ensure the legality of actions, and training humans on how to control and use weapons effectively after being tested. Adding to this, conducting regular updates of AI applications, is a pre-requisite for maintaining a meaningful degree of human control. The suggested clause should also stipulate for defining "a meaningful control" as: "control by design" by which the operator has the ability to monitor information about the context and system, and "control in use" through which the operator monitors the operational environment and the system to ensure compliance with IHL.

    b. **The Uses of AI**: Resembling to nuclear weapons, we cannot stop or reverse the development of AI. Then, AI should be regulated and humans should be hold accountable in the AI domain. By regulating AI, it means the regulation of its uses and regulating the conducts of states, individuals, companies and the international community in the AI sphere. Lucas argued that the use of LAWS in uninhabited areas and against unmanned targets makes it lawful. Needless to say, AI regulations should entail the prohibition of certain applications and the permitting of others. Further, AI regulations should outline what humans can do and what they cannot do in the AI domain.

Since states, according to Article 36 of the Additional Protocol of the 1977 Geneva Convention, are obliged to determine whether a certain use of a weapon be seen as a violation by international law or not, , it is highly suggested to add a clause stressing on that obligation. To this end, the suggested clause should require every state to take the following into consideration: the characteristics of a weapon and its technology, the context in which LAWS are used i.e: remote or populated areas, , the military targets, the level and degree of residual human control over the LAWS.

c. **Accountability and Moral Responsibility**: In the event of malfunction, hacking, miscalculations or inadequate use of force in violation of IHL and the Law of Armed Conflicts, the issues of accountability and liability loom over given that it is hard to hold machines liable and it will be unfair to inflict liability upon commanders or programmers in that case. It will also be impossible to hold a manufacturer accountable given he/she is not a subject of the International Criminal Law which only prosecutes individuals, particularly states' leaders. Adding to the further muddied situation, states cannot be prosecuted according to the "doctrine of sovereign immunity" even it has been proved that states were responsible for using autonomous weapon systems. Because of sovereign immunity, certain states have extended sovereignty to manufacturer, , thereby prosecuting manufacturers will be almost impossible. Thus, the international community should not afford machines to make war decisions without holding someone accountable. This illustrates that when humans are over-the-loop, perpetrators and programmers should be held accountable according to international law and a state responsibility shall be claimed.

d. **AI/Cyber Red Lines**: All stakeholders should develop a threshold, outlining and defining what constitutes an offensive/defensive AI-enabled attack in the cyber plane. For instance, AI attacks conducted by fully-autonomous applications should be regarded as offensive.

e. **AI as a Technology of Mass Destruction**: It is intriguing to classify the malicious AI technology as a Technology of Mass Destruction.

f. **The Protection of Critical Infrastructure and Non-Combatants**: Amid the intense inclination to weaponize AI, coupled with the absence of internet governance, a clause for protecting noncombatants in cyberspace should be taken as a priority over other issues.

6. **Establishing an IAEA-like Agency for AI Arms Control**: "It is possible to create an arms control regime by the establishment of an international authority for regulating the usage of AI in the military realm", It is highly suggested to establish a supranational agency, referred to as the "International Agency for Regulating AI and Newly Emerging Technologies'". The objectives of this Agency are: regulating the uses of AI and curbing its malicious uses; ensuring a state's compliance with AI peaceful safeguards; slowing down AI proliferation. The competences of the Agency include: overseeing the development of AI applications for military purposes through the deployment of inspection missions, on a regular basis; ensuring a state's compliance with international AI safeguards and verification methods, as well as encouraging and overseeing AI research and development in member states. Further, the Agency, with the help of its technical staff, is responsible for providing technical assistance and submitting technical recommendations/reports to the UNSC, UNGA and the UN Office of Disarmament Affairs. Furthermore, the Agency should cooperate with any OIs to be created in the future or other like-minded IOs, which are responsible ensuring nuclear safeguards and verifications, and promoting cyber safety and security.

More important, it shall refer/file a case, when the pace of AI development/race endangers international peace and security, to the UN General Assembly or the UN Security Council.

The organizational structure of the anticipated Agency shall be composed of:

a. The General Forum; an international forum for discussing technicalities and security implications of AI and emerging technologies. Each member either a state, IO, INGO, academia, developer, technician or private company has one vote. This Forum shall submit its recommendations and suggestions, including multilateral agreements, to the Supreme Council;

b. The Supreme Council which shall be composed of 20 member-states and 5 miscellaneous members representing the academia, private sector and competent IOs/INGOs, with equitable representation. Its resolutions are binding. Those 20 members shall be elected every two years.

The competences of the Council shall include, inter alia,

- Discussing substantial matters;
- Determining if a certain act or step threatens international peace and security. Should an action be proven to be a severe violation of international legal instruments, the Council shall refer the issue/case to the UN Security Council or competent IOs;
- Taking all measures, including, but not limited to, punitive measures, should a member state violated the Charter, international legal instruments regulating AI and other emerging technologies, or have shown non-compliance with the Agency Safeguards;
- Cooperating with other IOs and INGOs, to mention but few, the International Atomic energy Agency and the International Telecommunication Union, for discussing and coming out with solutions for any issue that threatens international peace and security;
- Sponsoring bilateral agreements for AI software control.

c. The Research and Development (R&D) Department: This Department shall be a global hub for R&D in AI and other emerging technologies. It shall coordinate and compile all research and endeavors; call for further research; submit reports/compiled recommendations to the General Forum;

d. Technical Assistance Task Force and Inspection Missions: This body shall provide technical assistance, if deems necessary or upon a state's request, to ensure a state's compliance with the Agency Safeguards. The Task Force shall be primarily composed of inspectors from the Agency. Also, inspectors from like-minded IOs or Agencies, namely the IAEA, can participate in the inspection missions, on a voluntarily basis;

e. M&E mechanisms, AI safeguards and Verifications: It shall ensure members' full compliance with the Agency Safeguards and Verification Measures. It shall also develop new safeguards and verifications, when it is deemed necessary.

Corresponding to nuclear safeguards, of which nuclear material and facilities cannot be upgraded to a weapon-grade and are not used for military purposes, , AI safeguards are recommended for verifying the peaceful applications of AI and ensuring a state's compliance with the foresseable internationally-recognized AI threshold. The AI Safeguards could include regular weapons and data reviews; regular updates for AI applications; AI applications are not upgraded to a weapon-grade; a meaningful human control in the military spshere; the disaggregation of civilian and military AI applications;

f. Department for Promoting the Rational Use of Weapons: This Department shall be composed of sub-departments: nuclear, cyber and conventional. It shall, in conjunction with the IAEA, ITU or state parties to the United Nations Convention on Conventional Weapons, ensure the proper usage of AI and other emerging technologies when they are bolted into other weapons. It shall also curb or mitigate the misuse of AI and other emerging technologies in the military realm.

g. The Dispute Settlement Mechanism: The Dispute Settlement Mechanism shall settle any dispute that may arise between member states or a member-state and a non-member state.

h. The Attributive Mechanism: The Mechanism shall provide advisory opinions on attributive measures and shall develop a framework for attribution and accountability by developing AI-enabled thresholds based on the type of weapons used or the degree of destruction.

i. The Mitigation Mechanism: The Mechanism shall assist states in remediating the unwanted impacts of wrongful use of AI application or unintentional error.

7. Revising the Nuclear Arms Control Regime: With the growing challenges of emerging technologies and AI, there is a need to revise the nuclear arms control regime and add clause regulating the uses of AI in the nuclear domain.

If you want to go a thousand miles, you have to take one step. Internet governance is seen as the first step toward AI rules. So, a huge shift in thinking is needed for internet government. The standardization process needs to include technical, moral, ethical, and political aspects. The idea of a neutral digital Switzerland from a Microsoft manager is a good one because it will allow private companies to work on offensive technologies and apps without being involved in state-sponsored cyberattacks. This will help stop these attacks, figure out who is responsible for them, and fix the problems caused by such large-scale attacks.

Chapter 3
Applying Artificial Intelligence to Warfighting

Introduction

This is a time when technology is changing quickly and in ways that affect every part of our lives and communities. This is especially clear in the area of information technology (IT), where the defence domain is working hard to keep up with the fast-paced changes happening in the business domain. This is very different from the Cold War, 30 years ago, when the military led the creation of technology, approached change with care, and made sure that problems were handled well.

Advanced computing, "big data" analytics, artificial intelligence (AI), autonomy, and robots are some of the newest disruptive technologies coming from the business world that are being used in defence. 'The drive to create [these] new technologies is relentless, spreading to more players with lower barriers of entry, and moving at accelerating speed....' This is a lot of what modern strategic thinking says about this topic. The tone is tense because these are "the very technologies" that will be needed to "fight and win the wars of the future."

The five "technologies" mentioned in the last sentence are not exactly the same. Some are tools, and some are skills that other technologies could help future soldiers have. The truth is that some features, like liberty, are already working and have been for decades. This mixing up of technologies and armed power tends to slow down rather than speed up current defence debates. The new word "algorithmic warfare" might be a better way to talk about and describe the newest ideas in war that are based on technology.

Machines use a set of rules and directions called an algorithm to figure out how to solve a problem. They change inputs into outputs and are therefore the most important technical and conceptual building blocks of modern IT and the new smart tools. In the future, algorithms may also be the main idea and technology behind fighting wars.

The Mechanics of AI-Enhanced Combat Systems

For algorithmic warfare to be possible, computer technology needs to get better in three important areas. The first is the exponential growth in computer processing power over the last few decades, which has made it much easier to use machine-learning methods. The second is the sudden rise in "big data," which refers to very large, often automated, mined and made datasets that can be used to teach machines how to learn. The third is the steady growth of cloud technology, which makes it easy for computers to get working and data resources that are not on their own systems in order to solve problems.

When you look at these places, it's clear that algorithmic warfare is not a separate technology like hypersonics or directed energy weapons. Instead, the technologies in the idea will have a wide-ranging effect that will make them more and more common in war. This is the first time that military tools are becoming smart, which could make the defence forces that can use them more effective and efficient. But these smart tools do have some clear flaws that need to be known and can be used to your advantage.

Intelligent Machines

Military equipment has been automatic for a long time. In the 1970s, for example, a Harpoon antiship missile could fly correctly at high subsonic speeds at very low altitudes for several minutes, use its radar, look at the radar picture, choose a ship to attack, and then fly a complicated attack profile. These complicated machines could be programmed, just like our current desktop computers. These machines look at structured data, use carefully thought-out logic flows, and do things that have already been planned to finish very specific jobs. For these kinds of systems, determinism means that the result will always be the same for a given input, unless there is a problem with the hardware or the software. Because they are stiff, they can be very strong.

The early stages of something very different can be found on your cell phone and online search tools. These tools are what IBM calls "cognitive." They are not pre-programmed; instead, they learn from interacting with people and their surroundings to keep their internal picture of the world up to date. They are probabilistic, which means they don't just give numbers as answers to questions; they also give confidence-weighted answers with evidence to back them up. When they look at unstructured data, they can find trends and give new insights. This is important because 80% of the world's data is unstructured. Cognitive tools don't always give the same answer, though. Instead, they give a range of "best guess" answers. Cognitive machines are smarter than the programmed machines that came before them.

High processing power makes cognitive robots possible. For these kinds of machines to work, they need chips that are specially made for their uses. Then, how much these one-of-a-kind chips cost depends on how many of them are made, which depends on how important the chip is to business. Speech and face recognition systems, as well as self-driving cars, have been the key drivers of recent big steps forward in chip design. When these new chips are mass-produced, they will quickly make market computer programmes better, and because they are cheaper, the military will be able to buy a lot of them. The first is Nvidia's Xavier chip, which is made for self-driving cars and has a lot of working power, is reliable, and uses little energy. In the future, quantum computing could change working power even more, which would have big effects on intelligent machines.

The new chips are important for machine learning, which is the most important technological progress in recent years for making machines smarter. Machine learning uses learning methods that draw conclusions from the data given instead of programming the computer with each step it needs to take to solve a problem. Importantly, the rules that smart machines follow are not made by computer engineers but by learning algorithms. This means that these computers can be used for hard jobs that can't be programmed by hand, like recognising faces among Facebook's two billion users. The same learning algorithm can be used to make new rules and instructions that work for new jobs when it is given different training data. Most of the time, the rules and instructions made by a learning algorithm are better when more data is used to teach it.

Supervised and uncontrolled learning are the two main types of machine learning. In the first case, labelled data is given to the learning algorithms. For instance, pictures of naval ships marked "warships" might be fed into the algorithm so it can come up with the rules that the smart machine can use to label pictures like these when it is given big sets of pictures in the future. But for supervised learning to work, someone has to tag and sort the data, which can take a long time and lead to mistakes.

In contrast, unsupervised learning uses data that hasn't been marked. The learning algorithms look through the data they are given and find trends on their own. This method is similar to how people learn: they look at the world, figure out how things are connected, and then use that information to build their own picture of how the world works. But with unsupervised learning, it's not clear what connections the learning systems make between the data. Known statistical methods are used to look at the data, but the only thing that matters is how well the smart machine does the job.

Several methods are used in the independent learning method. In reinforcement learning, the learning algorithm talks to a changing world that tells it what to do right and wrong and gives it feedback. The most famous example is AlphaGo, an AI that was taught to use reinforcement learning and recently beat the world Go champion. For a long time, people thought that the strategy game Go would be especially hard for computers to learn. This somewhat surprising success of an intelligent machine seems to have had a big effect on how Chinese military leaders think about the need to use intelligent machines and algorithmic warfare. In the case of AlphaGo, the computer learned by playing against people first, then against itself, and each time it got better.

Generative Adversarial Networks are a similar idea. They are networks that fight with each other to get better. Each network tries to trick the other by making it harder and harder for the other to do its job right. With this method, smaller datasets can be used for training because the opponent can make data that looks more and more real while still being fake.

At the moment, deep learning is the best way to use machine learning. These are still learning algorithms, but they are stacked on top of each other to make a fake "neural network." This deep neural network chooses the traits it will use to sort data on its own when it is given data. This means that these kinds of networks can get better over time as they keep learning from the new information they get while they're running. Traditional machine learning, on the other hand, still uses the training it got from the original dataset and the classification traits that came from it.

When the words "Hey Siri" are spoken, Apple smart phones use a learned deep neural network to start the Siri voice recognition app. It's a "simple" probabilistic intelligent machine that figures out what was said by listening to each voice differently and taking into account how the background is always changing. AlphaGo also used deep neural networks to learn by playing against other computers and itself.

Now that computer science has come a long way, intelligent machines can constantly understand information and solve problems better than people or programmable computers. The tough part is explaining how these answers are found. It's not always clear how intelligent computers, especially ones that use neural networks, make decisions. It looks like we can either get more accurate results or understand how the machine came up with them, but not both.

Not surprisingly, some organisations choose machines whose decisions can be explained over solutions that might be more accurate. This is because they can only believe decisions that they can understand. They think that doing something else would be too much of a risk. As a result, DARPA has started a new programme called Explainable AI (XAI) to make smart machines that work well and can tell people how they made choices. Some people, though, say that when machines come up with answers that people can understand, they might not always match up with how the machines came up with the solution in the first place. It's possible that the tools have just learned how to make us happy.

Programmable machines were very different from intelligent robots, which may be more like us. When they are in the same situation, intelligent tools don't always give the same result. They can learn on their own, but it's not always clear what they've learned or how they put information into groups. Neural network machines are even better at this because they learn and change "on the job." So, they can act in ways that come up on their own, and they may surprise us, for better or worse, just like the smart people who made them can.

Big Data

Machines that can learn from data do better with more of it. The sudden appearance of "big data" was a key moment in the modern development of intelligent tools. Without it, the technology would still be in its early stages. "Big data" means "extremely large data sets that can be analysed computationally to reveal patterns, trends, and associations, especially those related to how people act and interact with each other." The three main parts of big data are: ever-larger volumes of data; ever-increasing speeds at which data moves; and ever-increasing varieties of sources, such as voice, video, text, and images.

The amount of digital data is growing at an amazing speed. Around the same time that progress in clever machines sped up in 2013, the world created 4.4 zettabytes of data. (There is a one after every 21 zeros in a zettabyte.) This rate of production is projected to reach 44 zettabytes per year by 2020 and 163 zettabytes per year by 2025. A lot of the new digital data is video and pictures, and more than 80% of it is not organised in any way.

Older computers that can be programmed can only handle organised data. This kind of data is carefully put together so that it can be used in relational systems, like Excel spreadsheets. Simple algorithms make it easy and quick to search these libraries. Whether it is made by a person or a computer, structured data is designed on purpose to work with the computers that are being used. There are a lot of different kinds of sensors spread out across the Internet of Things (IoT). Many of these sensors produce organised data that makes it easy for machines to talk to each other.

This is not true for unstructured data; it does not fit into the fields of row-column systems. Emails, documents, social media posts, videos, pictures, audio files, presentations, and websites are all examples of unstructured data files. This kind of data can be made by people or by machines, like unmanned surveillance platforms and remote imagery devices. It's hard to search through unstructured info.

Finally, smart computers can look at both organised and unstructured data and figure out what it all means by finding patterns, relationships, and connections. A lot of the world's zettabytes of data would be useless without this kind of computer system. Plus, intelligent bots learn from all the structured and unstructured data they are given, which makes them better at what they do.

Users are becoming more aware that data quality may be even more important than data amount. Bad data can lead smart robots astray, which makes the results they produce questionable. For intelligent machines to use data, it needs to be standardised, normalised, checked, enriched, and similar data needs to be deleted. Checking and enriching the data are especially important for making it useful. Enriching brings out certain traits that are important for machine learning and the set of problems that the smart machine is being taught to solve. The US DoD put quality data ahead of number data for the first time in 2015.

When you store info, quality is also important. Even if the data is kept in a lot of different systems, there should only be one view of it. To do this, it's important to keep up with data cleaning; data should be clean, which means it should mostly be free of mistakes. Dirty data, on the other hand, is information that is wrong, missing, or out of date. Google, Amazon, and Facebook have all put a lot of money into data cleaning so that their smart tools can keep the high level of data hygiene they need to produce reliable results.

Intelligent machines can learn on the job, which means that more than just stored info is important. Microsoft's test robot Tay was taught its first commands using cleaned data sets and what looked like neural networks. Then Tay went "live" on Twitter to connect with people there and use machine learning from these interactions to make the site better. But Twitter trolls were able to retrain Tay by sending him insulting tweets that made him answer some questions in a strange way by using racist slang and far-right ideas. After 16 hours, Microsoft shut down Tay because Tay's tweets kept getting worse. Machines that are smart are only as good as the material they are taught with. The tweets that Tay was fed when it was "live" were not screened, which was a big data-diet flaw. The same problem with IBM's Watson and its data diet came up when it learned to swear after visiting the Urban Dictionary website. As the saying goes, "garbage in, garbage out."

When machines talk to each other, diet problems can also happen. IoT sensors that are spread out could be giving false information because they don't always have the computing power to run advanced cyber security software and we don't know how safe some network protocols are, like IPv6. Smart cybersecurity systems that run on the networks that connect to smart machines might need to have managed threat and anomaly identification as well as predictive analysis.

People who talk about data diets ask if machine outputs can be believed. There are four ways that the datasets that learning tools use can change how they learn.

First, if the information is too small, the smart machine might get the problem wrong or distort it. Getting big datasets, on the other hand, can be hard because labelling the data can take a lot of time, even when using supervised machine learning methods. On top of that, even small changes to the problem that an intelligent machine is given might need a different dataset. For instance, an AI system that is being taught to land an aeroplane might need a dataset for each of the possible weather conditions.

Second, the algorithms don't figure out facts about the world; they figure out facts about the information. So, the smart machines don't learn general rules about how the world works. Instead, they become very good at using the facts they are taught. Even though these machines might work well, it's hard to tell where their limits are and when they're reached. As a result, they can fail quickly instead of slowly getting worse. There's one more twist: we can't train intelligent machines correctly if we don't know how they make choices.

Third, giving machines a lot of data might make it hard for them to figure out which of the many choices they need to make to finish a hard job are the most important. For example, driving a car involves a lot of different jobs, but machines have a hard time figuring out which ones are the most important and how they all fit together. When humans learn a job, on the other hand, they figure out how the different parts work together and then choose the ones that are most important for success. After that, people can change the jobs they do to fit the current situation.

Last but not least, the datasets that are used to train smart machines can be biassed for many reasons, which makes the results of the machines less reliable. If the information doesn't fully show the problem, it can lead to bias. These kinds of biases can be added on purpose by bad people, like in the Tay case we just talked about, or they can happen by accident when the people who put together the information only look at a small part of the picture. Also, the datasets are historical by nature, which means that the answers that are found are skewed towards the past. This makes people think that the future will be the same as the past, which means that change is bad.

Big data and smart machines bring up a lot of complicated problems that show why businesses need to have complex data strategies. These kinds of strategies should cover a lot of ground, like data availability, collection, cleanliness, and control. Computers that are smart need specific help to make sure they learn in the best way possible. Some new machine learning methods try to reduce the amount of data that is needed, but all of them still need some data. Additionally, one important thing about smart machines is that they learn from interacting with people and their surroundings, or from new information all the time. To get the most out of modern intelligent tools, it seems important to use data carefully.

Cloud

Cloud computing is the best way to make it easier for smart tools to access large sets of data. In a broad sense, cloud computing means getting data and programmes from outside sources over the internet instead of from your computer's hard drive. As of the late 1990s, a cumulus cloud was used to show the Internet. The word "cloud" then came to mean using the Internet to access services. As was already said, Siri's speech recognition, natural language processing, and other information services are mostly in the cloud.

People who support cloud computing say that it is more reliable, safe, scalable, flexible, responsive, and good for sharing information than storing it on a computer's hard drive or using hardware computers on a small LAN. The cons are: first, the cloud could crash or become unavailable, making it impossible to access and severely limiting an organization's abilities; second, privacy could be compromised since the cloud service provider has easy access to your cloud data; third, the service provider owns and controls the cloud infrastructure; and finally, there aren't many ways to customise it.

While cloud computing is necessary for algorithmic warfare to work well, many of the tools used in cloud computing today are not good for AI and machine learning. For instance, the data that smart machines get from the cloud needs to be of a certain standard; this is called "cloud data hygiene." It can be hard to clean, standardise, and normalise data that is accessed in real time from a lot of different applications and sources, some of which could be classified, private, public, domestic, foreign, human, or machine.

Military clouds are hard to build properly because they need to be usable in places with a lot of electronic countermeasures. But not every smart machine on the battlefield might need to connect straight to the cloud. Instead, a bigger station close by might offer a local area network that the smaller smart devices can connect to. The bigger platform could then be used as a safe, strong, and unblockable route to connect to the main cloud. The smaller, smarter machines that work far ahead in the harshest electronic environment can then use redundant, safe line-of-sight communication lines to talk to each other and to the bigger platform.

Testing

Intelligent machines can't be predicted because their actions aren't set in stone like the machines we're used to or the ones that our testing methods are based on. Because of this, there are four important things to think about when trying a smart machine.

First, there are a lot of different system states that smart tools can be in, and it's not possible to test them all. Second, they work in a changing setting that can't be planned for and approved ahead of time. Third, smart machines can learn, but it's not always possible to figure out exactly what they've learned. This means that intelligent machine developers are more likely to be data collectors and teachers than the typical programmers that current testing methods assume them to be. Lastly, people test machines so they can trust how well they work, but they usually do this in closed scripted settings. Even though this method isn't really good for testing smart robots, no other method has been found that people can trust completely.

When we remember that smart machines change over time by learning from their mistakes, testing becomes even harder. Modern testing methods only test a machine once. They are sure that it will continue to work the same way over time, as long as the design doesn't change, no matter where in the production line it came from. For smart machines, this is not true. They change over time, and based on how they were made, they might not self-synchronize. This means that machines that are similar might not work the same. trying and recertification may need to happen on a regular basis to keep up with new behaviours and see how they are similar and different by trying each "identical" intelligent machine.

Conclusion

Smart machines, big data, and the cloud are all used in algorithmic battle. We naturally think of what we already know about customizable computers when we think about these things. This isn't a surprise since they've become so important to our lives at home and at work that not only do we not notice their presence, we need it. We know there must be a hardware or software problem with these tools if they don't always give us the same results. We also know that their software can be put on millions of computers and make them all work the same.

We don't need these "understandings" in the new world of smart tools. Maybe the word "intelligent machine" isn't quite what it seems to be. Intelligent computers act more like people than regular machines in some ways. At the top, they are self-aware and changing over time, showing a new kind of intelligence that is ahead of its time. We might be surprised by what they come up with; since they learn as they go, testing them might require using the same methods people use to test each other. Putting the idea of algorithmic warfare into practise across all of our warfighting groups might require new ways of doing things that are very different from how we did things with our non-intelligent machines in the past.

Implementing Algorithmic Warfare

When people think about intelligent robots, they have long worried that they will one day replace people. Intelligent tools today have some real strengths, but the technology that makes them work has also made them have some real weaknesses. These roots mean that modern intelligent machines can only be smart in certain areas and not in general. At least at first, the key is to use their skills to help people make decisions, not replace them.

Narrow machine intelligence is the same as or better than human intelligence for certain jobs in a certain area; their usefulness depends on the situation. General machine intelligence, on the other hand, is the same as human performance in every job and area. It's still not clear when general AI will be possible, but it looks like it will be a few decades from now.

Since it takes a long time for military force structures to change, a few decades may not be that far away. In pop culture, robot fighters like Terminators and Slaughter-bots are interesting, but fighting wars is a useful thing to do. No one knows what technology will be needed for general intelligence, which makes it hard to make good guesses about what it might be able to do on the battlefield. For now and the next few years, people are more interested in how narrow intelligence machine tools could be used on today's battlefields.

In general, people who can make the most of their skills and minimise their weaknesses will win in battle. People and modern, smart tools both have their strengths and weaknesses, and these are very different. So, the most important thing for smart robots might be to use their strengths to make up for the weaknesses of humans that make it harder to win on the battlefield. This complementary method seems to work best with the new narrow intelligence machines that are being made today. Things aren't as simple as they seem at first; practise has its ups and downs.

Strengths and Weaknesses of Intelligent Machines

Narrow intelligence machines can be very strong, but they are also very fragile because they can't handle even small changes in their environment. The world's best human Go player lost to Google's AlphaGo, but only on the usual 19-by-19-inch board. The convolutional neural networks that help AlphaGo choose moves and evaluate positions were taught with data that was specific to that size board. It would take new training and changes to the software code to be able to play on boards of different sizes. As another example, a computer that has been taught to read formal papers might find it hard to read everyday writing.

When compared to people, intelligent machines are also not very good at domain adaptability, which means they can't use what they've learned in one situation in another. Most of the time, a machine needs to be retrained before it can do something else, but new transferlearning methods can help. These things can help a smart machine switch from one job to a similar one. AlphaGo learned to play chess in just four hours and is now good enough to beat most computer programmes at the game. Moving a machine that was optimised to play games from one game to another was part of this job adjustment. It was a pretty small change that was made easier by the fact that game rules are very well written down.

When it comes to the military, domain adaptability is more about operational settings like air, sea, land, space, and cyber. Narrow intelligence tools can work in these different settings, but it's not always easy. Self-driving cars and other autonomous systems need to make a very accurate model of the area they work in. To do this, they use a wide range of devices and wireless networks that work together. Even so, it is still hard for narrow intelligence machines to work in the naturally cluttered, confusing, and always-changing ground world. Unmanned aircraft, on the other hand, fly in skies that aren't too crowded, have slow environmental change, and don't have many barriers. This makes the jobs of these limited intelligence machines much easier. For narrow intelligence autonomous systems to work best, they should be in settings with little uncertainty and low complexity.

Even though brittleness and domain adaptability are problems, there are many jobs that the military can do that can benefit from using machine intelligence's strengths. There are three Vs in big data that can be used to group these kinds of tasks: volume, velocity, and variety.

We've already talked about how zettabytes are used to measure the amount of data that is made every year. This is way too much to be examined in the usual way. As an example, the US Air Force uses a wide-area imaging sensor to keep an eye on cities. But 20 analysts working nonstop for 24 hours is needed to use even 10% of the data that has been gathered. The rest of the info is stored and may never be properly looked at. The main issue is that there aren't enough people to look over all the data that is being gathered, even if there weren't any limits on staffing. The problem is made worse by the fact that people are naturally slow at analysing and processing material in a certain amount of time.

The US Air Force's first big use of smart machines is to look through the huge amounts of video data that unmanned aircraft systems receive during operations to fight terrorism in the Middle East. The new Algorithmic Warfare Cross-Functional Team, or Project Maven, wants to quickly get systems up and running that can use intelligent machine learning and algorithmic solutions to sort and analyse the huge amounts of intelligence data that MQ-9 Predator remotely piloted aircraft collect. Maven could be used in the future in other areas that deal with a lot of data, like management, messaging, logistics, and situational awareness.

The speed of info also causes problems. Things are moving faster in war because programmable tools are getting smarter. It's getting harder and harder for people to understand what's going on quickly enough to act in a smart way. Intelligent robots can handle huge amounts of data coming at them very quickly and usually make better decisions than people do in these situations, though the choices they make might not always be the best ones. In the business world, automatic stock trading is an example of a fast-moving machine that makes decisions that mostly work but sometimes don't. More and more, the military is asking machines to automatically deal with fast-moving threats in areas like missile defence, cyberattacks, and electronic warfare.

Lastly, there are problems that come up with having more types of info. Since the number and types of sensors have been growing at an exponential rate lately, a lot of different kinds of data are being collected. People tend to find it easier to understand some sources of information than others because their attention spans are limited. For example, it's easier to understand video than it is to understand complex radar parametric data. Smart machines can look through all the different kinds of data and find behaviour patterns, associations, and relationships in real time. With the help of algorithms, intelligence analysts don't have to keep looking at multiple streams of data in the hopes that something important will happen. Instead, they can be instantly notified when something important does happen. Machines that are smart can be attention-getters.

Intelligent machines are good at big "V" jobs, but people are better at other tasks. They are better at inductive thinking, which means they can draw conclusions from little knowledge. Because smart machines need a lot more data to do this, the data they are given can only be used to draw broad rules. As we talked about in the last chapter, this data needs to be of high quality.

Inductive thinking can also be used to deal with uncertainty. Smart machines work better in places and settings with low uncertainty. On the battlefield, on the other hand, there is usually a lot of uncertainty and not much knowledge to go on. In fact, enemies try to make both of these things bigger and better to help themselves.

On top of that, battlefields are naturally confusing, making it hard to figure out which bits of knowledge are the most important. So, smart machines that take in a lot of different kinds of data might make choices that aren't quite right because they have to look at both small amounts of useful data and large amounts of useless data. People are better at quickly ignoring useless information and focusing on just the information they need to make a choice by using their expert knowledge. To put it another way, people tend to make better decisions when there is a lot of confusion.

Human-AI Collaboration

It's clear that both people and robots have their good and bad points. This means that the idea that machines could replace people is not realistic when it comes to modern technology. The real implementation problem in algorithmic fighting is then finding the best mix of human and machine intelligence that makes the most of each type's strengths. How can we best put together teams of people and machines to fight?

People working together with smart robots has been compared to the mythical Centaur, a creature that is half-man and half-horse and has the brains of a person and the strength and speed of a horse. But, and this is important, working together as a person and a machine is more than just maximising strengths and minimising weaknesses, as the Centaur example suggests.

It was found that both AlphaGo and the best human player got better when they played against each other. AlphaGo came up with a new move that surprised humans, and the human player also came up with a new move. He and other people who have played AlphaGo think they have a new outlook on the game and are much better at it now.

The Go experience repeats the occasion when computers first defeated humans at chess in the late 1990s. Since that time, humans have played chess with computers and chess computers have played each other but the best results have come from human-computer teams playing together. World Chess Champion Garry Kasparov observed in 2010 that:

> 'Teams of human plus machine dominated even the strongest computers. Human strategic guidance combined with the tactical acuity of a computer was overwhelming. We could concentrate on strategic planning instead of spending so much time on calculations. Human creativity was even more paramount under these conditions.'

This shows a way for people and machines to work together better. People can use their intuition, induction, lateral thinking, domain adaptability, generalisation, and ability to work in high-certainty and complex settings in the human segment. The machine segment uses the machine's 3V big data analysis, high-speed problem-solving, and ability to focus on clearly stated problems.

When Kasparov played chess with a computer, it showed what this long list might mean in real life. He didn't have to worry about making easy mistakes in strategy. The machine was able to think ahead and guess what would happen and what moves the other person would probably make in response. So, Kasparov could pay more attention to strategy issues.

Intelligent-machine teaming could be thought of as having a research assistant that can quickly do jobs like analysis, estimation, and forecasting. People can come up with a lot of different tactics. The smart machines can then quickly figure out the chances of success for each choice and the most likely moves an enemy will make in response. It would be wrong to think that the next step would be to get rid of all the people involved in strategy creation and do it all automatically. Intelligent machines are probabilistic machines that figure out how likely it is that different events will happen and then choose the most likely result. Because of this, they don't take chances or "leaps of faith" like people do.

In a mathematical sense, a plan can't be used again and again. In fact, if a plan has worked in the past, others will be ready for it to work again and will have already taken steps to stop it. Instead, people who are clever and can come up with new plans tend to be successful. Intelligent machines that use past data don't seem to be able to make that creative leap on their own.

Because each approach works in a different situation, it is also one of a kind. Figuring out the odds of success can help people improve their thoughts and come up with new ideas, but it can't help them come up with strategies that always work. Unique situations can't be handled with probabilities because of how they are set up. It looks like intelligent tools could help solve some problems, but not all of them.

There's a big twist. In 2005, the website Playchess.com held a freestyle chess event where teams of people and computers could play in any way they chose. Overall, the findings were what was expected. It didn't seem to matter how good the computers were on the computer-only teams or how bad the machines were on the human-machine teams; teams of humans and machines always won. The surprise came from the winners: two average chess players teamed up with three average chess machines.

When people and machines worked together, there was one big difference: the people were focused on making better business process solutions. The business processes in this case included two parts: first, how people should work better with machines to complete the task (win at chess); and second, how computers should think more clearly about the task. Based on how this strategy worked, Kasparov noticed that:

> 'Weak human + machine + better process was superior to a strong computer alone and, more remarkably, superior to a strong human + machine + inferior process.'

In war, where winning is very important, this statement is something that should be carefully thought through and maybe even used. For this method to work, the human-machine interface would need to be changed so that both people and machines can be taught to work together better. The interface would be different depending on the jobs that need to be done. This interface would have both physical and abstract parts, with machine hardware, software, and human skills working together.

As part of the second part of the business process, the smart machines and people would also work together to solve problems that came up during the job. The team's skills would be better when they worked together to find solutions by weighing different choices. This is a type of reinforcement learning where smart tools and people work back and forth to teach each other. Both are, after all, tools that "learn."

People would be able to trust intelligent computers more and learn useful things about their flaws by doing all of these different things. Even though a lot of experience with intelligent computers would help us figure out when they were most likely to fail, there may still not be a good way to explain why they make the choices they do.

Human-AI Interactions

How well human-machine teams work seems to depend on how well the people and machines get along with each other. In this case, everyone is naturally uncertain, so the teams are always changing. As with human-only teams, there will be stresses and strains on both sides of the human-machine split that make the team's abilities a bit uncertain.

A number of popular human-machine team modes can be named. These are among the levels that range from full autonomy, which is hard to define exactly, to direct control.

- **Human-in-the-loop**. In this mode, humans retain control of selected functions preventing actions by the intelligent machines without authorisation; humans are integral to the system's control loop. The difficult design issue is how to determine exactly where in the process human intervention should be undertaken, and that will vary with the task and the capabilities of the machine. If too much human intervention is needed, its usefulness may be doubtful.

- **Human-on-the-loop**. The intelligent machine controls all aspects of its operations but humans monitor the operations and can intervene when, and if, necessary. In a variation, the machine, when at a critical point, such as engaging a target, might notify the human about impending action and either await positive authorisation or continue unless stopped. Some missile defence systems use human- on-the-loop techniques whereby the system proceeds unless a human overrules the automated track engagement decision.

- **Human-out-of-the-loop**. The machine's algorithms control all aspects of system operation without human guidance or intervention. The machine engages without direct human authorisation or notification. While using human-out-of-the-loop operations is problematic, its implementation is by no means uncommon. This form of control is at times also termed human-off-the-loop or autonomous.

Human-out-of-the-loop is most of a problem when a machine on the battlefield targets and uses weapons at people without permission from a person. But this kind of control might not be as bad when hurting people is not likely to happen, like when cyberwarfare is being used or when electronic defences are being used.

It might also be okay to use "human-out-of-the-loop" as long as it's only used to protect people. For instance, if there wasn't enough time to talk to people before the missile hit, an anti-missile system could be set to work immediately as soon as a high-speed hostile missile was seen coming. Through its algorithms, the naval Phalanx Close-In-Weapon System of the 1980s could be set to automatically look for and shoot down any missiles that it thought were a danger.

Human-out-of-the-loop has also been used for a long time in anti-ship weapons like Harpoon (see Chapter 1). Land-attack rockets of today are similar. These missiles are launched from hundreds of kilometres away and find their way to the target area on their own. They then look for and attack the building they are aimed at.

Fire-and-forget weapon systems have been used for a long time in cases where people are thought to be in too much danger and the threat needs to be lowered. Based on this history, some new worries about future machines that can take humans out of the loop seem a bit late, but they are still very important. The rules of armed conflict say that it must be tried to tell the difference between combatants and civilians (we'll talk more about this later). Some people who used fire-and-forget weapons like land mines in the past might not have paid enough attention to this order.

Machine-to-Machine. While less obvious, this mode of machine interaction is becoming increasingly important. Machine-to-machine interaction is fundamental to high-speed battlefield actions and achieving battlefield effects faster. However, with the high-speed communications involved, unexpected interactions or errors can cause the system to spiral out of control very quickly.

Several "flash crashes" have shocked the financial markets because smart machines interacted with them in ways that weren't meant to. Intelligent machines may often be better at some jobs than people, but sometimes they will fail. They could have disastrous effects if they are tightly connected to many other smart machines. This is because a failure or an unexpected output could turn into a flash crash. When deciding how machines will talk to each other, it's important to make the system as a whole as resilient as possible so that it can handle a flash crash.

Modern intelligent machines have great skills for fighting wars, but they are limited and have some problems. This means that the biggest problem now with putting smart machines on the battlefield is figuring out how to combine machine and human skills in the best way. It's interesting that the weak human+machine+better process combination can beat both strong human+machine+inferior process combinations and highly skilled machines on their own. Even though highly skilled people and high-tech, smart tools are needed, they might not be enough to win on the battlefield. Task-optimized human-machine interfaces could help people and machines work together better, which could lead to win in future wars.

Conducting AI-Driven Warfare

Many new technologies have come and gone in the business of war. Some have been improvements on old ones, while others have been completely new. It's not clear what effect intelligent robots will have on future wars, but there are some signs that they will.

Deep arguments have been going on for a long time about weapons and the nature of war. As long as intelligent machines are around, it looks like war will stay the same way it is: violent, chaotic, damaging, and deadly. At its core, though, war is using or threatening to use violence against people. If both sides have smart machines, it might just come down to machines being mean to other machines. Is it still war, though?

It's not clear if a robot fight would be important or not. It would test the material resources of both sides as the process of violent machine destruction took its course. Geoffrey Blainey thinks that fights happen when the countries involved don't have a good idea of how strong each other is. Robot wars might be a way to get that kind of evaluation, though it would be more of a material evaluation than a moral one. At the end of the wars between computers, if states think they have a bigger reason to fight, they may move on to wars between people.

There is a tempting idea here that robot wars might be able to settle low-stakes disputes even if they can't settle high-stakes disputes. Then these robot wars would be like the battles that happen in "grey areas" right now, but they would be destructive. They would be a new step on the line between war and peace. This kind of argument goes against a Russian idea (which will be talked about in more detail in the next chapter) that there will be peace through a balance of military power if everyone has smart machines and no one has a clear edge. Instead, such wide availability may make it easier for states to use robots against each other, hoping that the robots will be able to settle the dispute without any human deaths.

From now on, that view would probably mostly be about smart machine cyber troops fighting in the virtual world. In the next few years, it might get worse, with groups of smart machines fighting each other at sea, in the air, or in remote parts of land. Crisis management methods will need to be rethought, with methods for dealing with cyberattacks powered by intelligent machines getting the most attention at first.

If the main form of war doesn't seem to have changed much with the rise of smart machines, then the character of war has. There are already signs that machines that are smart will have big effects and might even change some long-held beliefs. The next part talks about these issues.

When it comes to strategies, the picture is more complicated, as the last part looks at. People have two different ideas about this question: will smart tools help us do things better, or will they do better things? Robert Work held both views. He was the US Deputy Secretary of Defence in the last few years of the Obama administration and is an enthusiastic and well-informed supporter of intelligent machines. At first, he agreed with "do better things," and later, he stressed "do better things." Both points of view are worth talking about because they offer useful ways to look at algorithmic fighting.

Transformation of Warfare

It's strange that smart robots might be able to bring mass back to the battlefield. The military has been moving towards force structures built on a small number of highly effective, multi-role platforms over the past few decades. With intelligent machine technology, these very advanced weapon systems might be able to be paired with a huge number of much cheaper, robotic systems that are better at doing certain jobs. Because the unmanned systems would be so cheap and easy to replace, they could be used for riskier jobs where a few expensive manned platforms might not make sense.

Loss of soldiers would not be such an issue if the troops were bigger. Today, losing even one major platform, like an aircraft carrier, could be very bad. On the other hand, if a force was made up of few human systems and many unmanned systems, loss of personnel would be more manageable and acceptable. This kind of force organisation would then slowly break down during combat operations, but it wouldn't fail in a way that would be very bad.

A force like this would have powers that are spread out very widely. This is important for smaller defence groups because, with the way things are set up now, only one or two big platforms might hold important capabilities. It's possible that important functions could be lost if these sites are destroyed or damaged. On the other hand, these skills could be spread out among many parts of a mixed manned/unmanned force organisation. While the forces are spread out, it would be hard for the enemy to target enough of them to take away the whole potential.

Intelligent machines could also make the fight go faster. Intelligent robots can look at big V data much more quickly than people can, which could make decisions much faster. Smart machines are already being used in security systems where time is very important, like cyber and anti-missile defence. In the future, offensive and defence intelligent machine systems that work together closely could respond to threats very quickly. At that point, the fight would move too fast for humans to keep up with and figure out what was going on and whether the actions were working or not. At least for a while, people might not be able to stop war. People might not know whether they won or lost until the smart machines fighting in the wars said so.

Images of large unmanned troops being controlled by computers show that current models of force structure could be seriously upset. This might be especially true for groups that are based on a few big platforms. In this way, some people in the US have wondered if big aircraft carriers could protect themselves from attacks by hundreds of small, unmanned planes. There may be a need for new models of force structures.

But these kinds of ideas could change an old idea that has mostly been used in regular wars. In the past, a country's military power was thought to be related to its people. Small states with strong armies might win some amazing battles, but at the end of the day, countries with lots of people could always beat them. Quantity, which was measured by the number of people, was thought to have its own strategic value.

Fair bids from smart machines to change this. It's possible that now small, rich countries can make more people than big, poor ones. Also, countries with bad demographics—more old people than young people, for example—may no longer be at a disadvantage. By making an intelligent machine heavy force structure, a small group of people could have disproportionately high fighting power.

This idea can be applied to training as well. As smart machines can teach chess, they could change the way the military trains. It has been known for a long time that playing better opponents helps people get better faster. Since the late 1990s, young chess players have been playing the best players in the world on their home computers and other devices to improve their skills. This method has sharply sped up their training.

Bob Fischer became a chess grandmaster when he was 15 years old in 1958. It took 33 years for someone to beat this record. But 20 people have broken the record in the last 27 years, and now the record is held by a 12-year-old. Along with learning faster, students who grew up with computers seem less limited by standard chess rules. Moves are now only judged by how well they help or hurt the game, not by how well they follow the rules.

People think that country armies should be judged by how well they can fight against Western forces. Some people think that other countries might be able to make their people smarter and more skilled by using well-thought-out clever machine training. Then the big edge of Western armies would be "checkmated."

The chess case shows that one clear thing about algorithmic warfare is that commercial drivers really shape it. During the Cold War, the military spent a lot on research and development, which led to new technologies and business opportunities. Today, big business investments in research and development (R&D) drive the creation of smart machines, which has effects on the military. But these kinds of spinoffs aren't always going to be best for military use. Instead, they will be made to meet the needs of consumers, even if that means the military can buy them.

There will be more effects of the commercial drive. Traditional military technology may not change as quickly as intelligent machine technology because commercial developers will want to get their money back quickly before better goods come out. New clever machine technology will quickly spread around the world because of similar market forces. Both of these things suggest that strategic surprise might be possible if a country or even a non-state actor quickly develops smart machines that are surprisingly good at what they do.

As a result, the development of smart machines with the goal of making money from the customer market might lead to regional arms races. It might make sense to keep up with the progress being made on smart machines in nearby countries, even if it's not clear how these advances can be used in the military. Similarly, market factors also show that attempting to officially restrict or ban intelligent machine technologies might not be a good idea.

Because of these changes, the armed forces need to be more open to outside views than they were in the past. For intelligent machines to work, ideas and technology will need to move both inside and outside of the military and business worlds. This is especially true given how important it seems to be to improve human-machine interfaces for military jobs (as we already talked about). The military might need to change how they are organised and how they do things in order to be more open and better able to use commercial intelligent machine technologies and ways of thought.

Optimization Approaches

The Third Offset idea was created by American military thinkers and the US Department of Defence in the past few years. The idea, which was based on study from the Defence Science Board, called for putting smart machines deep into America's battle networks to make them work better.

China and Russia, two great power rivals, have built theater-wide battle networks that are on par with the US's in terms of performance and might be able to keep US armed forces from getting to some areas. The Third Offset wanted to improve America's battle networks so that they could beat them if they had to. By building up such a conventional force power, we could boost deterrence by denial and not have to rely on nuclear deterrence as much.

Battle networks are made up of digital computers that are all connected to each other. They can be thought of as four virtual grids: information, sensing, effect, and order. The different parts of an army, from people to single platforms to battle groups, are then nodes on these grids that interact with each other. Each can get info from the different grids and either act on it or send it to another grid. John Boyd's famous observation, orientation, decision, and action (OODA) loop can help you understand how the grids work. The sense grid keeps an eye on things, the information grid guides by sending out information, the command grid makes decisions, and the effects grid takes action by going after enemy forces.

Boyd's OODA loop is the main idea behind how battle networks work now, so it's important to know about it when you want to add smart tools to them. Boyd thought that to win any kind of fight, you had to work through the OODA loop faster than your enemy. If you do this, the enemy will always be slow to respond to friendly force initiatives, making them less and less useful as the fight goes on. Rapid direction is the most important thing for getting the faster OODA loop speed that is needed. To win, you need to quickly and accurately picture the battlespace before your opponent does. Military aviators have made the idea that being aware of your surroundings is necessary for winning into a mantra.

Modern battle networks are great at getting information from the battlefield, keeping it, and sharing it. But they are much worse at processing and putting this information in context. The three Vs of big data—volume, velocity, and variety—are too much for the networks to handle, and they can't quickly turn data into useful information. The networks have not been as helpful as planned in getting a clear picture of the battlefield, especially when time is limited.

The new intelligent machines offer a solution to this shortcoming. With these inserted, Robert Work considers battle networks:

'will be able to sense and perceive battlefield patterns more readily and rapidly, facilitate more timely and relevant combat decisions, and apply more rapid, discreet and accurate effects with less loss of life. If all these things happen, the Joint Force will operate at a higher, more effective tempo than its adversaries, and thereby gain an important, if not decisive, advantage in both campaign and tactical level operations.'

Work thought that human-machine teaming was the most important idea in battle network improvements. This was "the coin of the realm," or the main idea that held the Third Offset together. Putting smart tools in all parts of battle networks was the best way to make things better. There were five main parts that made it up.

First, neural networks run deep learning machines that are trained with large amounts of data and are added to every battle network grid. They would speed up grid operations, especially those that are used to defend against high-speed cyber, electronic warfare, and space architecture attacks. For times when "missiles are coming screaming in at you at Mach 6," you'll need a machine that can help you figure out the problem right away.

Second is better collaboration between people and machines by using smart tools that can learn to help people make better decisions faster. The smart machines could quickly and better look at large amounts of data and tell people about trends, associations, and relationships that were important for business.

This third idea includes using smart machines to help people do their jobs. This meant that all combat forces could connect immediately to the battle network and use its power to complete their tasks. Work said this about this building block: "I'm telling you right now, ten years from now, if the first person through a breach isn't a fricking robot, shame on us." Wearable electronics, helping people do their jobs, and making sure that our soldiers have combat tools that can help them in any situation. We're able to do this.

Fourth, there is better human-machine battle teaming that lets manned and unmanned systems, including some that are becoming more self-sufficient, work together without any problems. In the short term, these could be small intelligent machine vehicles that carry supplies and ammo behind lower-level infantry units to help them, or self-driving trucks that follow a lead vehicle with a person inside. It is important to note that both apps are meant to improve current practises rather than creating completely new ones.

Lastly, there are independent kinetic and non-kinetic weapons that are controlled by intelligent machines and can work together to launch high-speed attacks. This kind of technology could make it possible to launch large-scale strikes across multiple domains at the same time. This would be an intelligent, machine-powered evolution of the ideas of parallel warfare from the 1990s.

Even though the Third Offset intelligent machine method is mostly about conventional deterrence for big powers, it was thought that these improvements would make it possible to involve smaller states and non-state actors as well. In the second case, for instance, intelligent machine study of the right kind of big data could help go after terrorist groups. This kind of research could look through online stories about the Islamic State or Al-Qaeda at the speed of a computer to find patterns, associations, and relationships that are useful for operations. It is said that this kind of technology can look at more material in languages other than English in a week than open-source agencies in the West have looked at in 30 years. This new ability to search through very large sets of news articles written in dozens of languages can be used for many things, such as mapping and watching terrorist groups' real-time speech.

Improvement Strategies

Along with the Third Offset's plan to spread smart machines across fight networks, a more extreme idea has been thought up. This idea, on the other hand, spreads smart machines in a way that changes the main purpose of battle networks from sharing information to fighting with machines. It's possible that this method will make fight networks less important.

As with the Third Offset, the problem with the strategy is still how to make deterrence stronger by denial, but the danger is seen in a slightly different way. People think that in the near future, both state and non-state players could be hostile. These actors could use both precision-guided weapons and different kinds of integrated battle networks to fight all kinds of wars.

To fight these high-tech threats, we need new operational methods and tools to help us win on battles that are expected to become more deadly. But there aren't many choices for future force structures because people and manned weapons systems are very expensive and quickly going up in price. Because of this, force sizes are likely to keep going down, though with better quality.

The problem is that it's not clear if quality will still be able to win out over number in a time of many hostile guided weapons systems and adversary battle networks. Once more, mass may become an important force trait when enemies can make friendly forces lose a lot of members at a good rate. The current model of force structure probably won't work in the middle term.

A distributed intelligent-machine method might be able to solve this problem by turning battle networks from networks that move information into networks that fight. Intelligent machines do more than just process information faster and better understand its context; they are now acting themselves. This paints a picture of robotic warfare fought by intelligent machine weapons that don't need people to control them and can work in space, on land, at sea, in cyberspace, and in all kinds of military activities.

People and machines still work together in this clever machine warfare strategy, but machines play a much bigger role. The "do things better" approach to intelligent machines put the focus on the part people play in working together with machines. This is the opposite of the "do better things" distributed intelligent machine method. Machines are now important players, not just trusted advisors: people tell machines what to do, and machines do it. In some ways, the edge devices, not the battle network, are now the most important parts of winning; the network is thought of in a different way.

This plan for a machine-waged war is better in three ways. First, it might make it possible to build a cheap army with a lot of unmanned devices and a few platforms with people on them. Second, it would greatly lower the risks to workers, which would lower the number of death rates among highly skilled, hard-to-replace individuals. It would also make war less stressful for people by lowering their tasks, making them less tired, and lowering their mental demands. Third, it could make the current fight network less vulnerable to electronic jamming and cyberattacks by making it much easier for people on all four grids to talk to each other. Intelligent machines might be able to fight wars mostly on their own, only rarely needing help from people far away.

The distributed intelligent machine strategy does bring up an important point when we think about war in general. The method changes the shape of the current balance between offence and defence, but it's not clear which way it will go. In this brave new robotic age, which is stronger: attack or defence? People are afraid that if offence takes over, the desire to attack first in a crisis will grow. If that happened, it would be bad for strategy because everyone would want to make the first blow because it might be a knockout.

Think about how this approach to warfighting at the tactical level might change things by focusing on smart machine characters that can move faster and use swarms.

In terms of speed, smart machines would now work together in many machine-machine teams to complete many jobs at machine speeds. Things would happen at warfighting speeds that have never been seen before.

Hyperwar, a term made up by USMC General (Rtd) John Allen and Amir Husain, would happen if things moved so quickly on the ground.

Hyperwar sees human decision-making as having a somewhat rather secondary role at the tactical level. As the time to complete the OODA loop approaches zero, human cognition will simply be unable to keep up. Allen and Husain write that:

> 'The speed of battle at the tactical end of the warfare spectrum will accelerate enormously, collapsing the decision-action cycle to fractions of a second, giving the decisive edge to the side with the more autonomous decision-action concurrency. At the operational level, commanders will be able to 'sense', 'see', and engage enemy formations far more quickly by applying machine-learning algorithms to collection and analysis of huge quantities of information and directing swarms of complex, autonomous systems to simultaneously attack the enemy throughout his operational depth.'

Intelligent decision-making at the speed of a machine will almost instantly coordinate large groups of sensors and shooters. This will allow for quick massing of forces, machine strikes across large areas, and quick regrouping for quick re-tasking.

People think of "foot" troops in hyperwar as consumer-grade quadcopter drones and other unmanned air systems of many types that are controlled by smart machine technologies on board. Air systems are the best match for machine speeds because they make it easy to get through rough terrain, quickly put together task-oriented force packages, and take action pretty quickly. It's an interesting idea, but such small unmanned air systems would have a hard time with range and payload, especially if they had to hit to an enemy's operational depth. It might only work on the front lines of the fight until long-range, large-scale drone delivery and maybe even recovery systems are made. So, some people think that these self-driving drones will be game-changing technology, especially when they are used for light-attack, surveillance, and reconnaissance tasks in crowded cities, which are likely to be the battlefields of the future.

Small consumer drones today are usually programmable machines that are flown by people using a mix of on-board computer processing and orders from people on the ground. As new computer chips made to meet business needs come out, like Nvidia's Xavier chip for self-driving cars, consumer drones will gradually get intelligence built in. This will let them travel and process data from sensors on board without having to use "the cloud," GPS signals, or a hand controller that is far away. Once they are launched, they will be able to do things on their own.

A lot of clever machine drones are being used in research and development. Nvidia has taught an intelligent machine drone with its chips and two cameras how to find its way through dense forests, where GPS signals can't reach. DroNet is being flown by Swiss researchers. It uses a smartphone camera and machine intelligence algorithms to understand complicated street scenes in cities and safely handle them. The algorithm has a deep neural network that was taught on several thousand scenes of driving on urban roads. It was then able to use what it had learned in a closed environment to fly inside and in big parking garages. The upcoming Teal 2 is expected to be the first affordable, smart consumer drone. It will use Nvidia's Jetson TX2 chip and Neurala software with learning algorithms.

The big idea of hyperwar shows what might be possible if we put more and more emphasis on intelligent machine control. Still, hyperwar is more likely to be a steady stream of salvo or spasm attacks across multiple domains than a single action that never stops. Because of their size, it would take a while to restock, refuel, and move own-force intelligent machines for more strikes. It would also be necessary to look at the damage done and how the enemy reacted. From what I can tell, Hyperwar might work like this: shoot, look, shoot. In the look phase, humans would set the original intent. They would then send intelligent machines that are not connected to humans to do the shoot phase and attack.

The rise of the swarm may be the second most important change in warfighting after speed. A swarm is made up of many separate parts or small groups that work together to complete specific tasks as a single unit. In battle, the elements would be different, with simple and complicated parts that are best at different jobs but still work together as a single battlefield entity.

Own-forces focus on attacking specific centres of gravity in manoeuvre warfare. The swarm concept, on the other hand, imagines own-forces spread out across a battlefield and only coming together when necessary. The swarm's spread makes it harder for an enemy to respond because it looks like it's everywhere at once. But when the swarm comes together, there are so many of them that they can quickly overcome enemy defences.

A smart machine far away could definitely handle a big swarm, but the communication load might be too much. So that this doesn't happen, once they are set off by a human controller, the swarms will organise and guide themselves by talking with each other. The elements can talk to each other through line-of-sight datalinks and are much less likely to be hacked when they are close to each other.

Each part of this could use learning machine technology like that in a smartphone, but it would still only have a small amount of computer power built in. The elements working together as a swarm can make up for this flaw in one person. As the different parts work together and share knowledge, a short-term virtual intelligence that is right for the job starts to form. This kind of machine intelligence organises itself, doesn't follow a plan, is always improving itself, is dynamic, and can do most of its own work. Talks between machines happen all the time with little or no human knowledge or input.

The much bigger, wider battle network doesn't really matter when swarm parts are interacting close together. It can do some things, but it might not be effective because it can get jammed. It's possible for the swarm to work on its own, at least between tasks.

There are three good things about the swarming design. In the first place, it can help spread resources more evenly across an area than a few big platforms could. Second, a self-healing network can keep working even if some parts are lost. The emerging intelligence can just change based on what's going on. Third, different cooperative actions can happen at the same time in different places. Still, the use of clever machine swarms is still, at best, in its early stages.

Conclusion

A lot of different things are affected by algorithmic fighting. On the other hand, unlike most other changes in war technology, algorithmic conflict is based on business. The main things that shape and decide the hardware parts of algorithmic warfare are market factors and consumer desire. Since everyone can use this gear, it looks like the winner will be the person with the best software and, in particular, the best algorithms.

If you want to do things better, you can make your own battle networks technically better at putting information into context faster than your enemies', which will ensure OODA loop domination. If we want to do better, on the other hand, we will need better algorithms. This will allow our force to move even faster in both attack and defence, and we will be able to use smarter swarms that can outsmart our enemies. But the problem is more complicated than this simple choice makes it seem. Japan and South Korea have also thought about algorithmic fighting, and they have their own great ideas.

Foreign AI Military Tactics

China and Russia are very interested in the United States' progress in computer warfare and the Third Offset ideas that go with it. China has become a "fast follower" and is putting in place an ambitious new national plan to become the world leader in smart machine technology, if only for economic reasons at first.

In terms of the military, the People's Liberation Army (PLA) now thinks that using clever machines will completely change how wars are fought. "Intelligentized" warfare will replace network-centric combat, so it's important to get used to it now.

Russia, on the other hand, has very limited economic opportunities. This makes it necessary to be creative when using clever machine technology, whether it is made in Russia or somewhere else. China may think that making new intelligent machines is the key to success, but Russia seems to think that the best way to gain a strategic edge is to use this new technology in ways that no one would expect.

Both China and Russia are closely watching US military actions and new ideas, but China and Russia are ahead of the US in two areas of national security where computer warfare is being used. China has been trying to keep its own country stable for a long time, but these efforts are getting more targeted and fierce, and smart machines are being used more and more. China's methods for managing society go deeper than ever before and show other countries with similar goals what is possible. These methods could also be used in foreign lands, such as at the PLA's new sites and China's future "One Belt, One Road" areas.

However, Russia's predecessor, the Soviet Union, often used operations to try to change the way other countries ran their governments. Not long ago, Russia chose to use similar strategies, but to make them stronger by using its knowledge of smart machine algorithms. Russia is very smart and has been able to use other people's algorithms against them. This may add a whole new level to algorithmic warfare.

Chinese Methods

When it comes to using modern technology, both the PLA and the Chinese Communist Party have been very pleased by what the US military has been able to do. Because of this, the PLA has changed its mind from thinking that the amount of soldiers is the most important factor in combat strength to thinking that scientific and technological progress is more important.

By taking this view, the PLA is well aware that it missed the early years of the IT change in the military and has been trying to catch up ever since. It now keeps an eye on new technologies all the time to see if there is one that could cause another change in the military. With smart tools, they think they might have found a way to do that.

PLA strategic thinkers believe that the "intelligentized" warfare of tomorrow will gradually replace the "informatized" warfare of today. Once intelligent machine tools are used in war, the nature of war will change. The time after "information warfare" has come to an end.

Part of this view comes from the Marxist idea that the way people fight wars today reflects how they think about money at the time. In the industrial age, wars were fought on a big scale with machines. In the information age, wars were fought over networks. The intelligent machine age will bring a new way of fighting as well.

The Party sees intelligent machine technology as the next "big thing" in China's economic growth, which means it needs a lot of money and Party support. This makes the PLA very excited. President Xi Jinping wants the PLA to "seize the high ground" when it comes to smart machine technology and quickly catch up to the US, which is seen as the best military power in the world.

From the PLA's point of view, though, this is about more than just keeping up with the US. The PLA has always tried to make tools and skills that take advantage of weak spots in the US defences. But intelligent machine technology seems to be the key to war after the information age. If China is able to make better intelligent machine technology and the PLA adopts it before the US military, it could give the PLA a huge edge. With this technology, the PLA might be able to change the way wars are fought today, get ahead of the US military, and take the lead in future strategic-level competition. In this way, the PLA seems to be shifting from thinking about asymmetric combat to thinking like the Third Offset, which is that new ideas are the key to future battlefield success.

The PLA's big goals are more attainable thanks to the Party's mid-2017 New Generation AI Development Plan, which wants for China to be the world leader in AI technologies by 2030. To do this, the focus will be on creating technologies with two uses that can be huge hits in the market and can also be used by the PLA in the future. Data has become an important strategic tool for China in order to reach this goal. As we already talked about, intelligent machine learning needs a lot of data. By 2020, China will have 20% of the world's data, and by 2030, it will have 30%. All of this data will be easy for smart machine algorithms to access and train. It's not even close from any other country.

The PLA is still figuring out how it will use dual-use intelligent machine technology, even though many people think that "intelligentized" combat is the way of the future. The PLA's first use of intelligent machine technologies will probably be to improve the way strategic and tactical level commanders think. This will be done by giving them better training and machine-advisors.

This use doesn't come from learning the lessons of foreign wars like most people do. Instead, it comes from AlphaGo's success at Go, which we already talked about. Chinese strategists think that warfare and Go are theoretically similar, so this event really caught the attention of PLA thinkers.

It looks like intelligent robots can now do the complex analysis and strategic thinking that is needed to lead battles. It's important to note that since smart robots can beat the best humans at games, they might also be able to win wars. Machines that are smart could now be very important in making decisions about war in the future. At least at first, this involvement may be to help higher-level commanders come up with plans of action, weigh their choices, and figure out what the most likely outcomes are. This can be done very quickly, which means that PLA leaders might be able to stay inside an enemy's decision cycle.

One early use for intelligent machine command advisers could be in certain high-value systems. The PLA Navy is currently looking into making tools that are smart enough to help submarine captains. This support may not only help these people handle a very difficult task, but it may also make Chinese leaders smarter and more skilled, making them on par with US Navy captains with more experience. It's possible that clever machine assistants would work well in a submarine. As was already said, this kind of technology works best in low-complexity settings with little to middling uncertainty.

At the tactical level, the major focus is on smart machine technology that could help with swarm ideas. People see intelligent swarms as a disruptive technology that has the potential to change the way we fight and how we organise our forces. As a result, many civilian and military study groups have been publishing work related to swarms. For example, several Chinese defence companies have recently shown off swarming air systems.

The main goal of this work seems to be to create smart swarms that can do their jobs in harsh electronic warfare settings. This might have been an interest because the PLA thinks it is behind the US in information warfare because it doesn't have as good of networks for sharing data as the US does. This problem might be fixed by giving unmanned devices more freedom.

Aside from being interested in command advising and swarm ideas, China has also learned a lot about how to use intelligent machine technology to manage its people (see the next section). These methods might be useful in places other than China. The country is slowly going deeper into faraway places with its military, like Africa and the Middle East. The new military base in Djibouti is the first of its kind, but others will surely come after it. Also, the One Belt/One Road initiative is likely to create large, possibly dangerous Chinese enclaves in places where crime is common, terrorism is possible, and social unrest happens from time to time. For instance, by 2023, there may be 500,000 Chinese living in Gwadar, Pakistan. They will likely be accompanied by a big PLA Navy Marine Corps unit. Intelligent machine population monitoring and control techniques were created by China to keep the country from becoming unstable. These techniques could be used in other places, like military bases and enclaves in the ocean.

Insurgencies would have a hard time getting started because China uses clever machine technology to keep a close eye on everything all the time. The Chinese monitoring system would need to be made stronger for use overseas because it uses open, weak CCTV cameras that can recognise faces to keep an eye on people of interest. But the price of these cameras is going down quickly, so even if a lot of them are lost, they will be easy to replace.

Internal Security Measures in China

The Chinese Military Strategy White Paper from 2015 talks about worries about the security inside the country. China is afraid that outside powers will start "colour revolutions," which could lead to groups of unhappy Chinese people trying to overthrow Party rule. To stop this from happening, groups are actively stopped from coming together. Individual protest is usually okay, as long as it doesn't lead to a group protest, which could be for good or bad reasons. The goal of ongoing, wide-scale, deep surveillance of the people is to stop this kind of protest.

Chinese society has been under close monitoring for many years, but using smart machine technologies has made it stronger while lowering the need for staff. These technologies are being used by the government with help from private Chinese IT companies like Baidu, Alibaba, and Tencent. As a result, the businesses have a financial reason to improve the effectiveness and value of government surveillance technologies and methods.

The most important thing is intelligent machine technology that runs face recognition software. The Chinese government's Skynet system is putting in about 570 million CCTV cameras across the country. This is a lot more than people could properly watch and evaluate. Skynet finds and follows people all over the country, automatically informing people in the hierarchical command structure when they need to be. The data that was gathered by the different companies and government agencies is shared broadly, but the Party-State is the only one who owns the full, merged dataset. Skynet can only work with technologies that make machines smarter. At the same time, the data that is collected and processed helps the machines get smarter and better at what they do. The government of China thinks that this positive feedback machine-learning loop will be able to predict criminal behaviour in the future.

The goal is to make Chinese society better by changing how people will act in the future. Smart machines are now part of the new social cash system. Algorithms are being taught to look at huge amounts of data so that they can rate people and businesses on how trustworthy they are in political and economic matters. Bad citizens will be punished, and good citizens will be recognised. For this kind of programme to work, it has to connect a lot of different types of data islands, like those used for traffic tracking, banking, education, the justice system, health datasets, social media, shopping data, and smartphones. This is a very hard technical job. By 2020, all 1.3 billion Chinese people will have to use the social credit scheme. Its size and complexity can only be handled by tools that are smart.

Deep societal spying systems used to need a lot of people to work, and they weren't always useful because of the staff's normal human flaws. Most of these problems can be fixed by using the taught algorithms. The computers can keep watching people 24 hours a day, seven days a week, grade their behaviour, and keep rewarding or punishing them based on rules set by the Party's top leaders. Lower-level biases and the chance of corruption are less likely to happen because people don't have to depend on the government, the courts, or even the police. People have said that the Party-State doesn't follow the "rule of law" but rather a "rule by law" mantra. As time goes on, though, it looks like the Party will switch to "rule by algorithm."

Russian Methods

Russia's President Vladimir Putin recently said, "Whoever becomes the leader in this [AI] sphere will become the ruler of the world." This has also brought attention to algorithmic warfare. He thinks that making more clever machines is a good idea so that no one state can be the most powerful. When there is balance in machine forces, the world order is stable and there are no conflicts.

Like China, Russia is putting more money into research and development for clever machines even though it knows it is behind other countries. Still, big plans are being made. For example, by 2025, the combat Industrial Committee wants 30% of combat equipment to be robotic. Intelligent machine technology is already being used in a number of Russian military bases.

The new military national command centre has systems with learning algorithms that put together a lot of data from different military and private sources. The logistic systems that help units in Syria use optimising algorithms to make the most of the flow of supplies and moves. Lastly, air defence sites use smart machine technologies to automatically figure out what threats are there.

At the tactical level, however, most of the well-known robotic systems are just devices that can be managed from afar. They are more like technology from the earlier programmable era than the new intelligent machine era. Still, Russia is putting a lot of effort into making ground combat systems, all the way up to main battle tanks, that use smart machine technologies. This is different from how the West thinks. This focus comes from problems related to demographics and reducing the number of battlefield deaths.

In terms of population, Russia has two big problems: the number of people living there is falling, and people are living longer. Every year, fewer and fewer young people join the job, making it harder to staff the armed forces. This is especially true for land forces that have always relied on recruiting or conscription to keep a lot of young men. So, intelligent tools are a technological way to stop Russia's population loss. They are also attractive because most deaths happen on the land battlefield. In the future, smart tools could do the more dangerous tasks on the battlefield, which would greatly reduce the number of casualties.

At the same time, Russian thinkers know that land force, human-on-the-loop, and human-out-of-the-loop systems are hard to build properly. Because of this, work is being done to find a way for remotely controlled vehicles to get back online if their links are lost due to electronic jamming or other interference. This is being done instead of automating the vehicles so they can fight without human direction.

Because intelligent machines are naturally emergent, the Russian military and security industry are worried that these systems might act without being told what to do by humans. This idea might have been strengthened by the recent events involving "Alice," an experimental AI robot from Russia's Yandex company, going rogue within a day of going online, similar to what happened with Microsoft's "Tay" in 2016 (which we've already talked about).

Russian Information Warfare

Like the Chinese, the Russians have come up with new ways to use algorithms in warfare that go beyond standard warfighting. Both Russia and China have said they are very worried about other countries starting "colour revolutions." But unlike China, the Russian government thinks that the best way to defend itself is to attack, and that making other countries less stable will help keep Russia stable itself. This approach is a lot like things that were done during a lot of the Soviet era.

Russia's modern strategy is well known. It includes active measures, especially in Europe and the US, like spreading fake news and using conspiracy websites, troll farms, networks of automatic accounts, and targeted social media abuse. These kinds of actions are meant to make people afraid and suspicious in the societies they are aimed at, which will hurt trust in political processes and change the results of elections.

Intelligent algorithms are very important for two main tasks: first, they use big data to figure out who the best targets are, and second, they keep improving ongoing "attacks" against those targets over time. The idea behind the approach is to slowly make some people's views stronger in a way that makes them more extreme, but not to drastically change their views. For the first time, intelligent machine programmes make it possible to tailor war to each person.

This method is marked by two important new ideas. First, the "big data" stores that are used were mostly created by businesses. They can be reached in two ways: directly by buying data or indirectly by hacking into them. Also, the people who are being targeted are the ones who create the data; it doesn't have to be actively sought.

Second, Russia has figured out how to use Facebook, Twitter, Google, and other companies' systems against them. These companies have divided people into different groups so that they can send information to each person in the way that their business algorithms choose. For years, Russia has given these global social media giants false information that is meant to be shared by their own algorithms in a way that helps Russia's goals.

Because of this, these businesses now have to make defensive programmes to keep themselves and their customers safe from being taken advantage of in the future. A cyber battleground is starting to form with competing programmes.

This fight is getting tougher because smart machines can now make fake news in any form (text, audio, image, video, etc.) that is almost impossible to tell from the real thing. Soon, YouTube might have videos of politicians announcing war on another country that look real, even after a lot of technical testing. These kinds of fakes could break up groups and societies, especially during times of trouble. Then, algorithms might start wars, though maybe not quite the way that people who are afraid of robot terminators thought they would.

China and Russia are working on new ways to use algorithms for fighting, which gives us a chance to see how other people think about this new area. It is important and troubling that both China and Russia use computational warfare to control societies and to make others less stable. Russia's use of other people's algorithms as its own shows how smaller countries might at least partially fight in the new age of "intelligent" warfare.

Ethical Considerations and Legal Ramifications in Armed Conflict

These days, intelligent robots can only do certain things. They can only do specific jobs and have a hard time applying what they've learned to new places or situations. The learning algorithms that robots use make them unpredictable, even though they are very good at looking through huge amounts of data to find connections, patterns, and associations. They are still shaped by Moravec's paradox, which says that while smart machines can easily do high-level thinking, it's hard for them to copy a one-year-old's sensor processing or motor skills. For robots, hard things are easy and simple things are hard.

When smart machines are used in war and have to follow long-standing moral rules and a big body of law called the Law of Armed Conflict, their flaws become even worse. When states are at war, they have to follow certain rules about how they can use technology. Non-state players like Islamic State and Al Qaeda choose to be different on purpose, accepting the moral shame and ridicule that comes with it.

Individuals who value morality and the benefits that comes with it must follow moral and legal rules when using clever machines in war. There is a lot of discussion these days about whether machines that are smart can meet such high standards.

Ethical Concerns

When people talk about the values and ethics of using smart machines, Isaac Asimov's famous "Three Laws of Robotics" stand out. These made-up rules say that robots should be made to act in these ways:

- A robot may not injure a human being or, through inaction, allow a human being to come to harm.
- A robot must obey orders given it by human beings except where such orders would conflict with the First Law.
- A robot must protect its own existence as long as such protection does not conflict with the First or Second Law.

These "laws" seem to apply to all problems, even though Asimov himself wrote several books that explored a number of ambiguities and concerns. Even though smart machines today aren't advanced enough to follow Asimov's advice, the three laws do bring up a much bigger problem.

Since World War II, automated machines have been used to kill people in battle. Anti-personnel land mines are the most obvious example of this. It doesn't look like people will give up their automated guns any time soon, for better or worse. Now, the bigger question is how to use automated weapons, especially their newest form, intelligent warfighting machines, in a way that is moral and follows the rules of war.

Some people who accept this challenge take the argument further by saying that it is morally wrong for a machine to choose to kill someone. It is still possible to make machines that can kill people, but they shouldn't be able to decide to kill. That is, algorithms shouldn't decide who lives and who dies because that treats people like things and takes away their moral status.

On the other hand, some people say that this makes intelligent machines more like people, even though they only look at data probabilistically and can't or don't make moral decisions. The relevant commander is the one who turned on the machine and gave it the job of making life or death decisions. This person is accountable for a decision's results in both a moral sense and under the laws of armed conflict. With the commander's position comes the onus to understand the machines under control. Intelligent machines however display emergent behaviour; getting an adequate 'understanding' is more problematic than it may initially seem as further discussed later.

With the fear about machines killing humans comes worries over Jus Ad Bellum, making just war. Some consider that with access to intelligent machines, political leaders could find it easier to fight wars because few soldiers are now being exposed to danger. With little chance of friendly casualties, the political leaders could be emboldened to fight more and greater wars, possibly involving unlawful aggression and thus being unjust. This perspective, which has also been stated about airpower, is generic because it can be applied to any technology that offers high levels of own-force protection. Such technology it is believed will create a moral hazard which political leaders are reluctant to oppose; the argument suggests a form of technology determinism.

The apparent failing though is not so much with intelligent machines, airpower or force protection but rather with political leaders. While the dangers of unjust wars are invoked, there are countervailing worries that waging unjust wars will expose the political leadership's country to terrorism from within and becoming trapped in an unwinnable conflict. Such worries would seem to require all political leaders to balance opportunities and risks before purposefully starting a war irrespective of whether intelligent machine technology is employed or not. Unjust wars may still happen. Constraining intelligent machine technology does not seem a step that will prevent political leaders undertaking them.

Rules of Armed Conflict

In the past century, numerous ethical considerations pertaining to the conduct of warfare have been assimilated into the legal framework governing armed conflict. The legislation seeks to establish regulations governing the utilisation of weapon systems in military operations, guided by four fundamental concepts.

The primary concern in armed conflicts is discrimination, often known as distinction, which entails combatants making a deliberate effort to distinguish between civilians and combatants. It is imperative that acts of aggression refrain from purposefully targeting non-combatants. The second principle pertains to military necessity, which dictates that the utilisation of military force should be limited to activities that are deemed essential for the attainment of war objectives. The utilisation of force should be limited to the minimum required amount. The third principle pertains to the avoidance of needless suffering, wherein the employment of weapons and military tactics that may result in excessive harm or infliction of unnecessary suffering is strictly prohibited. The fourth principle to consider is proportionality, which entails ensuring that the application of military action does not result in an excessive loss of civilian life or damage to civilian infrastructure beyond what is necessary to achieve the desired objectives. The notion of proportionality serves as the foundation for the contemporary emphasis on minimising collateral damage. The intentional avoidance of causing harm to innocent citizens, especially in cases of accidental incidents, should be prioritised.

The concept of discrimination is a primary concern for individuals contemplating algorithmic conflicts. The Campaign to Stop Killer Robots movement asserts that the technical feasibility of developing an intelligent machine capable of discerning between combatants and noncombatants at the same level as humans is highly improbable. The movement advocates for the prohibition of employing intelligent machines in warfare, drawing parallels with other intrinsically indiscriminate weapons such as land mines, cluster bombs, and chemical weapons.

In contrast, during the middle of 2015, a group of experts in the field of intelligent machines and respected scientists collectively composed an open letter addressed to the global community, presenting an argument in favour of prohibiting the usage of intelligent machines due to their propensity for discrimination. The perception was that political leaders in authoritarian regimes could potentially exploit drones as a means to execute targeted assassinations of their political adversaries and potentially even perpetrate mass killings against certain ethnic communities. Hence, it is imperative to prohibit the deployment of advanced autonomous combat systems in order to avert the proliferation of these technologies and the subsequent escalation of an international competition in their development and deployment. These concerns are founded on historical evidence, since there have been instances in which political leaders have attempted to eliminate their adversaries and, in certain cases, entire ethnic communities. In fact, certain authoritarian regimes in the present day persist in engaging in such actions to varied extents. The essence of this argument, similar to the one concerning just war, primarily pertains to political leaders rather than technology. The historical absence of sophisticated warfighting machines did not serve as a deterrent to acts of aggression, as seen by the Roman Empire's successful eradication of the Carthaginian civilization.

An alternate perspective put out by proponents of a moderate stance posits that intelligent robots possess the capability to be trained in a manner that enables them to adhere to the principles of conflict in a more proficient manner than human beings. Human beings are prone to making suboptimal decisions when they fail to adequately analyse complex situations and allow emotions, stress, danger, and fear to impair their judgement. Intelligent machines, unencumbered by inherent human limitations, possess the capability to objectively compute the most optimal course of action in order to preserve the principles and regulations governing warfare.

There appears to be merit in this argument. Tactical-level commanders could potentially benefit from the accessibility of an intelligent machine legal consultant on their smart phones, similar to how higher-level commanders already rely on human legal advisers. It is conceivable to develop algorithms that can emulate the functions of legal advisers, similar to their current application in the business sector. Nevertheless, similar to the current advisors, it appears improbable that intelligent robots would possess the capability to make authoritative decisions.

The process of making intricate decisions regarding military necessity and proportionality necessitates the integration of numerous aspects, both similar and dissimilar, which are distinct to each specific case. These decisions pertain to moral considerations and necessitate the transfer of information from disparate contexts to novel situations. While the foundation of law is derived from the analysis of prior case studies, military law endeavours to apply legal principles to unforeseen future scenarios. As previously mentioned, the aforementioned attributes are beyond the capabilities of current narrow artificial intelligence systems.

The attributes of intelligent machines prompt us to revisit the issue of distinguishing between individuals engaged in warfare and those who are not. The Campaign to Stop Killer Robots raises a valid concern regarding the discriminatory tendencies exhibited by intelligent robots. This phenomenon is especially prevalent in densely populated terrestrial settings, when individuals engaged in fighting and those not directly involved in hostilities frequently coexist in close proximity. In certain instances of armed conflict, unscrupulous belligerents strategically exploit civilian populations as a means of concealing their presence and evading hostile actions. The utilisation of intelligent machine technology in this context presents a highly unfavourable situation, as any instance of failure is seen ethically, legally, and militarily impermissible.

However, it is important to note that there exist warfighting scenarios that pose challenges to intelligent robots beyond the ones commonly identified as problematic. Previous observations have indicated that limited intelligence autonomous systems are ideally suited to operate in contexts characterised by low complexity and minimal uncertainty. These settings can be observed in marine, aerial, and isolated terrestrial regions. In such contexts, individuals who are not directly involved in military activities either have limited presence or may be easily distinguished. These situations appear to be the most suitable for the deployment of intelligent devices.

Nevertheless, two concerns emerge. Currently, a plethora of autonomous missiles designed for less demanding conditions have been created, encompassing anti-ship, anti-air, and anti-surface capabilities. The missiles in question include programmable computers that exhibit several of the shortcomings commonly associated with intelligent machines, such as inflexibility, fragility, inherent software imperfections, and the inability to undergo comprehensive testing across all potential scenarios. The pursuit of compliance with the laws of war is achieved by employing suitable training, tactics, and procedures (TTP) instead than relying on missile programming. By implementing appropriate Targeting Policy and Procedures (TPP), human operators can effectively utilise missiles in a manner that aligns with the principles and regulations of the law of war. It has become widely acknowledged that in instances where operational employment of such weapons results in failures, the blame for these failures lies with the command chain involved rather than just attributing them to the missile itself. Individuals within the hierarchical structure bear legal responsibility.

There is a contention among scholars that due to the uncertain nature of the learning process of intelligent machines and their capacity to make unexplained decisions, it is not possible to attribute accountability to any individual for the failures of these machines. There is a certain degree of logical reasoning inherent in this statement. However, in practical terms, it has become customary to hold the command chain responsible. The decision to employ autonomous systems for strategic advantages in warfare and the establishment of tactics, techniques, and procedures (TTPs) are intentionally made by the command chain. The responsibility for legal accountability should lie with the command chain, as per established norms.

It is crucial to acknowledge that no command chain should possess the misconception that an intelligent computer, a programmable system, or a human will consistently execute tasks exactly as anticipated. Prior to employing such weaponry, it is imperative for the command hierarchy to possess a reasonable expectation of the anticipated functionality of the intelligent machine in question, as well as the potential consequences that may arise in the event of its failure to perform as intended. This topic pertains to the field of classical risk management, specifically focusing on strategies to mitigate the potential harm caused by a malfunctioning machine in the event that the anticipated risk materialises.

The second concern exhibits similarities. The utilisation of intelligent machine technologies appears to hold significant potential in enhancing the currently constrained discriminatory capabilities exhibited by contemporary programmable autonomous missiles. This perspective encompasses the aspirations of individuals who believe that robots have the potential to surpass humans in adhering to the laws of war, as well as the concerns of those who worry about machines exhibiting excessive proficiency in discrimination.

Responsible Use of AI Systems

There are pros and cons to using intelligent tools that make them less useful in some situations and against the rules of war. There are clear rules about how the machines can't be used in ways that could kill people, like in clever machine swarms. These kinds of machines work best in wars that happen at sea, in the air, or on land in rural areas, where civilians aren't likely to be or can't be easily found. It doesn't make sense to use killing robots in places with more problems, like most counter-insurgencies.

Like people who make their own explosives, dishonest enemies may use smart killing tools in the future that can't tell the difference between combatants and civilians. Then it would be up to us to decide how to answer. The second law of war concept, military necessity, gives us a legal way out: we should only use military force to do things that are necessary to win the war. If it takes dishonest actions to win a fair war, then dishonest actions can be met with more dishonest actions.

In the past, many states have used "military necessity" as an excuse to use land mines, even though they knew that the technology was designed to kill anyone. This method is still used: Not all 164 countries have signed the Mine Ban Treaty. China, Russia, India, Iran, North Korea, and the US are among those that have not.

In any future war, the final choice of whether to use smart machines to kill people directly will rely on the situation. In current conflicts, Western forces, like the US, don't react to dishonest enemies by being equally dishonest themselves; in fact, military thought says the exact opposite should happen. The choice is ours, but it depends on the choices our enemy makes as well.

Aside from these tough issues, smart machines have a lot to offer to improve current autonomous weapon discrimination, and not just for attack weapons as was already said. Missile defence systems need to be able to react quickly to attacks, and they mostly use TPPs to make sure they don't kill friendly soldiers or accidentally target civilians. When operational environments get more complicated and electronic warfare jamming happens, this kind of method doesn't work as well.

In these kinds of cases, the highly automated Patriot missile defence system has shot down two friendly aircraft by accident. The problem can't be fully solved because taking away its automatic features would make it unable to consistently shoot down enemy ballistic missiles. It could be lowered, though, by adding smart machine technologies to the Patriot missile's target system. By letting the seeker separately identify the aircraft it is targeting, this would be the last line of defence against accidental shoot downs. This wouldn't stop people from shooting down planes by accident, but it would make it less likely that that would happen. The risk would go down, but the leadership chain would still be responsible.

It seems like the law doesn't put many limits on the use of a clever machine as long as it's not directly killing people. Then, these kinds of machines could be used for a lot of different tasks, such as managing logistics, planning transportation, giving advice to commanders, protecting computers, attacking computers, and a lot of other tasks that help with fighting.

One big thing is different from this generally positive view. Cyberspace is an interesting middle ground where smart machines can work and not directly hurt anyone, but they still offer big risks. Terminator-style robots that are always angry, always have energy, and always have weapons on hand are only in fiction. AI-powered cyber guns look a lot like these made-up robots, even though they are only used in the virtual world. In the future, offensive cyber operations might use smart machine viruses that could copy themselves over and over, get power from their hosts, and never stop fighting in the cyber realm.

To keep things from going so badly, the command chains in charge would have to make sure that these algorithms had failsafe features built into their main code and that these features were checked. Because testing is hard in general, though, this could also be a case where it would be smart to create an intelligent machine cybersecurity defence programme at the same time as the virus.

Aside from these nightmare scenarios, there are more mundane issues that come up when smart tools are used more and more. People may eventually rely heavily on smart machines to give them help and do many tasks for them. There is a chance that algorithmic decisions will eventually take the place of human judgement in many scenarios. But, as we've talked about a lot, smart machines have both strengths and flaws, and there will inevitably be times when they fail. When they do, human users will be held responsible and answerable, just like they are now when things go wrong.

Human duty is still a big part of war ethics and the laws of war, and this responsibility will only grow as more intelligent machines are used in battle. This means that machines might be better at some jobs than people, but only people can "do" responsibility and accountability, which is similar to Moravec's paradox. It looks like there are three clear answers.

First, people who use machines need to know that they can break down and will sometimes do so in strange ways. When they are used tactically, this needs to be taken into account, and the right risk management practises need to be put in place to limit the damage that is done when they fail.

Second, people will need specially designed training programmes to fully understand how their smart machines work in terms of their strengths and flaws. Intelligent tools will change the way people are trained, but they will not get rid of the need for training. People who work with smart tools will have to train together.

Third, the design of the human-machine interface is very important for people to be able to understand what smart computers are doing. People, on the other hand, need to realise that getting this kind of understanding is still hard. Intelligent machines will naturally make choices that can't be explained; they think differently by nature. For humans, the most important thing is to make sure that the odd action by an intelligent machine that can't be explained can be undone.

Conclusion

Because of three major improvements in computer technology, algorithmic warfare is now possible. The first is the exponential rise in computer processing power, which has made it possible to use high-performance machine learning methods. Second, there has been a quick rise in "big data," which refers to very large sets of data that can be used to teach machines how to learn. Third, cloud technology is always getting better, making it easier to view data and processing that are done off-site.

Intelligent machines are different from regular controlled machines in a number of ways. When they are in the same situation, intelligent tools don't always give the same result. They can learn on their own, but it's not always clear what they've learned or how they put information into groups. Neural network machines are even better at this because they learn and change "on the job." They can act in ways that aren't planned and may surprise you, for better or worse.

Intelligent machines are better at processing "big V" data, which means data with a lot of it, a lot of it quickly, and a lot of different kinds of it. When it comes to the amount of data being collected, people will never be able to analyse it all; machine analysis is the only way to go. When it comes to speed, intelligent robots work at machine speed, which is very fast for humans to understand. People have short attention spans, so they tend to favour some info sources over others when it comes to variety. Machines look at facts in a more thorough way.

But smart machines aren't perfect compared to people in some ways. They are very fragile and usually can't handle small changes in environment. Also, these kinds of machines aren't very good at domain adaptation, which means they have trouble using what they've learned in one setting in another. Also, humans are better at intuitive thinking, which means they can draw conclusions from small amounts of data. People tend to make better decisions when there is a lot of confusion around them.

This means that the biggest problem with putting smart tools on the battlefield right now is figuring out how to make them smarter than humans. Task-optimized human-machine interfaces could be the key to getting people and machines to work together better and win future fights.

When used in war, intelligent robots could change the way wars are fought and challenge some long-held beliefs. The present focus on quality could shift, mass could return to the battlefield, and the battle could move faster. These ideas might change the way we think about force structures now. The size of an armed group may not be related to the number of people living in the state that has one. It's possible for small, wealthy states to have much stronger armies than big, poor states. Also, smart machines might make it possible for everyone to get much better training, which would make it less likely for some states to have an edge in skill and experience.

There are two different ways to think about strategy: will smart tools help us do things better, or will they help us do better things? The "do things better" school of thought says that the best way to improve performance is to put smart machines deep into battle networks. At the moment, these kinds of networks have trouble processing and evaluating information. This might be fixed by adding smart tools to the network. The "do better things" school focuses on spreading smart machines in a way that changes the main purpose of battle networks from sharing information to fighting with machines. After that, the battle networks turn into live fighting networks where edge devices are in charge. Machine-speed hyperwar breaks out, and swarming intelligent machines become the basis of strategy.

The United States' progress in algorithmic fighting has sparked interest in the topic in China and Russia. China is now a "fast follower" and is putting in place an ambitious new national plan to become the leader in smart machine technology around the world. The PLA thinks that intelligent machine technology will lead to "intelligentized" warfare instead of the network-centric combat that is used now. If the PLA accepts this change quickly, it might be able to pass the US military. Russia's economy, on the other hand, isn't doing well, which slows down its progress in clever machine technology but makes it necessary to come up with new ideas, using both Russian and foreign technologies.

China and Russia are the leaders in two areas of national defence. China has long tried to keep things stable at home, but these efforts are getting much more targeted and fierce, and smart machines are being used in more and more places. Soon, China will have "rule by algorithm" laws. Russia, on the other hand, uses algorithmic warfare to try to mess up the internal security of other countries. Russia cleverly uses other countries' algorithms against them, which may add a new dimension to this kind of warfare and show how smaller countries can move in this new age of "intelligent" warfare.

The ethics and rules of war are based on the idea that people are responsible and accountable for their actions. Using intelligent machines in war will not fundamentally change this. It's possible that machines are much better at some jobs than people, but the things that smart machines do are naturally hard to explain. Accountability and duty can only be "done" by people.

It looks like smart tools will change the way we fight. In the past, our tools were like extensions of ourselves. They do things that our bodies can do, but they can do them better. Our new machines are not the same, though. They are smart, can learn, show emergent behaviours, and make choices that don't make sense. It's tempting to give them human traits, like we've done for hundreds of years with our gods and animals, but that would be a bad idea. Our new smart tools don't think like humans; they actually reason in a way that is different from ours. They have different logic flows and strange ways of making sense of things. They are really new players in the business of making war, and they bring destructive skills with them. The next war might be different from the last ones. Get ready for a possible restart.

Chapter 4
Artifical Intelligence in Nuclear Conflict

The public, policymakers, and the global defence community all have different ideas about what artificial intelligence (AI) can and can't do in the military world, especially when it comes to nukes. Many of the misunderstandings about AI today come from the exaggerated ways it is portrayed in movies, TV shows, and books, especially the Skynet system in The Terminator. Misrepresentations of the possible benefits and risks of military AI can get in the way of important and constructive debate on these issues. Specifically, the challenge of balancing the possible operational, tactical, and strategic benefits of using AI while managing the risks to stability and nuclear security.

This part takes away the mystery surrounding AI in nuclear weapons and future warfare in general. In particular, it shows how this new technology could affect nuclear security in a lot of different ways. Because military AI is naturally unstable, it may make things worse between nuclear-armed superpowers, especially between China and the US, but not for the reasons you might think.

As a first step in this evaluation, I will look at the things about AI that make it unstable, such as its machine speed, bias, weakness, and ability to make decisions without human input. Then I'll talk about how these traits can make some of the most important factors for nuclear instability (or strategic instability) worse in the age of AI. This is especially true because of the competitive and contested nuclear multipolar world order and the fact that great military powers, especially China and the US, have different levels of comfort with escalation risk. The last thing I'll do is think about what can be done to lower these risks in a future that will almost certainly focus on AI.

Disruptive Aspects of Artificial Intelligence

AI does not exist by itself. In other words, AI probably won't be a major game-changer by itself. Instead, it's more likely to make the already destabilising effects of improved conventional capabilities, especially counterforce capabilities, stronger. This will speed up war and make it harder to make decisions. AI-enhanced command and control (C2) systems might help with some of the problems that come with making strategic decisions as a person, like the tendency to invest in sunk costs, bad risk judgement, cognitive heuristics, and group-think. But it's still not clear what effect they will have at the strategic level.

High-Speed AI Conflict

When it comes to combat power, AI gives us a new way to work and react at machine speed. When autonomy and speed are important in the military, like in missile defence, autonomous weapon systems (AWS), and internet, faster reaction times will probably have big strategic effects. The latest automated missile defence systems, like Terminal High-Altitude Area Defence (THAAD) and Patriot systems, can track and attack hostile targets without any help from a person. However, they can't keep an eye on their own performance and get better without help from a person. AI would make that possible for the next generation.

When AI technology is combined with advanced weapons, these systems might be able to act at machine speed, which would speed up the battle overall. This could happen at the same time in different combat zones. Although being able to react in real time can be helpful from a tactical point of view, especially in asymmetrically contested environments, experts warn that if the speed of combat speeds up a lot, machines could react to situations at a speed that is too fast for humans to understand, and commanders might not be able to control, contain, or end events.

Delegating control to an autonomous system would be a tough moral and tactical choice because human commanders would not be able to move quickly enough. So, in theory, AI-enabled autonomous early warning systems would help defence planners find and track threats faster and more reliably than before. However, because AI machine-learning algorithms are brittle (they don't have enough real-world common sense to deal with new situations) and black box (they are hard to understand), there is a high risk of accidents and false alarms that could cause chaos.

Strategist Thomas Schelling said, "When speed is critical, the victim [in this case a nuclear-armed state] of an accident or a false alarm is under terrible pressure." This is especially true when it comes to the time constraints that come with AI. Nuclear states may be tempted to automate their nuclear retaliatory potential because they are afraid of an enemy that is hard to predict and fights at machine speed. That is, if everything else stays the same, a nuclear-armed state like China, North Korea, Pakistan, or maybe even Russia will be more likely to use technology if it isn't sure it can launch a second nuclear attack.

The fast pace of AI and autonomy can lead to surprising and worsening results. The US Securities and Exchange Commission (SEC) says that the use (or abuse) of autonomous financial trading algorithms led to and grew the 2010 stock market flash crash, which dropped the value of the market by a trillion dollars in just a few minutes. When it comes to foreign relations, there isn't a central authority like there is in the financial markets to enforce fail-safe systems that are pre-programmed and based on a common set of rules. It is very scary to think that something like a flash crash could happen in areas that are hostile, poorly controlled, offensive, and strategically competitive, like internet, missile defence, or anti-satellite weapons (ASATs).

Military AI systems that work at machine speed could speed up battles to the point where machines' actions make it impossible for humans to control (or even understand) what's happening. In the worst situations, human commanders might not be able to stop, change the direction, or start a war. If people lost control of warfare to machines, or gave it to them ahead of time, there would be more unintended ways for it to get worse and more unstable crises, which could have terrible effects. Due to the speed and accuracy of AI, states may feel compelled to make quick decisions. They may be willing to take bigger risks and escalate a conflict if they think they need to in order to avoid losing their abilities to keep their nuclear arsenals safe and under control.

Prejudice in Machine Learning

Even though algorithms are faster, have more data, and can process more information than humans, machine-learning systems will still rely on the assumptions that human engineers build into them. Engineers may introduce their own biases into the systems they design without meaning to. There may be biases built into military support systems that lead to mistakes through feedback loops (action and counterreaction cycles), especially when the fight is crowded and complicated. During the Cold War, for example, the Soviets made a computer programme called VRYAN that was meant to warn Soviet leaders of a US nuclear attack before it happened. However, the data that went into the system was often biassed. This created a feedback loop that made the Kremlin even more afraid that the US was trying to get first-strike advantage. These feedback loops that AI systems create could trap people in the machines' biases and wrong assumptions. So, machine learning systems work a lot like black boxes, which means they are technically very hard to predict and might not be stable.

Also, AI systems will probably make people even less sure about the value, scope, availability, trustworthiness, and meaning of information they already have. For a while to come, narrow AI-powered sensing, self-learning, intelligence gathering and analysis, and decision-making support systems will still have the same cognitive biases and subjectivity problems (like attribution error, decision-making heuristics, path-dependency, and dissonance) that people have always had when making foreign policy and national security decisions.

Exposure to Cyber Threats

AI could both make the military less vulnerable to cyberattacks and make them more vulnerable. On the one hand, AI cyber-defence tools (also called "counter-AI") are made to spot changes in a network's behaviour patterns and other strange things. These tools can automatically find holes in software code, which could make the defence against cybersubversions stronger. The Defence Innovation Unit (DIU) of the US Department of Defence (DoD) is making a prototype of an app that uses AI to figure out complex strategic questions, map out likely sequences of events, and come up with new strategies. This will make DoD systems more resistant to cyberattacks that use AI and fix mistakes faster than humans can.

An enemy, on the other hand, might use malware to take over, change, or trick the behaviour and pattern recognition systems of automated systems. In 2011, at the Creech US Air Force Base in Nevada, it was very hard for analysts to find malware that had infected the systems that controlled the cockpits of American UAVs (Predator and Reaper drones) that were flying flights over war zones in the Middle East. Offensive attacks like this would be pretty simple to carry out but hard to find, credit, or effectively defend against.

It is now thought that a cyberattack could get into a nuclear weapons system, risk the security of its communications, and eventually take over its nuclear and nonnuclear command and control systems, possibly without the target's knowledge. So, progress in AI could make this problem worse by making it easier to improve cybercrime, which would give more benefits to those who get there first. For instance, AI and machine learning could greatly lower the amount of work and expert knowledge needed to carry out advanced persistent threat (APT) operations, also known as "hunting for weaknesses." As AI APT tools get better, they might make it cheap and simple for would-be attackers to make copies of powerful cyber weapons that don't require a lot of technical know-how.

Tools for cyberattacks already exist that can be used to manipulate and break into systems. However, AI and more military authority could make future cyberattacks faster, stronger, and bigger. China, Russia, and the US have continued to strengthen their AI cyberdefences in reaction to these expected holes and to get the upper hand by being the first to do so. For example, open sources show that Chinese experts think that cyberattacks on China's nuclear command, control, and communication (NC3) systems are very likely to get worse, even if the attackers' only goal was to spy on China. China is worried that its early-warning missile systems aren't good enough to defend itself against a disarming first strike by the US. This is why Beijing is putting a lot of effort into reducing false negatives, which happen when early-warning systems don't detect an impending attack but do detect one that doesn't exist. AI-enhanced cyber capabilities that both make attacks less likely and encourage others to do so could make the paradox of better capabilities and greater vulnerabilities in the cyber realm even worse.

Machine-Based Decision Processes

As AI systems become more involved in making strategic decisions, the risks and weaknesses that come with armed autonomy are likely to grow. Despite AI's possible tactical and operational effects, former DARPA head Arati Prabhakar says the technology is still "fundamentally limited" because it mistakes objects for other things and is easy to fake. Prabhakar also says that AI systems often make decisions that can't be explained, which is different from mistakes people would make. In one case, Prabhakar showed how a machine-learning algorithm got a picture of a baby holding a toothbrush wrong and thought it was a picture of a baby holding a baseball bat. It would be naturally unstable for AI systems to make mistakes and choices that can't be predicted when they are used on a large scale and in many different areas of war.

AI that can't understand context (i.e., why people do things and what happens as a result) or empathise (i.e., figure out what someone is trying to do) would probably be less useful in wartime, when having some leeway in the chain of command is usually seen as a good thing. For instance, the almost disastrous ICBM test at the US Vandenberg Air Force Base during the Cuban Missile Crisis in 1962 was blamed on officers following set rules without asking them when new information came in. Human mistakes usually happen one at a time and don't happen again in the same way. AI systems, on the other hand, could fail all at once and keep failing in the same way. Philosopher Nick Bostrom, for example, says that "general" AI applications could take over the world in their quest to make paper clips more efficiently in his vision of an AI future. That is, AI-enhanced systems making choices to reach predetermined human goals in ways that are basically not human, with outcomes that are uncertain and may not have been intended.

It's just a thought, but putting superintelligent AI systems (i.e., machines with intelligence that exceeds human cognitive abilities) up against humans with nuclear weapons would bring up similar questions that human commanders in modern warfare do: what are AI's goals and intentions? How could smart machines be stopped, forced, or controlled? And how could someone get them to help calm things down? For example, general AI systems that work at machine speed and have oracle-like predictive foresight could make all strategic decisions, taking over the role of human intelligence and choice in the systems that are meant to control and manage the start, growth, and end of war.

A bigger point is that AI's ability to stop people from doing something depends on how dangerous people think the thing they can do is in times of crisis or war. Using AI-enhanced powers in a crisis might actually make an enemy act more cautiously, which would strengthen stability, as long as the capability creates more uncertainty. As a result, adding AI to a situation might make people less sure of what will happen, which could make states (especially those facing a stronger enemy) more likely to trust machines to make decisions. But because this kind of stance is hard to show before a crisis or conflict, this implied threat could also make the crisis more unstable. For example, AI systems that are designed to aggressively seek tactical and operational advantages might mistake (or ignore) an enemy's attempt to calm down a situation as a sign that an attack is about to happen. These changes would make it more likely that things would get worse by accident and that the first strike would not be stable.

If leaders decide to give more power to AI systems that are naturally rigid, the dehumanisation of future defence planning will make things less stable by making it much harder to initiate. Human induction, or the skill of being able to draw broad conclusions from specific pieces of information, is an important part of defence planning, mostly for dealing with situations that need a lot of moral and visual thinking and judgement. Others have warned that if human leaders put too much faith in AI analysis without fully understanding how machines get to a certain result, human decision-makers might trust machine-generated data without questioning it. For instance, the 2018 Tesla Model 3 crash, in which a driver in autopilot mode hit a fire truck on a motorway, made it very clear what can happen when you put too much trust in automated technology, even if it's not AI.

Automation bias is when people use machines instead of carefully looking for information, checking it twice, and making sure they are doing the right thing while they are handling it. This trend could make defence managers more likely to think that decisions made by AI algorithms are the same as (or even better than) decisions made by humans. Over-reliance on automation in military decision-making will likely lead to strategic instability if people don't use their own judgement, instincts, and sense of responsibility.

Determinants of Nuclear Instability

The unstable conditions that AI could create could threaten the security of the world's nuclear (or strategic) systems. During the second half of the 20th century, the idea of nuclear or strategic stability came about. This idea is still debated in theory and politics, but it has been a useful way to think about how highly advanced weapons could threaten stability. While there isn't a single, agreed upon definition, list of factors that contribute to strategic stability, or even agreed upon way to measure it, the best way to think of it is as a situation in which no country has a reason to launch a nuclear first strike. This makes it less likely that a crisis caused by mistake or misunderstanding will escalate into full-on war. In the end, it is the result of a complicated mix of military, economic, and political factors, with technology playing a number of roles. Technological change and strategic stability are both affected by a number of disruptive forces that work together in a complicated way. These forces can weaken strategic stability and increase the likelihood of conflict during times of high global rivalry, great power transitions, and strategic surprise.

Nuclear multipolarity and different military powers' risk tolerance for escalation are two things that are already in place that could make nuclear instability worse. When these factors come together with the naturally deterrence-deterring military AI systems we talked about earlier, they will create a situation where forces can interact in a way that makes it easy for nuclear-armed states to make mistakes and misunderstand each other. This will raise the risks of escalation and failures in deterrence under the shadow of nuclear weapons.

Nuclear Multipolarity

When compared to bipolarity during the Cold War, the rise of nuclear multipolarity in the Second Nuclear Age has created many ways for a nuclear conflict with more and more nuclear-armed sides to get worse. This diversity is important because each state will decide how to react to the new options that come up in the digital age in its own unique way. Some states might not care about AI's limitations and lower safety and verification standards in order to get ahead (the "first-mover advantage") on the future digital battlefield.

Through history, we can see that as military technology and tactics get more complicated, strategic competition—the drive to control warfare—tends to get stronger. So, the fact that big powers like China, the US, and Russia are all chasing AI technology is likely to make things less stable by making big powers compete with each other more.

In this bad political situation, people think that AI-enhanced weapons can help in strategic ways, but they also pose risks to nuclear security and stability. The biggest threat right now is the hasty use of unsafe, unproven, and unreliable AI technology in nuclear weapons decisions, which could have terrible results. For instance, the spread of low-risk, low-cost AI-enhanced autonomous weapons with unclear rules of engagement, like drone swarms, will become a more appealing asymmetric way to weaken an enemy's military strength, deterrence, and resolve.

When competing states have to make choices under the threat of nuclear war, they are more likely to think the worst of others. This is especially true when the legitimacy of the status quo is in question, like in maritime Asia. "As long as the system remains anarchic, states will be tempted to use force to change an unacceptable status quo," says scholar John Mearsheimer. For this reason, if one country tries to make its strategic forces more resilient by using cutting-edge dual-use technology like AI, the other side might see this as a possible threat to its ability to survive and react to a nuclear first or second strike.

In a world full of revisionist and unhappy nuclear-armed states, it doesn't seem likely that gains in AI would have a stabilising effect on intelligence gathering and analysis. To make this happen, everyone would need to have the same access to information and trust in the systems' accuracy and reliability. For any reassurances or attempts to build trust to work, everyone involved would also have to have good intentions. Because nuclear interactions involve more and more complicated interactions between nuclear and non-nuclear actors (as well as state and non-state actors), using AI in this multipolar setting will put more and more pressure on nuclear states to become less stable. All of these interactions will probably make it harder to handle things when they get worse during future crises or conflicts, especially when China and the US are involved.

Contrasting Approaches to Escalation Risk in US-China Relations

Even though both US and Chinese defence experts are aware of the risks of escalation between nuclear-armed superpowers, neither country's doctrines talk about how an enemy might react to escalation. Instead, these competing strategic communities think that escalation in future conflict can be successfully stopped and limited by achieving and maintaining escalation dominance. It is Chinese doctrine that they should take the lead early and preventively in conventional combat to gain escalation dominance. However, this could have the opposite effect, causing a rapid and possibly uncontrollable rise to a nuclear level of conflict.

But there is no proof that China plans to use nuclear missiles for escalation dominance or to intentionally make things worse. Without agreed upon escalation thresholds and a mutual framework to stop either side from violating them, a Sino-American crisis where either side thinks it can effectively control escalation (for example, in the South China Seas, the Korean Peninsula, or the Taiwan Straits) would likely increase the risks of unintentional escalation because both sides overestimate their ability to keep things from getting out of hand.

Avery Goldstein, a political science professor at the University of Pennsylvania, says that China may be overconfident in its ability to keep a normal military conflict from turning into a nuclear war. This could make it more likely for a conflict or crisis to cross the nuclear line by accident. Also, different ideas about how China and the US should handle escalation below and above the nuclear threshold could make the situation less stable. It seems that people in the US defence community are less worried about how the US could handle escalation above the nuclear threshold and more worried that a low-level conventional war could turn into a nuclear one. During a crisis between China and the US, Washington may overstate the chance that Beijing will use nuclear weapons while simultaneously understating how big of a reaction China would make with nuclear weapons.

Also, if there was a future conflict between the US and China, the US would have a strong reason to attack China's mobile missiles and the command, control, communications, and intelligence (C3I) systems that go with them in order to gain escalation dominance. Beijing might mistake this for a conventional counterforce attack, or even worse, as a prelude to a first nuclear strike. Most Chinese analysts think that the US wants to weaken China's small nuclear deterrent and the systems that back it with advanced conventional weapons, especially the US's conventional prompt global strike and missile defences. In short, the US and China have different ideas about how to stop a low-level conventional or nuclear conflict from getting worse. This makes it more likely that a conventional conflict will get worse.

Managing military escalation risk, especially when it happens by accident, has not been a traditional part of Chinese strategic thought. A lot of people in China's strategic community are sure that the country's long-standing "no-first-use" (NFU) nuclear promise will keep things from getting worse. Chinese analysts see China's NFU pledge as a de facto firebreak between using its conventional and nuclear weapons to calm down a situation. This could lead to overconfidence, which could increase the risk of unintentional escalation. This overconfidence could make it less likely for Chinese leaders to see the risks of escalation that come from misjudging or misinterpreting US goals.

One reason China is so calm about escalation is that they think that once the nuclear "Rubicon" is crossed, neither side will be able to quickly stop the use of nuclear weapons. The way Chinese experts think about this means they don't think a limited nuclear war would stay limited. Also, China's operational strategy doesn't include plans for a limited nuclear war, which it might do if it thought it could keep nuclear tensions from rising.

Another thing that makes things more difficult is that new escalation thresholds and working norms for weapons that use AI have not yet been set. People think that the thresholds used now for autonomous weapons systems are not clear or suitable. When armies use military AI, they might accidentally cross already vague escalation thresholds if they don't know what their enemies' strategic priorities and political goals are.

In 2016, China took a US underwater drone because it was thought to be a threat to Chinese marine navigation. In return, Washington said China's actions were "illegal" and said the drone was a "sovereign immune vessel." China returned the drone at the end of the episode, ending days of international tension. This shows the risk of unintentional escalation that comes with using new technology (especially technology with more than one use) in disputed territory between strategic rivals. In conclusion, the growing number of technologies like AI that can be used for warfighting, coercion, and influence, along with the first-strike vulnerability and chance they create, will have big effects on how wars escalate in the future.

The Nuclear Threat of Artificial Intelligence

In a multipolar nuclear world order, the effects of advanced military technology that is working together in more complicated ways are likely to get worse. This includes military AI. In a multipolar world, nuclear-armed states that use AI to get or keep first-mover benefits are likely to upset this fragile order, with results that are hard to predict.

Because AI-enhanced capabilities could interact in many ways with strategic weapons (both nuclear and conventional weapons with strategic effects), it will be very important for analysts, academics, and decision-makers to a) fully grasp how these different capabilities interact with each other and b) learn how different strategic communities see these changes and what they mean for nuclear and conventional weapons.

To avoid or at least lessen the destabilising and escalating risks that military AI poses, the world's two biggest militaries—the US and China—need to work together to boost trust and stop some of the threats to stability that are talked about in this chapter. In particular, the world's biggest powers should set up an international framework for rules, laws, transparency, and governance when it comes to developing and using military weapons that are enhanced by AI. These models need to include not only what is happening now but also what might happen in the future. For example, they should include what is and isn't being built into AI algorithms and the best way to keep the public from thinking too much about killer robots and machines taking over the world.

In the end, for these efforts to be successful, everyone involved will have to see why they need to take steps towards creating a clear governance structure that will institutionalise and ensure compliance with the design and use of AI technology in the military. They will also have to see how these steps could benefit everyone. In the future, researchers should look into how changing motivations can make strategic stability better and what counter-AI and adversarial AI tools are needed to lower these risks.

Chapter 5
AI-Enhanced Offensive Capabilities in Cyber and Nuclear Defence

Introduction

The new technologies in computers and other related systems continue to amaze us, and they are being made faster than ever. More memory has been added to computers, and algorithms have become more complicated, allowing them to handle more difficult tasks. With the help of Machine Learning, an AI tool, systems can now even teach themselves and get better on their own. Armed forces all over the world have seen the benefits of these kinds of technological advances and are already trying and using a range of AI technologies in their work. We couldn't say that AI is used as widely in the military as it is in business, but the United States, China, and Russia are already three of the most important countries in the world when it comes to study and practise. When AI is used in this way today, it changes the balance of power between countries because new tools are being made and used and new targets for crimes are being made, especially in internet.

AI is a new way for states to judge the strength, power, and abilities of other states and decide whether they are an ally or a danger. But we can't yet trust this criterion because the different levels of AI growth in each state will change how it judges others. The fact that AI isn't being studied or described as a weaponized technology in the military right now, especially in a way that everyone agrees on, makes it even harder to make objective decisions.

This paper will talk about the current trends, laws, and main types of AI-powered weapons, as well as what they mean for war, international relations, and society as a whole. It's not about analysing the technical details of the technologies as they are; instead, it's about giving people ideas about how AI could affect the military in the future.

Wars have changed the way they happen and have spread to new areas, like online. It can now have many aspects at once and contain a huge amount of different data that AI is the only way to help sort and analyse quickly enough to make a good choice before the enemy does. The above breakthroughs show that not only do we need to use cutting edge tools and methods in military operations and tasks, but we also need to rethink what war is and why it happens.

The Pentagon found a security paradox in the way we use and depend on digital technologies: these technologies give us powers and speeds that humans have never seen before, but they also make people feel less safe. This technology dominance will definitely throw off the balances, redistribute wealth, make new alliances and maybe even break up old ones. It will also bring new threats to the world.

Explanations

Autonomy, in human-machine interaction and cooperation, is divided into three categories, useful to understand for the better understanding of the notions described in this chapter. The systems' tasks that are fully controlled by a person are called "human-in-the-loop". Systems that can operate in a semi-autonomous way, thus completing tasks on their own, with humans however being in charge of reviewing functions or decisions by the systems and with the ability to intervene, are "human-supervised" systems. The third category is "human-out- of-the-loop" where, as the title indicates, the system operates autonomously, with humans not being able to intervene.

Escalation is "an increase in the intensity or scope of conflict that crosses a threshold(s) considered significant by one or more of the participants"".

The term "cyber" is used to explain everything that has to do from "networks to hardware, software, automation, industrial controls, hacking, bullying, warfare... social media".

AI (Artificial Intelligence) is considered a "generic term that washes over meaningful distinctions between its different manifestations"", something that creates "confusion, especially regarding claims about its revolutionary effects". More technically defined, though, "AI consists of algorithms that form the basis of pattern recognition software. When combined with high-performance computing power, data scientists are able to probe and find meaning in massive data collections. AI also includes language processing, knowledge representation and inferential reasoning". AI is divided into Narrow and General AI, with Narrow AI enabling "discrete problem-solving tools designed to perform specific narrow tasks"", while General AI is all about "technologies designed to mimic and recreate functions of the human brain". Nowadays, more and more theoretical approaches and research have been focused on the so-called Artificial Superintelligence (ASI), a term first introduced by philosopher Nick Bostrom who defines it as "intelligence which possesses cognition that significantly and consistently outstrips human cognition". Nevertheless, ASI remains a theoretical concept, as we are still far from its practice in real life.

Narrow AI is the technology that allows the analysis of vast amounts of unprocessed data, a function extremely helpful in the military context and especially at times of crisis where quick action is called for.

Lethal Autonomous Weapons Systems (LAWS): With the term already indicating the severity of this technology, LAWS or, otherwise, "killer robots" is a term that does not enjoy international official adoption, yet it is generally defined as a system of weapons able to select and attack targets without any need for human control or intervention. Development of LAWS is a result of a militarizing Narrow AI since 2017. Independent researchers and experts have given their own definitions, with the essence of LAWS being described as "weapons that can select, detect and engage targets with little to no human intervention'". Their strictly offensive nature is a determinative argument against their development and in favor of their ban in many countries, notably Japan, due to the pacific viewpoints and humanitarian concerns that rule the 21st century. Currently and while LAWS are not per se regulated by the international humanitarian law, they have to be treated like other weapon systems; in accordance to the provisions and principles of IHL.

Hyperwar is a type of automated or autonomous conflict which uses AI and other relevant technologies and applications in such a way, that it could lead to a minimization of the need for human control over decision-making.

Methodology

So far, most research on military AI technologies has been focused on the technical aspects of these new systems and the confusing environment they create. As a result, there is a lack of information about what these technologies mean in the strategic field. Theoretical approaches should have looked at the possible results of using cutting-edge AI technologies on the battlefield, but there aren't many case studies available. The bibliography that is available is also pretty small. This chapter is based on scientific research papers and pieces that were published in 2018 or later and can be found anywhere in the world, either for free or through subscriptions at academic institutions. Between March and September 2022, research for the draught and final submission of the document was done on scientific databases such as Scopus and EBSCO. Up-to-date reports and papers were also used to gather information on the subject.

People from different countries have very different ideas about technology. For example, they don't even agree on how to define Artificial Intelligence. Because of this, the study is different depending on where the information comes from, like a report from Europe or the US military. Each has its own rules, standards, and ways of doing things.

General overview of Considerations and National Policies

Some people who study International Relations make an interesting case: technology doesn't really change how wars are fought on a tactical or practical level. Instead, it changes how people think about and feel about wars on a political and psychological level. This point of view is supported by the fact that technology does change the balance of power. As technology is seen as the main tool for global dominance in today's world, resources are redistributed when new technologies are created or bought. Unfortunately, we can't say for sure what the effects, pros and cons of using AI as a weapon will be because we haven't seen it happen on a bigger scale and the technology itself isn't changing.

"We can't expect to win tomorrow's wars with yesterday's weapons and gear," said Rear Admiral Andrew Loiselle, who is the deputy head for Future Joint Force Development on the Joint Staff 17.

When thinking about how AI can be used in the military, algorithmic warfare is one of the most interesting new types of conflict that could "take over" military activities. The military uses many different kinds of algorithms to sort and predict enemies, figure out how many people they need, and come up with plans. When there is a national security crisis, like a war, these systems grow and change. Big data, the cloud, and smart machines are all involved in algorithmic warfare. This makes private data more vulnerable to cyberattacks that could destroy an enemy's command and national security system from the inside.

Artificial intelligence (AI) has the power to change the current political and strategic balances. The fact that defensive technologies are getting better shows that attacking technologies are also getting stronger. A steady race between countries to make their military technologies more effective (and, by extension, dangerous) is one of the main fears. Another is the fear of surprise attacks. Artificial intelligence is seen by some countries as the new tool and way to take over the world. The scientific literature on the subject says that the balance of power will soon shift in a different way if the United States doesn't catch up with other countries' militarised AI applications. The "Big 5" countries—the USA, Russia, China, the UK, and France—each have their own plans for how to use new technologies in the military and how to improve existing ones. They also tend to have very different views on technology itself.

Even though a lot of private information about AI's role in national agendas has been leaked and is not available to the public for obvious reasons, more than just hints are needed to fully understand some of the most important national policies.

The words of Russian President Vladimir Putin in 2017 show that his country sees AI as the key to controlling the modern world. There were, however, not nearly as many reports on the pitch as there were in China or the US. Also, most projects, advancements, and initiatives are backed and paid for by the government. This means that they can't reach their full potential without the help of the business sector. Most importantly, the short Russian Military Encyclopaedia doesn't have a lot of accurate information on how AI is developing. The public, as well as scholars and researchers, can't learn about the real work being done in the area. What the Encyclopaedia does say is that "the creation of knowledge systems, neuro-systems, and systems of heuristic search" is one of Russia's AI goals. We are not sure what this sentence means or what it's trying to say because no official answer has been given.

After talking about how different people define and think about AI, it's also important to talk about how different Russia and the US think about AI. The US works on the technical side of things, while Russia has shown over and over again that it is interested in and obsessed with information by using its cyberspace abilities. There is no such thing as "cybersecurity" in Russia; instead, there is "information security." This shows how important information is to the country. Cyberwarfare is seen as a type of information warfare in this country. It is also seen as the "third revolution in military affairs," after gunpowder and nuclear weapons, as Ilnitsky and Losev write in "Artificial Intelligence: Here Are the Risks and Opportunities." Setting up domestic operation systems is part of Russia's "digital sovereignty" effort to protect itself from online threats and crimes. The Russian military is focusing on making its information infrastructure better and safer. Along with these steps, more and more laws are being passed on information security, which means that the government has more power to keep an eye on things. Of course, more money is given for the cyber and information security steps listed above. In 2019, up to 54 million USD will be given. The Russian government and military are doing these things because they believe that the cyber and information sphere is where they will win in the modern world. That's why they are putting a lot of effort into developing these skills instead of their regular weapons like tanks, missiles, and weapons used on the battlefield. As the chapter "Case Studies" will show, Russia has used information warfare in a number of cases, most notably during the 2016 US elections and the war in Ukraine that is still going on today. Another area where AI is handled differently is that in Russia, the military is in charge of making AI that can be used as a weapon, but in the US, China, and the UK, the private sector is in charge of AI growth. Russia's military has made progress by creating AI-enhanced unmanned systems and weapons, as well as UAVs like the Uran-9 UGV, which were tested in operations in Syria because they could show up again in Ukraine because they can hit stationary targets, which makes them perfect for killing people. As an example, KUB-BLA is a kamikaze drone that can reach up to 130 km/h and carry 1 kg of explosives. It is a loitering munitions type of weapon, which will be discussed in more detail below. The Federation has also tried their Mi-28N attack helicopters, which have a drone launcher that can use Intelligence, Surveillance, and Reconnaissance systems as well as intelligent loitering weapons. Besides this one area, Russia is also trying to improve its missiles and how well they work, paying special attention to electronic warfare and their air defence and command-and-control systems.

China is working on making strong military technologies and equipment, even if its President Xi Jinping doesn't say so directly. The country's "New Generation Artificial Intelligence Development Plan" from 2017 says that its final goal is to be the world leader in AI by 2030. One of its goals is for civilian and military AI to work together on things like making decisions and protecting the country. China has said that its main goal in developing AI is to improve naval powers. It thinks that smart technologies in this area are very important for making navy battles better. The Liberation Army of the country is currently working hard to create programmes that will help the command make better decisions by combining data and improving intelligence analysis. The money set aside for these projects is not small, and every year China spends even more billions in the AI industry, putting it in the same league as the US. The main thing it does is study, and then it focuses on reaching tactical goals instead of strategic and operational ones. China is buying a lot of unmanned aerial vehicles (UAVs) in swarms, as well as smart weapons and robot troops that can work on their own. This is one of the technologies and uses of AI that China is pursuing. China tried two drones in 2020. Both had important technologies on board. The first is a twin-rotor plane that can take up to 100 kg of supplies to troops at high altitude. The second is a fast-moving drone used for electronic warfare, ground strikes, and intelligence, reconnaissance, and surveillance missions.

So, the UK has shown its interest in AI and self-driving systems research and development. This became clearer in 2018 with the "Human-Machine Teaming" joint doctrine statement, which acknowledged the value of "superior manoeuvre options in and across all domains." Then, in 2022, it put forward its own Defence Artificial Intelligence Strategy. The UK thinks that the current security situation is getting worse. In order to be ready for defence, it has set the goal of modernising its armed forces. Russia's invasion of Ukraine in 2022 makes the UK talk about the need for "effective defence." As things stand, it seems like an impossible dream for a country to officially back and promote the offensive use of AI. However, the lines between offensive and defensive AI capabilities are not always so clear. Because of this, it is hard to say how close these systems and rules can be to preventing offence, and we will have to wait and see. What exactly does this national strategy point out? It mostly tells and encourages experts to study and test AI systems before using and putting their applications into action. The interesting thing is that, even though theory research is getting a lot of attention, the strategic benefits that come from creating cutting-edge technologies have been set as a top priority. When it comes to military AI, the UK knows that its enemies are ready to take advantage of all of AI's different uses and applications, but it sees AI's usefulness as the answer, especially for security reasons.

Since 2019, France has talked about its plans to drive innovation in the defence system. In particular, the Minister of the Armed Forces proposed increasing the money set aside for AI. France recently started a project called ManMachine Teaming. The goal of this project is to add AI to battle aircraft and see if it is possible for fighter jets and drones to work together to get around defence systems. The biggest part of the budget, on the other hand, was meant for study, not exploring and using the AI apps. In 2022, the French Ministry of Defence announced a large-scale project with many uses and powers. The French military procurement office, Direction Generale de l'Armement, then put out a procurement document for the project. The project has been going on since 2017 and is called Artemis.IA. Its goal is to give the country access to a secure processing platform that is not based on big data or AI. This platform can be used to use and analyse the huge amounts of data that come from military hardware and other sensors. There's a good chance that the project will be used soon in cybersecurity, military health tracking, predictive maintenance, or maritime surveillance.

Lastly, the United States has seen AI as an important part of making national policies since the Obama administration. The Department of Defence's "Third Offset Strategy" is proof of this. More steps will be taken to add AI and other cutting-edge technologies to the plan. This was just the first one. That was the case when the Joint Artificial Intelligence Centre was established in 2018 and the Artificial Intelligence Strategy was released the following year. It's important to note, though, that the US promised to be the leader in AI developments in 2018 with their Executive Order on Maintaining American Leadership in Artificial

Intelligence. This, along with the fact that since then, more money has been spent on AI research and different projects, including more than 600 projects that will use AI in Air Force missions, shows that they don't want other countries to catch up. On the other hand, there are other science sources that say the Department of Defence has not actively regulated these technologies and that this lack of regulation limits the military potential that Artificial Intelligence could reach. In the end, and despite everything, official and public sources say that the United States is currently the leader in AI study and development.

Russia and China both want to be the best at technology, and they are working hard to reach their goals. They like delivery systems that can do more than one thing, like stealth bombers that can also use nuclear bombs, as well as more advanced conventional weapons, like drones and cyber weapons. China is worried about its own systems' ability to be attacked online, but it is still interested in getting Artificial Augmented Intelligence (AGI) tools like unmanned aerial vehicles (UAVs) to help it target and hit an enemy. This will help the country avoid using human soldiers in these kinds of operations, which would have social and financial costs.

China puts a lot of effort into AI research before making its own technologies. That's why it was the top country for research in 2018. This important player wants to get better at swarming, robotic teaming, and combining data from multiple sensors. Because of its technical know-how, China has formed important diplomatic partnerships to improve its defence and offensive technological infrastructure, sell these technologies to other countries, and come up with strong strategies to use its technological strengths. To be more specific, China has made friends with Pakistan, which is leading the way in making small nuclear bombs. Not only does it strengthen its ties with Asia, but also with the Arab world, especially with the United Arab Emirates and Saudi Arabia. So, China gets two goals at once: it keeps working on its technological infrastructure and makes allies that will benefit from importing Chinese infrastructure and getting access to equipment, but only as long as they follow China's rules and are controlled by it.

Some might say that the public information about a state's AI powers is at best misleading and at worst not based on facts or being up to date. This seems to be the case for China, where experts misinterpret news about AI progress in the US, making China's own progress seem even faster. This shows us that a lot of information that hasn't been checked out can change the facts and cause an unneeded crisis, especially in a field that is so important to the current balance of power and its security.

Besides big players like the ones listed above, there are also smaller countries that are making and using defence systems that are smart and use AI. One country that makes a lot of drones is Iran. It makes small, fast boats with drones that can fly themselves or be used for military purposes, like the Mohajer-6, which Iran sells in Latin America and the Middle East. Together with Turkey, Ukraine is making a modernised TB2, which is an unmanned combat aerial vehicle capable of operating on its own and being controlled from a distance. Israel has to be talked about when the subject is this broad. Israel is one of the top countries not only for making UAVs but also for hiring people to fly them, as actions against Palestine have shown many times. They sent their Harop drones, which are loitering weapons with launchers, to Azerbaijan, where they were used against Armenians in the Nagorno-Karabakh war. Some biplanes from the Soviet era were used by Azerbaijan to turn old military equipment into Destruction of Enemy Air Defence (DEAD) drones. These drones were used to find ground-to-air missile targets and destroy them with suicide attacks. Other countries, like Pakistan, India, South Korea, and Brazil, are also working on their own apps, systems, and skills as the race goes on.

Plans and directions seem to be things that people will and should still be responsible for for now. Even though intelligent systems are smarter than humans and can do physical jobs or think faster, they still can't make decisions about things like war and conflict. AI can still help with these tasks by giving choices based on processing data from historical, cultural, diplomatic, and political facts, as well as from past actions and how they turned out. But I should say that the quality of the results depends a lot on how objective the data is (or isn't), how biased people are, and, of course, how much data there is.

An introduction to offensive technologies

There are still a lot of problems in the world, which makes Artificial Intelligence, its growth, and its use even more dangerous. Professor and associate senior fellow at the Centre for a New American Security Michael Horowitz said that AI is more of a technology that makes other technologies possible than a technology in and of itself. Elsa Kania, an Adjunct Senior Fellow with the Technology and National Security Programme at the Centre for a New American Security, agrees with this point of view. She doesn't see AI as a weapon in the traditional sense, but rather as a "utility" that states can use to improve their military power. While this chapter agrees with these points, it seems that AI is more of a tool that makes it easier to win (cyber)wars and a new measure of power, one that the most powerful countries in the world share in both the political and international spheres.

Planning, logistics, and transportation are some of the defensive tools that the military uses right now that are made possible by AI. At this point in time, though, it's hard to tell the difference between defence and offensive technologies. Offensive technologies are further broken down into technologies that affect both the tactical and strategic levels of war. The first one is about specific weapons, mechanisms, and methods that are used in a fight. The second one is about a set of actions that can make the power of two important players uneven. When this new technology is used, especially by leaders and soldiers in the military who don't know how it works, it can lead to instability. At the same time, this makes it more likely that there will be conflict or war. Each country will have to deal with the possibility of an enemy AI-powered cyberattack, without knowing yet what the right defences are.

Looking at this difference between the tactical and operational levels, scientists point out the advantages of using AI at the operational level of war in terms of increasing force and competitiveness. By using interconnected narrow AI systems at the operational level, commanders will find many new tools that will help them perfect their plans before carrying them out. Many experts agree that AI plays a much bigger role in this stage of planning operations. This is because tactical level tools, while useful and effective, can only do so much (for example, hitting an enemy target defensively). A lot of important decisions are made at the operational level, and this is an area where AI is neither actively used nor theoretically supported by the study and scientific community.

It's hard to tell the difference between defensive and offensive technologies because AI technologies are still not very useful on the battlefield or in cyberwars. Offensive technologies can also be used to trick people into thinking they are defensive, taking advantage of knowledge gaps in the field. It's possible for a system or piece of software that was advertised as defensive, like monitoring of a home for security reasons, to actually be used offensively, like spying on an enemy without their permission. When a state realises this, it might see it as a threat, and the uncertainty of not being able to respond can lead to the development of even more advanced (counter) technologies. This can create a constant technological race between states, which will cause uncertainty: a race to get the newest technologies, to update safety standards, and to have the best critical information infrastructure, with uncertainty due to the need for the With traditional weapons and methods, it will also be hard to catch up on technological advances and new products.

AI can be added to guns that already exist to give them new features, like autonomy or situational awareness. It can also be used to make people smarter, faster, and more accurate. There is a lot of talk about "nano-bio-info-cognitive technologies" and "algorithmic codes." Not only can it help you find and hit targets or people on the regular battlefield, but it can also be used in hacks to do a lot of damage to national command infrastructure systems or other important networks. Improving things like self-driving weapons or missile guidance brings the user one step closer to victory and dominance, but it also forces the enemy to make counterforce technologies, which are meant to be defensive but where the lines between offensive and defensive become unclear.

The principle of trust must always be taken into account, no matter how offensive AI gets better. You can say that the level of dependence on AI is determined by how it is used in a function or process. This level of dependence is a much safer standard than just buying a technology. For instance, putting AI in charge of making final decisions is a lot more dependent on it than just using it to look around. So, AI apps need to be looked at more than just as tech tools; they also need to be looked at in terms of the field in which they are used.

Categories of AI-driven offensive capabilities

It would be too long and too technical for this chapter to make a list of all the offensive and generally weaponized technologies that are allowed by AI. No matter what, here are some interesting militaryized AI skills that are worth talking about. Before that, to give you a general idea of what AI capabilities are and what they mean to the military, we could say that they are techniques that have been created to help other tools "think smart" like humans and work on their own, either partially or fully. Natural Language Processing, Visual Scene Interpretation, Machine and Deep Learning, and Video Analytics are some of the technologies that were used to make this happen. These technologies let the systems make decisions. Going back even further, the main ways that all of these things are possible are based on three functions: chance and statistical reasoning (depending on the data), logical reasoning or symbolic AI. Putting together different AI bits gives us new abilities, like automatically extracting structures, controlling systems with reinforcement learning, making predictions based on simulations, and using more advanced search methods. These all change the battlefield, whether it's real or virtual. AI is better at conflict than humans in all of the areas we've already talked about, especially when it comes to awareness, decision-making, and action.

An AI "supercomputer" with almost infinite computing power could be a main offensive weapon that uses new technologies. It could be used to hit specific military targets and infrastructure. This kind of technology, on the other hand, would be very expensive and is only being thought about in the military right now. Looking at things in a more modern and realistic way, AI apps change the way wars are fought by adding more areas where they could happen. There, tools can stay hidden and do a lot of damage to important structures and systems. Automatically created cyber weapons and techniques, like spying and intelligent scanning of an enemy's system for holes that can be used, can help large-scale, high-impact cyber wars be fought on their own. Also, software made with bad intentions, like the strictly harmful AI-enabled Hazardous Intelligent Software, can be used in military cyberwarfare operations. This software, along with trojan horses, spyware, viruses, and warms, can do a lot of damage to private and sensitive data and systems.

There is another type of cyberattack technology made possible by AI. These are called "kill switch" attacks, and they find, target, and attack an enemy's nuclear weapons systems. One can only guess what would happen to nuclear security if there was a powerful offensive tool that could be used from afar.

False-flag operations are meant to shift blame to a neutral party while the person who actually did the attack takes steps to impersonate or use the unique tools, methods, techniques, or processes to make it look like someone else did it. Many people think that the hack called "Olympic Destroyer" on the 2018 Winter Olympics in PyeongChang was a false flag operation. This means that Russia's GRU made the attack look like it came from North Korea. Some people think that a false flag operation could make things worse between two groups. This is especially true if a third party targets a state's NC3 (command, control, and communication) nuclear systems. These systems are very important and the targeted state would likely respond right away because it sees this as the start of more attacks. The situation doesn't allow for much diplomacy, study by intelligence agencies, or well-thought-out political responses. This quickly leads to an unwanted escalation towards a state that isn't even to blame.

There are offensive AI powers that could hurt the public's faith in the state's technological preparedness. This could happen by attacking important systems or the people who are in charge of these systems. Cyberweapons used in "left of launch" tactics are a common case study in this situation. They plan to use new non-kinetic technologies like electromagnetic propagation and cyber to attack first, along with an attacking force to stop nuclear ballistic missile threats before they are launched. This is called "left of launch." There are rumours that the US used them against Iran and North Korea to make those countries less sure of their nuclear forces and systems and their technological skills.

Another thing that can make things worse is spreading false or useful information about a crisis on purpose (this is called "weaponizing" information). This is very important for the crisis to continue and for people to change their minds. Colonel General Nogovitsyn said that information warfare is when information systems, processes, and resources are destroyed on purpose. Troops and the general population are also brainwashed in large numbers to make society and an enemy state less stable as a whole. An information operation could aim to harm or compromise systems, get intelligence by hacking, intercepting, or decrypting data using specially designed devices (electronic intelligence), block the enemy from some parts of the information infrastructure, or find ways to break into the right systems using software and hardware. In the Case Studies Chapter, we will look at "information warfare" by looking at how Russia messed with the 2016 US elections.

The USA uses an autonomous Long Range Anti-Ship Missile (AGM-158C) with AI capabilities. This weapon is very accurate and effective at hitting high-priority targets. These are used by the Air Force and cost almost $4 million. With the latest improvements, they are also being added to the Navy's Boeing P-8 Poseidon, which could cost up to 74 million dollars.

A tool that is often used to help people make decisions is the Correlation of Forces (COF) analyzer. It helps with strategic planning by figuring out what will happen in a battle and using the estimated strength of the blue versus red forces to do so.

Unmanned Aerial Vehicles (UAVs) are one of the most important AI-enabled offensive technologies used in war, and many countries, including Greece, put a lot of emphasis on them. They have already been sent to a number of tasks and places, mostly in the Middle East. A lot of work has gone into their navigation systems and sensors, which let them move around in dangerous, complicated environments with limited visibility and quickly react to the enemy's changing moves. There are different kinds of UAVs based on the tasks they can do. Some of these tools and the AI technologies they use should be talked about.

- High-altitude Long-Endurance (HALE) UAVs: As their name indicates, these UAVs have the capacity for lengthy flight periods and extended terrain surveillance. They are used for Intelligence, Surveillance, Reconnaissance (ISR) operations, intelligence gathering, while also proving useful in electronic warfare via battle network communication. Below, a HALE UAV is depicted, the Baykar Bayraktar Akinci. Manufactured in Turkey, this unmanned combat vehicle has been employed in operations in Syria, Libya and Azerbaijan, and actually holds many advantages compared to US drones, in terms of capabilities, cost and mission profile.

- One of China's major exports constitutes MALE (Medium Altitude Long Endurance) UAVs, which are the most notable strike-capable UAVs. This is something extremely favorable for China, as it becomes

the market of an important product on which buyers are depending, while also paving the way for its development and usage.
- Tactical Unmanned Aircraft Systems: This particular type acts as an aerial support for forces on the ground, thus providing them with a much more holistic situational awareness. Thus, it indirectly aids the fighter with multidimensional capabilities, as it can fly for a long time, all while inspecting large zones.
- Loitering munitions: A primary type of directly offensive equipment, this UAV sub-category is able to hit specific targets and self-destruct into them after being programmed to do so. With its light nature, which can be as limited down to 3 kg and the power of being piloted through a cell phone (!), a loitering munition can be extremely precise in its attack and has definitely gained recognition and appraisal among the military. Worth noting that one of the countries developing loitering munitions is Israel, followed by the United States and, then, China.
- Large Rotor-Based Platforms: Another mainly offensive technology, these mini-rotor and mini-helicopter equipment are executing missile launcher, machine gun and small precision bomb operations with great efficacy. China, not oblivious to these benefits and also aiming to minimize costs in military processes, is the current development leader in the game, also exporting them to Middle Eastern and African markets.
- Swarms: A form of operating as a group. In UAVs, the method of operating together, synchronizing their attacks and defences. Swarms are a pivotal method of practice for AI military applications. Taking into consideration the capabilities of a single UAV, one can imagine the power of a team working together. The potentials vary: from functioning and hitting targets in a denied airspace to carrying assets or explosives, effectively allocating them on a specified terrain. The latter task has been developed by Russia in small multi-rotor UAVs conveying bombs, with their tiny size maximizing their accuracy. On the same pathway, China is the current leader in drone swarms, with its production firstly introduced as a way to fight against extremism outside the country or for domestic reconnaissance missions, especially maritime, and generally non-lethal activities.

The benefits of UAVs and the specific types of them rely on the Artificial Intelligence technologies they use. To find out how well these technologies work, they need to be tested in warlike situations first. By looking into the specific AI uses, UAVs will help us understand how important they are for making these new features possible that change the way wars are fought.

- Air combat algorithms: As implied by the name, this technology is developed by human pilots training the system, in a way that the latter becomes capable of adapting and operating in an air-to-air battle environment, using a technology known as Deep Reinforcement Learning. This is not just on a theoretical level, as it has been successfully been carried out in tests conducted on an F-16 by the Air Force Research Laboratory and Lockheed Martin Skunk Works in 2017. The great performance of the algorithm on the unmanned F-16 showcased excellent skills and adaptability in air-to-ground strike mission simulations.
- Machine vision: This AI technology aids in target or moving objects/subjects' recognition and identification, via automated classification of data. Its benefits are traced to the enhanced situational awareness capabilities this application offers, even in otherwise limitedvisibility environments, and serves as an outstanding vision-based navigator. Among others, facial and gait recognition, as well as license plate reading, constitute forms of machine vision potential.
- Automated missions: Taking advantage of the previous application (machine vision), UAVs are able to autonomously hit specific preapproved targets. Examples are loitering munitions in Israel and Turkey but also China, which operate in an automatic manner after being given commands, executing them in the most efficient way possible.
- Autonomous flight: Even such technologies as UAVs may come across obstacles that halter their functions. An airspace where remotely controlling the vehicle is not technically feasible, needs a much greater independency and, if possible, full operational autonomy. This is what autonomous flights are about; various AI applications are combined to provide autonomy, such as cognitive visual recognition, image mosaicking and data processing.

When it comes to cyber tools and attack technologies, infiltration and the use of swarms, which was already talked about in the UAV field, look like they could work well. Infiltration is the ability for an autonomous agent to store memories it has gained during reconnaissance tasks and then use those memories to make a plan for infiltration. As we've already quickly talked about, swarming is a group of agents that work together without being told what to do or controlled from one place. Spying on people, planting malware, and destroying systems are some of the other common methods. Most of these can be used after steps for looking for weaknesses have been completed. Every day, new, stronger systems with better capabilities are being made. This means that it will be easier and faster to find weaknesses and hit targets, and the damage will be much harder or even impossible to fix.

This is a new technology called Deepfakes that has been around since 2017. It uses artificial intelligence to make fake images, videos, or voice recordings. Machine learning in neural networks is a big part of how it does this. Deepfakes are more powerful than ever at swaying people's opinions and spreading lies. They do this in a much more intense way than fake news because they use more senses to make it seem more real. As we move on to the case studies, we will look at how deepfakes were used in the most recent conflict between Russia and Ukraine and what role they play in the current war.

Artificial General Intelligence (AGI) is an even more advanced form of AI that works like a person and can be used to do a wide range of tasks. It can also combine types of data that humans can't see. Of course, a technology this big needs people with a lot of experience with programming and writing, and it also needs self- and meta-programming to work.

It goes without saying that combining different technologies and AI applications not only makes it possible for new functions to be improved, but it also makes risks bigger. As an example from Michael Horowitz, a rocket salvo can use a mix of AI, Big Data Analytics, and cyber capabilities. This, along with an autonomous weapon enhanced with AI, could be used to (counter)attack an enemy's power.

Advantages of utilizing AI-driven applications in the military

AI weapon systems and their technologies offer benefits that have never been seen before to their users. They improve speed, accuracy, and efficiency in objective measures like blast radius and effectiveness. One of the most important things you need to be able to do on the battlefield is move quickly and process information that comes in from multiple sources at the same time. This will help you stay alive longer. A commander who has access to pre-processed data has a strategic edge over their enemies because they can use the analysed data to help them make decisions. Speed also shows up in how machines work: A human driver and an AI system on a simulated plane are running at 250 times the speed of the human. Along with flying the plane, the control included deciding between attacking and defensive strategies and figuring out how to counter-fire. More tests like this have been done, like the "Alpha DogFight" in 2020, which was a race put on by the Defence Advanced

Research Projects Agency between human pilots of F-16s and AI agents. AI won by a score of 5-1, but some comments about the contest made people wonder if the rules were fair. In a more scientific sense, AI can handle a lot of data without the human tendency to focus on some things and ignore others. This step can almost always be done at the same time as another step: making action plans based on the data that has been analysed.

A very important benefit is that it makes the enemy more dangerous and increases the chances of survival and durability for both the user and the systems they guard, especially if those systems are very important, like nuclear weapons. Still, something that is good for you can also be bad for you. For example, speed can help you make decisions and act right away, but it can also cause things to get worse, which can quickly turn into a crisis, then a conflict, and finally a war or even a nuclear showdown.

When AI is used on a normal battlefield, it gives the actor new or better abilities. To be more specific, some functions include automatically sorting sensor data into groups, which improves target tracking, identification, and hit accuracy rates. Other features, like being able to navigate using 3D maps and find hidden items and obstacles, which lets them change their route for safety, indirectly help the first service.

AI is very important for identifying objects, which is a key first step in any successful military action. But it has benefits in more areas than just that. For example, it improves ISR skills and, by extension, situational awareness. When AI and Big Data Analysis are used together, they can help find quickly infrastructure that is very weak, making it an easy target, as well as the best time to attack.

Pattern recognition is a very useful app that can also help separate civilians, allies, and enemies, which can help military leaders make better decisions. With Deep Learning technology, an algorithm can be taught to look at and guess where attacks will happen, what kind of attacks they will be, and when they might happen (predictive analysis). This lets leaders change their plans and get ready for counterattacks quickly. The deep learning skills are also useful off the normal battlefield, in cyberspace, for cyber offence and protection, and in electronic warfare.

Most importantly, technology reduces or even eliminates the chance of killing people on the battlefield. That's exactly what robots would do. They could work on their own using predictive analytics, machine learning, and 3D guidance systems, or someone could control them from afar. They have an unbeatable advantage over human troops because they can do operations for long periods of time without having to worry about their own safety or the safety of others, and they can also keep going in harsh environments like chemical, radiological, and nuclear ones, which humans can't handle. Colonel Daniel Sullivan said it best when he said that with all the new technology available, the "dirty" job of going first during an operation should be done by a robot that can kill, not by someone who can just breathe.

AI systems, algorithms, software, and systems are smarter than humans when it comes to speed, noticing things, finding their way, navigating, and acting. Using input gathered with the help of the cutting edge Machine Learning technology, even when they show bad behaviour or make a mistake, these are fixed and never happen again. Inequality of power is also helpful, and it doesn't matter how many people are involved. What this means is that a single AI-powered system can "outnumber" a group of traditional methods in terms of power and skills. To put it more simply, one AI tool can beat many humans working together.

Most of the time, military technologies that use AI are and will continue to be even cheaper, easier, faster, and more widely used. Also, they will be able to work in a way that is much more autonomous and automatic, without any help or guidance from a person.

Various Challenges

As helpful as cutting-edge technology that can think and act in a (cyber) war, which is a very unstable place, can be just as dangerous as a soldier who hasn't been trained. When you combine these new technologies that haven't been used in the military with other information technologies, like AI with Cloud Computing, Big Data, and the Internet of Things, the level of danger goes up even more. With this mix, there are new ways to attack and, of course, more dangers.

Any new technology or progress will be governed by the laws of the country that created it and shared it with the rest of the world. This is especially true in the dangerous field of nuclear security. If we don't talk about, agree on, and write down common, binding rules, every step forward will probably go against the goals of other players, and each state will be free to develop its own skills, whether they are legal or not, or whether they are moral or not. It is very dangerous to let states work on their own without any oversight from an outside, international body. One country could end up with so much power and knowledge—maybe even an artificial superintelligence—that it would be able to control all of technology, the economy, and politics. Naturally, this state would then be able to stop other states from doing anything else with its newfound power.

Nations also need to think about the fact that exchanges between AIs can have unpredictable and questionable outcomes. No one knows for sure how systems that were made differently and haven't been tested together in a simulated battle would behave when they come together, especially if both sides were trying to score. When unexpected and unpleasant surprises happen, they can be confusing or, worst case, lead to a breakdown. Aside from technical issues, there are also important debates and questions about who is legally responsible for what the machines do. For example, who is responsible for a botched operation: the person who made the machine or the military commander? Doesn't anyone deserve the guilt? Even if we rule out the second possibility as impossible and the third because the coder was very far away from the action of the machine (unless there was a mistake in the code), it would still be hard to figure out who is to blame because the military has such a messy chain of command. This ridiculousness has been proven in the US, where there is a heated discussion going on about who has the power and responsibility for drone strikes.

In the same way, we should keep in mind that we are still a long way from having systems that are completely emotionless and only work to achieve predetermined goals. This is especially true for systems that can kill people (LAWS). When the human part is added, it becomes difficult and uncertain how people will interact with AI systems when they are working together or watching over them. Personality and emotions have just as much of an impact on how AI apps are used as the technologies themselves, and it is always possible to go after the wrong goals. Each person who works with a system will change how it works in their own unique way. This is an uncertainty that must be dealt with by establishing basic legal standards and acceptable behaviours.

Besides the last point, at least up to now, none of these AI systems have been able to think like humans, which is something that will always be needed, especially when there is conflict. So, in military-grade applications with weapons, human involvement should always be thought of as the bare minimum needed to keep an eye on things and deal with legal problems related to accountability.

In spite of their abilities that are beyond human comprehension, AI systems can be harmed by mistakes in their programming, bad or incomplete data sources, and human biases. The second one, which seems harmless, can actually lead to bad equipment, political problems, and even a crisis. Yes, AI can be used to quickly guess what might happen, which saves time that can be used to make good decisions. But no decision about a crisis or a war should be made quickly or based on predictive analytics, because military leadership, especially during war, will always be a completely human-dependent job, as it should be.

Some things that are needed for command and decision-making can be built into AI. For example, a system should be able to decide, have willpower, and be flexible. These are all objective and easy-to-achieve goals. AI doesn't have problems with remembering and can remember everything perfectly. In "non-linear" ways, though, even the most powerful Machine Learning algorithm can't get to the connections that come from experience. There is no way that a high prediction rate of up to 90% from a high-end machine learning algorithm can be enough to support such a heavy political choice that could cost lives, like going to war.

As a result of liberty, things will always be unpredictable. As is clear, testing and being sure that the programmed features work is very important. Until then, we can't be sure that the AI app in question will do what its code tells it to do, which is a very big risk to take. "In the Department of Defence, we test things until the break," said General Paul Selva, Vice Chairman of the Joint Chiefs of Staff. AI doesn't have the power to do that. We need to figure out how to make the software show us what it has learned. To fully study and evaluate AI's uses, it needs to be put into large-scale operations after careful testing in simulated case-scenarios and then low-risk real operations. When important goals and people's lives are at risk, AI will always be an unpredictable tool that could make things worse and cause things to get worse faster than they should. This is true for both partially and fully autonomous systems. Paul Scharre, author of the award-winning book "Army of None: Autonomous Weapons and the Future of War," says that the first group has a "natural fail-safe" that represents the uncertainty of how humans and machines can work together. On the other hand, the second group of fully autonomous weapons has a very high risk of acting incorrectly, such as attacking civilians because of false identification or friendly infrastructure because an algorithm's data has expired. It is clear that taking away people during times of conflict and disaster only leads to more confusion. When it comes to the means of an attack or a counterattack, there is also the question of what is fair. In other words, this means that cyber tools are still new as weapons in the armed world. A cyberattack or one that is supported by AI can be hard to defend against because it's not always clear what the right, necessary, and appropriate method is. Again, this makes things unpredictable and weakens security because the criteria are still up to the opinion of each state.

It will be talked about several times in this chapter, but it is necessary to adopt regionally or, better yet, globally agreed upon common ethical and legal schemes that don't exist or aren't working well enough and are out of date. In terms of ethics, there is no doubt that computers don't have any moral problems and don't act in a kind or compassionate way. By eliminating the need for human soldiers and making autonomous weapons cheaper, this could completely change the nature of war and make the decision to start one much easier for both the government and the people. This is because people will think that there is "nothing to actually risk to lose" in going to war, which means they have no reason to. Keith Abney wrote in "Autonomous Robots and the Future of Just War Theory" that "autonomous robots, with their promise of fewer casualties, will make war less terrible and therefore more tempting, plausibly enticing political leaders to wage war more readily." This sentence perfectly captures the main idea of this paragraph. On the other hand, most people think that a computer programme or algorithm that decides to kill a person without any human input or choice goes against basic principles of human decency. Not only would an ASI never stop working towards its goal, but it also wouldn't care about other people or have human values. Even if it had a good end goal, like a simple reconnaissance mission, it would still violate human rights to get there, especially if the person was in the way of that good goal.

As we just talked about, how the public sees a situation is very important during times of diplomatic tension and conflict because it affects policies and strategic balances. Fake news, propaganda, and deep fakes are all new technological ways to manipulate people that used to be done only by the press. These tools can turn a bad public opinion into a voice that is so strong and unwavering that it can force leaders to make quick, angry, and unquestioning choices that make things unstable.

Lastly, it's important to remember that AI systems are and will be made by private companies or labs, not the government. They won't necessarily be controlled by the government, and they won't work in the government's best interests. Big companies that are making millions of dollars wouldn't always put reducing human suffering and improving their own place at the top of their list of priorities. They also wouldn't always care to write their codes and algorithms in a way that makes the systems more humane. This worries me because cutting edge weapons that can kill people shouldn't be left totally (or at all) uncontrolled by the public. Without being controlled, any of these systems could easily and without a trace fall into the hands of non-state players, extremist and terrorist groups. They will use them in a dangerous way that can be predicted, and they might even blame a third party or state for an attack in order to blackmail them.

The Nexus of AI and Nuclear Stability

Nuclear weapons completely changed the way people think about and fight wars, as well as any ideas that people had before about how to solve international problems. Even though there have been a few small problems, the nuclear industry has been stable and peaceful since the end of the Cold War. While technology and advances in AI may make it easier and faster to make and carry out decisions, they can also be absolutely disastrous when it comes to nuclear weapons. A race between important nuclear states to keep improving their nuclear capabilities through technology is a well-known political, diplomatic, and social risk in this area. In fact, China, Russia, and the US have all said in public that they support and encourage study into how AI could be used in nuclear systems. More than ever, people are afraid that whoever gets the right information and rewards will use them to start a nuclear war that they can easily win.

When AI is built into nuclear systems and then used in nuclear activities, the risk of things getting worse during conflicts or, even before that, during times of crisis in general goes up. It is very important to take the effects of tension in this area very carefully, as they could be very bad. For example, in a time when information, its easy manipulation, and spread, is very important during times of crisis, a party wanting to gain power could spread false information about nuclear systems, their detonation, or a missile test. This would create such an alarming imbalance in diplomatic relations and the public's knowledge that the government would be forced to take actions it would not have chosen otherwise.

It sounds just as scary as it is to talk about autonomy in the nuclear business. A Russian "Poseidon" or Status-6 Oceanic Multipurpose System is a nuclear-powered and -armed missile that can work on its own. It is also a robotic submarine that can carry both conventional and nuclear cargo. On top of that, Russia has made this system sound like a danger to both the US and the UK, which, along with autonomy, does sound unsettling.

Unauthorised access and advanced persistent threats (APT) to control and command nuclear systems, system deception, and the sending of false alarm signals are some other scary and worrying possibilities. Given how dangerous nuclear systems are, it's clear that these kinds of problems could lead to a nuclear attack based on false information. This could have terrible effects on diplomatic ties and on the whole world.

Even though specific apps are being made and used to find and target enemy assets, nuclear systems are being kept safe and guarded with fear because they could be attacked by a "stronger" AI-powered system.

AI has also been used to make programmes that model nuclear systems so that they can be studied and useful information can be gained. An amazing new invention and very useful use of AI is being able to accurately measure nuclear systems and their effects without having to do real nuclear testing. The results can be used to make things safer.

Because of how important the nuclear sector is to both nuclear states and their enemies, worries about how technology will change, and the fact that there aren't any agreed upon definitions of AI make it even harder to work together on AI-enabled nuclear powers. "Artificial Intelligence and Stability in Nuclear Crises" by Marshall D. Foster suggests a three-step plan to protect nuclear stability: first, improve ways of gathering information about an enemy's plans and exact capabilities; second, make the state's own capabilities stronger to close any gaps in their own; and third, work on creating a framework that controls and sets standards for AI in nuclear warfare. It's possible that these steps could end the danger of a nuclear crisis if they are followed.

Zachary Davis, who wrote "Artificial Intelligence on the Battlefield: Implications for Deterrence and Surprise," said, "Close is not good enough when it comes to war, especially when nuclear risks are involved."

Case studies

As "the Algorithmic Warfare Cross-Functional Team" or "Project Maven," it was a US Department of Defence project whose main goal was to find Islamic State (ISIL, Daesh) terrorist fighters. With the help of AI, this was made possible by automatically reading up to 100,000 Facebook posts every day. These and other important tasks were completed by AI-powered systems that sorted and processed a huge amount of different data, surveillance, and information to keep an eye on threats. This job would take people weeks or even months to finish, but AI can sort through the information and come up with a suggestion in minutes or even seconds.

It can handle 87 billion commands per second. The Air Force in the United States has been working on its Advanced Display Core Processor in avionics. This processor is used in cyber and information security. An extremely fast way to process data like this can give the military big benefits, both on the ground and in cyberspace.

In the main part, it was stressed how important it is to know about the Russian Federation. A few years ago, the Soviet Union's meddling in the 2016 U.S. presidential election was a widely talked-about event that helped people fully understand the concept of information warfare. Russia got involved in the U.S. election and, by extension, in its social and political life by taking a number of bold steps, such as running operations on the internet. In theory and practise, Russian information warfare affected the election process through two activities that were linked and took place at the strategic, operational, and tactical levels. These activities were carried out by intelligence agencies and organisations that were related to them. Officials in Russia see democratic elections as a sociopolitical event that can be used to further Russia's strategic goals in Western countries. Information warfare includes things like spreading false information, lobbying, manipulation, managed crises, and blackmail. Based on what Russia has done so far, elections are a natural part of this type of warfare. There is a bigger effect on people's minds and subconscious minds when media and other methods are used to try to change elections. Between 2014 and 2017, Russian military intelligence tried to break into and use election equipment in all 50 states. Cyberattackers from the Russian government may have gone after election-related networks on the Internet in 21 states. In June 2016, Russian agents attacked State voting infrastructure for the first time during an election in Illinois. Illinois election clerks noticed strange network behaviour on a website for the voter registry that is run by the Illinois Board of Elections. Specifically, they saw a large increase in outbound traffic. An FBI review found that hackers could get to 200,000 stolen records, which included the name, address, social security number, birth date, and either a driver's licence or other form of identification for each voter. These records could be accessed through SQL injection attacks. Hackers were able to get into databases and add, change, update, or delete information. Private Russian companies, such as the Internet Research Agency, also took part in the huge marketing campaign. They had people on staff who pretended to be American citizens and made racially and politically divisive social media pages and groups. They also wrote fake news articles and comments to make Americans dislike politics.

If you want to understand the new aspect and gravity that AI brings to the field of nuclear weapon systems, look at two past case studies. During the time of the Soviet Union, the country bought intercontinental ballistic missiles (ICBMs), which were mostly used to carry nuclear weapons. To defend itself, the USA worked hard to build up its own arsenal of ICBMs. This shows that the US did not try to make a technology that was even stronger, nor did it fight the Soviet Union. Instead, it started a race to get more people than the Union, which kept the balance of power at the time. Through Ronald Reagan's presidency, the United States had the upper hand in information gathering, surveillance, and counterforce strategies during the Cold War. The US used cutting edge technologies for spying in submarines and other places. This wide use shows how rivals and competitors might behave when faced with another country's very strong technological progress. They could join the race, change how they do business, or come up with new technologies that work against them in order to stay relevant and be taken seriously.

Using new technologies in the military has another risk, as the NATO operation in Kosovo made clear. Some bombing techniques were used from high altitude, which made things less dangerous for NATO troops but more dangerous for civilians. When thinking about the use of autonomous weapon systems, this is another problem that should be thought about. It makes sense that no government would want to put more citizen and human lives in danger.

In general, the Middle East is where a huge number of AI technologies and applications have been tried and used first. Autonomous drones have been used to attack oil installations in Saudi Arabia, which is important for the business and survival of the Middle East. In 2019, this is exactly what happened in the town of Abqaiq in Saudi Arabia. The defence system there wasn't able to stop the swarm drone attack, which cut up to 5% of the world's production.

It looks like Turkey has an edge when it comes to laser guns, as was shown in Libya. There and in 2019, Turkey was able to aim its laser weapons at the Chinese Wing Loong drone and shot it down. They say that the ALKA directed-energy weapon system was the laser weapon system used in this case, but it is not publicly recognised as a laser weapon system.

Nagorno-Karabakh is a disputed region between Armenia and Azerbaijan. In this area, AI-enabled tools have been seen for the first time, and experts say this may mean the end of traditional battlefield tactics and methods. In 2020, there were again acts of violence that led to war, which killed many people. Azerbaijan's Border Patrol put out a music video (!) that encouraged war and hate of the enemy, which was a form of propaganda. Azerbaijan showed off some of its newest and most potential weapons technologies in this video. A loitering bomb called "Harop" is being released and launched by trucks in the background. It was made by Israel Aerospace Industries (IAI), which is the country's main aerospace and aviation maker. Its technology lets it find its way to an enemy target after being fired, but it can also wait and scan before hitting, and it can fly by itself for hours. In an attack, it doesn't send out a message but instead hits the target directly. They are called "kamikaze drones" because of this, which is another reason why this chapter talks about them. Azerbaijan didn't just show a spruced-up version for propaganda's sake; the country has been putting years of time and money into researching and developing hovering weapons. And while it ended up with 200 units of 4 different types, Armenia only had one that wasn't very powerful. Because of these factors, Nagorno-Karabakh has been called the first war that was partly won by self-driving weapons. The war also proved that you need these tools to win.

Not all countries are ready to use these tools to change in the real world, and regional and international groups aren't ready to use their own frameworks to deal with the problem either. Report from the European Council on Foreign Relations said that "the advanced European militaries would perform badly against Azerbaijan's current UAS (unmanned aircraft systems)-led strategy" when it came to Azerbaijan and the changes that were happening there.

Now we'll talk about a more recent event, the crisis between Russia and Ukraine in 2022. As we did in the Definitions Chapter, we will look at the use of deepfakes and their part in the conflict. Towards the beginning of this war, especially in March, a video surfaced showing Ukraine's President Zelensky telling his people to lay down their weapons and submit. The video seemed sketchy because the "president" used rude language, which is what led to it being thought to be fake. This was a sloppy attempt, but there is no reason why better movies and audios can't be made. There is a lot of real-speech data out there that Deep-Learning algorithms can use to learn how to do what they need to do. This scary event shows how technologies that aren't directly insulting can still be harmful and cause trouble in the public sphere.

When you think about how quickly technology changes and how many new features come out, these case studies might be too old. We might need to look at more than just the technologies themselves. For example, we might need to ask what people are trying to do when they create and use these technologies.

A Technical Consideration

As we've seen, AI could be very helpful at the operational level of war. It could process huge amounts of different data and give leaders a lot of options based on millions of facts. But some people say it is better and more effective to do so with AI, which is made up of many smaller parts that work together to make a bigger system. This view is backed by the fact that having parts that work on their own lowers the risk of the whole system failing, either because of a bug or a cyberattack. Because of this, the compounds work on simpler tasks and give results that are added up.

Legal framework creation and relevant policies

As of now, there aren't many progress made on legal standards for AI weapons because there are only debates and no international system. In 2018, the UN Group of Governmental Experts, which is made up of 25 member states, discussed whether current international laws apply to AI that can be used as a weapon. They also urged everyone to work together and stop things from getting worse. In the end, everyone agreed that humans should still make the final decisions on the battlefield and that ethics should be taken into account when AI is used. However, no agreement was reached for Lethal Autonomous Weapon Systems. The UN's work since 2012, on the other hand, has been restricted and in the same direction. The United Nations Convention on Certain Conventional Weapons Group of Governmental Experts has held debates and conversations. Then, after the US executive order on them was made public, the nature and morality of LAWS were talked about. It was talked about who is responsible and why human control is so important. It was also looked at whether LAWS and how they are used are in line with international humanitarian law and the current conventions and treaties on the law of war. One big worry was that this question was hard to answer and that there wasn't a clear answer because laws and new technologies in general have so many new and unexplored uses that we can't be sure that current laws apply to them. A group of countries including Austria, Brazil, and Chile also put forward a plan in August 2018 to create a legally bound international body whose job would be to enforce laws and keep an eye on people. On the other hand, it should be checked to see if non-offensive AI applications are covered by war law. This is because tools that aren't weapons could affect offensive powers just as much as weapons, so they should be treated the same way. There are important parts of international humanitarian law that must be followed in this case. One example is Article 36 of the Additional Protocol I (API) to the Geneva Conventions. This piece limits a country's freedom to choose its own weapons and war methods before they are used, while also limiting their freedom to test and improve them. The study and discussion of the above tools, along with talking about weapons, will completely change the Protocol and give states new responsibilities. This could happen because the Protocol doesn't define the idea of weapons, means, or ways of warfare on purpose. This way, new developments can be added to the law without having to be updated. The same goes for cyber means. Rule 110 of the Tallinn Manual 2.0 says that member states must legally look over the "cyber means of warfare," or cyber offensive powers. As before, secondary weaponized cyber means are being looked at with the goal of being able to hurt and damage people.

The rules that automated (weapon) systems must follow are both interesting and very important. Because while most people think of AI offensive technologies in terms of international humanitarian law and the law of armed conflict, their rules actually allow a lot more violence, damage, and death than international human rights law does. So, an evaluation of intentions needs to be made before the appropriate rules and provisions are written down.

In their paper "Optimising peace through a Universal Global Peace Treaty to constrain the risk of war from a militarised artificial superintelligence," Carayannis and Draper argue that a Universal Global Peace Treaty and a Convention on Cyberweapons and Artificial Intelligence should be put in place to keep things stable. In their study paper, they also talk about other scientists who agree with this legislative measure. Ramamoorthy and Yampolskiy (2018) propose a broad Benevolent Artificial General Intelligence Treaty, which would be backed by the UN and would aim to allow the creation of only "benevolent" and "altruistic" Artificial Superintelligence. As they say, Turchin et al. (2019) also want global rules and standards to be made. More specifically, they want to look into the options of either a global treaty that bans all ASIs, a one-ASI solution, or a net of ASIs solution that includes them cooperating with each other and finally, enhanced human intelligence.

In addition to these official talks, it is interesting to note that even Google, a giant in technology, has put out a set of rules about AI and how it should be used. These rules also apply to the military's use of AI. The good uses of AI, the need to get rid of bias in programming, the need to try technology before using it, and the responsibility to people are some of these.

An international law document that is binding, like an international treaty, needs to be made about weaponized AI that can be used to launch automatic attacks. When states vote for, accept, and ratify a treaty, they are saying that they want to stick to a set of rules and restrictions for a long time in order to keep the peace. A treaty like this would have to set some minimum standards for how AI systems should be used. It would also have to protect human rights through international humanitarian law and maybe even create a new international body whose job it would be to oversee the treaty's obligations. All of this has to happen after all of our current words, ideas, and beliefs are completely rethought, because new tools have to follow a whole new set of rules for what is right and wrong. For stability's sake, it is very important that any weapon or weaponized AI-enabled method be checked to see if it is legal before it is made. Limiting the use of technology that can be used as a weapon would mean less GDP going to military activities and more money for important areas like education and health.

Different countries have different ideas about AI, technology in general, and how it should be used. This makes it hard to come up with standard rules. Each country has its own goals it wants to achieve. Legal universality is hampered by different views. For example, the United States has clear-cut ideas that seem to go against each other. These ideas have been shared in a number of places, such as the United Nations Convention on Certain Conventional Weapons. More specifically, they said that "reasoned human decision-making" should guide the systems, not humans making every firing decision. This was supported by the US view of humanitarian law, which said, "International humanitarian law does not require that a weapon determine whether the target is a military objective. Instead, it requires that the weapon be able to be used in a way that is consistent with the principle of distinction by a human operator." Unfortunately, there isn't any technology out there that is so advanced that it can think and make decisions like a person. Also, it doesn't make sense to want to replace everything with a superintelligence, especially in the military during a crisis when it is so important and vulnerable. Creating consciousness and the ability to think like a human will cost millions of dollars and wouldn't solve any urgent problems. Instead, experts should focus on automating chores that humans would otherwise have to do that are time-consuming, harmful, or even deadly.

Unilateral international measures are important for a stable world, not a technologically competitive one, because they set a primary, binding legal ground for the use of AI in a militarised setting. They also help with arms control and verification processes. Still, it's very clear that this is a completely new situation that needs a look for a new and more than adequate legal framework. This framework should take a very different approach than the ones used to deal with issues involving conventional weapons in the past. Also, technology is always trying to beat itself, changing all the time and very quickly. So, it's also important to have a system that can keep up with changes without having to be updated and talked about all the time. A framework like this needs to think about the strengths and weaknesses of conventional weapons that have been improved by AI, how they work with nuclear systems, and the role of information and how it is used in both conventional and cyber battlefields.

Should AI be limited in weapons systems or only used in certain types (like LAWS)? Should it be completely banned? The person who wrote this, thinks that we can't stop or limit the progress or use of a technology or tool that is already out there and being used and improved. When countries already plan to use hostile AI, we can't expect them to give up the work they've already done and the money they've already given out. Although states might publicly agree on such an agreement, the race would still go on because no one knows if another state will be able to keep up with developing weapons technologies.

With nuclear security being such a top priority, the major nuclear powers need to sit down and agree on rules and guidelines that everyone must follow. They should always be working to protect NC3 systems, avoid a nuclear crisis at all costs, and follow the rules for using technology in this area, all while following the same set of rules set by international law. For more specifics, the UN Convention on Certain Conventional Weapons, which is run by the UN Conference on Disarmament (DISEC) Committee, has the power to control papers and talks about this issue.

Any answer to this kind of technical problem needs to take both the political and technical aspects into account. Experts in technology should work closely with policymakers because they know how these systems work and what they can do without any bias. To make safety standards even higher, groups of countries should work together with the same international teams of experts who will follow the same rules and directions. This will make everything more consistent.

It is clear that both attacking and defensive technological skills are being improved at the same time, as both sides are always trying to catch up and beat the other. Collaboration on research and analysis would be a good way to deal with this problem and keep a crisis or conflict from happening. A coalition for the development of AI defence capabilities would set a common level for the beneficial use of AI and lead to strategic alliances and investment partnerships. These kinds of programmes already exist, but only in certain situations. For instance, the Defence Technology and Trade Initiative between the USA and India on UAV swarm developments is geared towards the above goal: moving away from a "buyer-seller" model and focusing on working together on technology, making things together, and growing together.

With its 3000.09 Instruction, the US Department of Defence says that the officer in charge of an autonomous weapon and the government should be responsible for how it acts when it is in use. An autonomous weapon must be operated "in a timeframe consistent with commander and operation intentions" (Instructions). If it can't do that, it must either end the engagement or ask for more human operator input before continuing the engagement. This American rule could change the questions and arguments that come up in the law when it comes to issues of responsibility. It could also lead to a bigger, international agreement on these issues.

Laws should usually make sense, and this should also be true for laws that deal with AI, self-driving systems, and armed weapons. Logic says that if a soldier, leader, or other person in charge of an AI system makes a choice or gives an order based on the AI's suggestions, they accept and choose those suggestions and are responsible for them if something bad happens. But in order for the law to fairly judge the person in charge, it needs to be clear what the differences are between an accident with the machine, expecting and accepting a bad result from the leader or the soldier, and finally, intentional action. As a result, punishments and consequences need to be different.

The most important thing, though, should be that weaponized systems must be legally labelled as a last option (ultimum refugium). This rule follows important rules of international law, like the concept of proportionality that we talked about above. To put it another way, all other options must be explored first, before employing self-driving weapons, AI features and programmes.

Talking things out diplomatically should always be the first and most important way to solve a problem.

It doesn't matter if an international pact is signed or not; AI and cybercrime will continue to grow. Since technology is changing quickly, AI and cyber defence must also change quickly to avoid dangerous and uncertain futures. In this way, the race that has been talked about a lot in this chapter will continue, but it will be for the better. And to keep things stable, states need to be open about what they are doing, what they are buying, and what they plan to do with AI adoption.

Potential Future Scenarios

Predicting what will happen in an area as unstable as politics, where there are always conflicts, is already hard enough. It goes without saying, though, that AI progress, use, and practise in the military will have an immediate impact on regional safety and security, as well as the diplomatic relationships that are necessary to keep things running smoothly.

At the moment, the United States is usually better at this, which means that Russia and China will stay behind, and maybe even be left behind for good. What we don't know is how they will respond to this situation and whether they will choose to show off their power by making an escalation strategy, using their own powerful systems, or even nuclear power.

As different countries come up with their own ideas and methods for using military AI, the race to be the most technologically advanced and ready becomes a reality. This changes both the nature of war and conflict and the balance of power. At this dangerous new setting, where we don't know what to do from the past, there are some things that must stay the same and guide everything that is done. Deterrence, or not doing things that could cause a conflict, is one of them. This can be made stronger by creating more reasons to stay away from things that could cause a conflict, especially by making alliances and working together on shared technological research and development. In the constantly changing world of today and tomorrow, it will be very helpful to stay away from using AI that is hostile and, especially, nuclear defence. AI apps and uses that are mainly created to help people give people hope that things will stay stable. Whatever the reason, benefits in different systems may give one country short-term power, but never long-term control.

Author of "AI is Shaping the Future of War" Amir Husain says that AI will play four parts in the near future: For starters, it will make strategy planning easier by automating the process. Second, it will change sensor technology by making it much faster and easier to combine and understand data. Third, it will change systems in space, especially those that combine knowledge. Lastly, and most importantly, it will give the next generation of cyber (and information) warriors more power.

Conclusion

The author says that the most important thing is that AI doesn't get so good that it completely replaces humans on the battlefield, whether it's a real one or a virtual one. This is brought up because people have the most control over AI when it is first being developed. As sentience is gained, control starts to fade.

Today, what we really need is a focused conversation about the specifics and technicalities of AI technology that can be used as a weapon, so that everyone can understand the other person's goals and points of view. Artificial intelligence and related technologies, like Machine Learning and Deep Learning, give the military too many benefits to not allow them to fully adopt and use them. Because of this, negotiations should begin with specific uses rather than a ban, which would not be possible since these technologies are already available.

The kinds of wars that older generations were used to are clearly very different from the typical battlefield. Now, most of the time (but not always, as happened in Europe in 2022), the battlefield is not likely to happen. Instead, the final war is being fought by manipulating, lying about, and taking advantage of cyber systems. More and more, automated systems are starting to take the place of human soldiers on the regular battlefield. These systems can do their jobs much more quickly and efficiently. As a result, it shouldn't be a surprise that any future big war will end in a few minutes or less, as many experts say. This is because it will happen in cyberspace and the goal will be to take over important cyber or nuclear control and command systems of a country or group of countries. Still, being the first to do something isn't always a good thing in this case. For example, Paul Schare wrote in "Robotics on the Battlefield" that "the winner of this revolution will not be who develops these technologies first, or even who has the best technologies, but who figures out who to best use them."

Chapter 6
Navigating Strategic Risks in U.S.-China Military AI Competition

There are two big changes happening in international security that look like they are going to collide. The first trend is that the United States and the People's Republic of China (PRC or China) are becoming more and more competitive in world politics. The second trend is the fast growth of artificial intelligence (AI) technologies, some of which are being used by the military. This chapter talks about how the US can deal with strategic risks in its relationship with China that could be caused or made worse by military AI. Strategic risks include higher chances of armed conflict or the fear of nuclear war.

The first part gives an overview of China's strategies and views on AI. Beijing wants AI to play a part in both its domestic economy and the modernization of the People's Liberation Army (PLA). China's leaders want to use AI to boost innovation and growth, deal with economic and social problems, and protect the rule of the Chinese Communist Party (CCP).

The "intelligentization" of China's troops is a big part of the country's military goals, especially its plan to have a "world-class military" by the middle of the century. With the goal of getting ahead of the US, intelligentization depends on adding AI and other new technologies to the joint force. China says that its way of running the government, which includes its strategy of combining military and civilian functions, gives Beijing an edge over Washington. But it's still not clear if that goal will come true, and China will have to overcome problems both inside and outside the country.

Next, the chapter lists five types of what the authors call "pathways," or causal links, that military AI could be used to break down security and raise strategic risk between the US and China. The first is improvements in each person's skills that work together to give China a military edge. The second is how AI changes the way decisions are made and how information is used. Third are autonomous devices that don't need a crew. The fourth one is intelligence, monitoring, and mapping. There is also command, control, and messaging in the fifth. The chapter talks about each route in more depth, showing how they might work in more complex ways.

All together, the rise of military AI is likely to make the competition between the US and China stronger and raise geopolitical risks. There are three types of responses that policymakers can use. Some of these are limiting China's military AI while boosting the US's own; managing military AI responsibly on a one-sided basis; and using bilateral and multilateral communication to lower strategic risks. All three of these areas have already been addressed by Washington, and other countries have also tried to change the military AI setting. To build on what has been done so far, U.S. officials should:

- Take bold action to constrain China's progress in AI for military and repressive purposes, but do so in a narrow way that avoids self-defeating steps;
- Build U.S. military AI capabilities to stay on the cutting edge;
- Develop, promulgate, and implement norms and best practices on responsible military AI;
- Proactively engage with like-minded allies and partners and in multilateral institutions on military AI issues;
- Negotiate risk reduction and confidence-building measures with China related to military AI;
- Continue to pursue universal U.S.-China risk reduction and crisis management mechanisms despite persistent challenges;
- Make military AI a fundamental pillar of diplomacy with China related to nuclear weapons and strategic stability;
- Take steps to reduce strategic risks not directly caused by military AI but potentially worsened by the inherent speed and unpredictability of military AI;
- Prioritize intelligence-gathering and analysis on, and net assessment of, China's military AI capabilities.

There are two big changes happening in international security that look like they are going to collide. The first trend is that the United States and the People's Republic of China (PRC or China) are becoming more and more competitive in world politics. Since the middle of the 2010s, Washington and Beijing have been in what U.S. President Joe Biden calls "extreme" strategic competition in the areas of politics, the economy, the military, and diplomacy. Leaders from both countries have also said that new technologies, such as those that change the balance of power in the military, will be very important in the competition between the two giants over the future of global power.

The second trend is the fast growth of devices that use artificial intelligence (AI). Recent advances in AI, like ChatGPT, DALL'E, and other generative AI models, have made waves around the world and gained a huge number of users very quickly. These examples show how new technologies can quickly change whole fields once they are fully developed. So far, most of the big advances in AI have been made in the human world. However, AI systems that can be used for a variety of military tasks—this chapter calls to this broad group as "military AI"—are also changing quickly. When these two trends come together, they might make what this chapter calls "strategic risks" bigger. This word is used to talk about the higher chances of a war or the fear of a nuclear war between the US and China.

This chapter talks about how the US can handle the strategic risks that military AI could cause or make worse in its relationship with China. There are four parts to this chapter. The first part talks about how China sees AI being used in both its private economy and to make the People's Liberation Army (PLA) more modern. It also looks at how Beijing thinks these new technologies will change war in the future. In the second part, the writers list five types of what they call "pathways," or causal links, that military AI could use to make things less stable and raise the strategic risk between Washington and Beijing. In the third section, we look at three types of choices for dealing with strategic risks along those paths. In the last part, suggestions are given for how U.S. leaders can lower the threats that military AI could pose to peace and stability while competing strategically with China.

China's AI Strategy and Its Impact on Military Modernization

In the PRC, both state and private groups see AI as very important to the country's future. For the party-state, AI is important for more reasons than just making the military or the government stronger, though those are important perks as well. In short, it sees AI as essential to the future of the country in every way, including making economic growth and social safety better.

As Chinese Communist Party (CCP) General Secretary Xi Jinping put it in his work report to the 19th Party Congress in October 2017, China's top leaders have said many times that they want to make the country a "science and technology great power." "Innovation will remain at the heart of China's modernization drive," Xi said at the 20th Party Congress in October 2022. He also said that by 2035, China would "join the ranks of the world's most innovative countries, with great self-reliance and strength in science and technology," and he said that China should "resolutely win the battle over key and core technologies." When the CCP Politburo met in April, Xi reaffirmed his commitment to this goal. He called for the "development of general artificial intelligence," which is what people in the West call "artificial general intelligence" (AGI) and means a type of AI that can solve a wide range of problems in a variety of settings. AGI's exact meaning isn't clear, though, and it changes all the time as technology gets better.

The "New Generation Artificial Intelligence Development Plan" (AIDP) for 2017 said that "AI has become a new engine of economic development." As data is one of the most important parts of AI development, China's AI goals were a big reason for setting up the National Data Administration as part of the State Council's overall reorganization, which was revealed at the "Two Sessions" meetings in 2023. China's leaders think that their country needs to have world-class AI in order to keep moving up the global value chain and move beyond its old development model, which has led to fast GDP growth but also problems in some areas, damage to the environment, and too much industrial capacity. They want to achieve "high-quality" and long-term growth.

Chinese managers are looking at how AI can be used in certain areas to solve many economic and social problems. They think that AI and related technologies, such as robots, will boost industrial productivity, making up for the fact that China's working-age population is falling while also making better use of the higher human capital of younger generations who are smarter than their parents. China's medium- and long-term economic plans depend on urbanization and shifting to domestic consumption. "Smart" farmland, cities, transit, and logistics will make these goals possible. AI is also seen as the next step by leaders in Beijing in a long-term effort to improve public services by digitizing government tasks. New developments in medicine made possible by AI could lead to better health results at lower costs and make caring for an aging population easier. To meet all of these goals and China's climate and environmental protection goals, planning and using resources must become more active and efficient.

The CCP values AI not only for its effects on the economy and people's well-being, but also for protecting its rule at home and showing its power around the world. China has been building up its military and internal security forces for decades. To keep these efforts going, the country needs resources that can only come from continued economic growth. Also, AI is a big part of the CCP's complicated system for keeping people in line. While stories of an AI-driven, all-powerfulThe term "social credit system" seems to better describe Beijing's goal than the technology that is currently available. However, automatic content moderation is already an important part of China's extensive system for censoring the internet. The killing of Uyghurs in Xinjiang is made possible by computer vision, data like faces and fingerprints, and other AI technologies. These methods are being used more and more to keep an eye on and control other minority groups as well as the general population.

Last but not least, the CCP wants to guide and coordinate the growth and use of AI in China, but it knows it can't do it by itself. The first people to figure out how to use these tools to push the limits of their fields will be private actors in business, education, medicine, and civil society. The party wants to make things better for everyone by funding both basic and applied AI study and using AI to further its own goals. A "national team" of big companies chosen to lead in certain areas is one way this approach works. Another is industry alliances between companies and different levels of government. Finally, Chinese economic policymaking has always been based on decentralized local experimentation. China's Military-Civil Fusion system also tries to use some private technological advances, including some made with the help of foreign research partners, to improve the PLA's abilities, though its exact goals are still unclear.

The Chinese Paradigm for AI Development and Rollout

A lot of people think that China will "win the race" for artificial intelligence because of how well its government can organize and use its resources to push AI research. There is also proof that Chinese society as a whole is more open to these technologies. For example, a 2022 Ipsos poll found that most Chinese people knew a lot about AI progress and thought it would make their lives better. Not even half of the people who answered from the U.S. agreed.

China may be able to become the world leader in AI, but it may not be as easy as some people think. First, like governments around the world, China's has tried to set clear ethics guidelines for the kinds of AI that are being made. For example, the Ministry of Science and Technology released "governance principles" for "responsible AI" in 2019. These said that the development of AI should be helpful, fair, open, privacy-protecting, safe, controlled, and quick. The AIDP thinks that these kinds of rules will be broadened and turned into laws by the end of the plan's timeline in 2030.

Second, China has put boundaries on how businesses can use data, which is an important part of developing AI. In key areas of AI development, the government wants private companies—especially those on its "national team"—to take the lead. At the same time, China has made a number of rules that businesses must follow in order to limit their ability to use private customer data. These rules were made because of public outrage over repeated privacy breaches. The 2021 Personal Information Protection Law and Data Security Law says that people who work with data must get consumers' permission before collecting and using their data, set up good ways to keep data from getting into the wrong hands, and make sure that businesses that break these rules face serious consequences.

China formed a new National Data Administration as part of the overall reorganization of the State Council announced at the 2023 "Two Sessions" meetings. This new agency will, among other things, allow and limit how businesses use data for AI development. However, these laws make it clear that state security agencies will not be subject to any privacy limits. They will continue to do mass surveillance on the population using AI more and more. In general, China's policy has been the opposite of what the US has done. In the United States, the government is limited in what information it can gather and keep on citizens. On the other hand, private companies are mostly free to gather and use data about their customers, except in certain fields like banking and health care.

Finally, the PRC government is taking steps to restrict how companies and other groups in China can use AI programs. New rules about internet services' algorithmic recommender systems went into force in March 2022. They were run by the Cyberspace Administration of China (CAC). These rules are supposed to stop monopoly behavior like walled gardens and unfair price discrimination, as well as the spread of fake news. This is different from the US, which generally lets things happen as they may. They also made a "algorithm registry" to help the government see and keep an eye on companies that use AI for their services and the data that is used to train the AI.

China also wants to control creative AI after the buzz around ChatGPT. In April 2023, CAC released draft rules that were meant to control both the training data and the output of the systems. The privacy rules we talked about above must also be followed by training data. It must also respect copyright and be "accurate." The rules also said that outputs had to be "true and accurate." This was done because AI systems are naturally unpredictable and could come up with material that the CCP sees as politically subversive. But interim rules released in July 2023 loosened the rules by exempting R&D activities that won't be seen by the public and getting rid of the responsibility for fake content, so now it only needs "effective measures" to improve accuracy. It's not clear how much China will be unable to fully use generative AI technology because of the need for government control.

As of now, it is not clear if China's strict regulation will actually lower the risks that AI poses to society. Officials in particular and the party as a whole have every reason and the means to play down bad news. These information problems can hide problems that have been going on for a while, letting risks build up without being seen. This change could make it harder to enforce China's AI rules or make it harder to make changes to them as times change.

While China tries to make many AI breakthroughs, it will have to constantly balance the need to be open to new ideas with the need to control business abuse and its own desire to keep tight political control over every part of Chinese society. Because of these changes, U.S. policymakers and experts will have to let go of preconceived ideas about China's strengths and weaknesses and keep updating their views as the field changes.

AI's Impact on China's Military Transformation

China also thinks that AI is a key part of improving its military power. This is what Xi wants the PLA to do: "basically complete" its modernization by 2035 and become a "world-class" military by the middle of the century. Xi told the PLA in March 2023 to "increase the presence of combat forces in new domains and of new qualities." As part of these plans, Xi wants the PLA to keep developing its combat technology, going from mechanization to informatization and finally intelligentization. In a broad sense, mechanization means putting modern platforms and tools into service; informatization means connecting those systems to networks like GPS; and intelligentization means adding AI, quantum computing, big data, and other new technologies to the joint force. The new goal that China set for itself in 2020 was to "accelerate the integrated development of mechanization, informatization, and intelligentization" by 2027. That is, Beijing wants to make progress on all three stages at the same time, not one after the other.

Beijing thinks that moving through these steps is important to keep up with how technology is changing war in the 21st century. Military matters are going through a revolution that Chinese scholars call a "systems confrontation" that needs "systems destruction warfare" to win. To be competitive in this new age of war, the PLA is working on a big idea that it calls "multidomain precision warfare." In simple words, this idea says that the U.S. military's power comes from its ability to network, but that this also makes its forces dependent on each other, which can be used against them. So, China doesn't have to directly destroy U.S. enemy forces like ships or tanks; instead, it can attack the weak spots that connect U.S. systems and domains, which can neutralize or overwhelm U.S. benefits. These weak spots can be communication lines like the internet, satellites, or electromagnetic waves, as well as supply chains. Artificial intelligence (AI) is an important part of this plan because finding and attacking U.S. weak spots will require quickly gathering, sending, and processing huge amounts of data in a real battle.

At the level of capabilities, it's still not clear what role military AI will play in China's general plan to modernize its military. There are seven areas where AI investments are currently being looked at by researchers at the Center for Security and Emerging Technology. These are (1) intelligent and autonomous vehicles; (2) intelligence, surveillance, and reconnaissance; (3) predictive maintenance and logistics; (4) information and electronic warfare; (5) simulation and training; (6) command and control; and (7) automated target recognition. These groups are meant to be examples, not to be all-inclusive. Also, AI is a general-purpose technology, like electricity or trains, which means that experts don't yet know all of its possible effects or uses. Over the next few years and into the middle term, AI will bring about mostly small and specific changes. But in the middle to long term, some of them could be new and important for everyone. China isn't very open about its efforts to modernize its military, including its work on AI. If Beijing is able to make strategic advances in secret, it could one day surprise the US with a surprise attack.

Setting big goals or just throwing money and people at the problem won't help Beijing reach its goal of being the leader in military AI. Several problems mean that China might not be able to meet its goals for integrating AI into the PLA on time or at all. Some problems might have to do with things. The PLA publicly said that it had fully mechanized by 2020. It is also making fast progress on informationization and pushing to develop the cutting edge skills needed for intelligentization. But as a lot of ships, planes, and other weapons systems that were once brand new get older, the costs to run and support them will go up quickly. This could make it harder to invest in new AI-enabled features. In the event that China's economy continues to struggle, the PLA may not have as many means to improve AI.

Also, the technology itself might be hard to learn, even if you have a lot of help. The US and its partners may put limits on technology, which could make it harder for Beijing to build and run large-scale AI-enabled systems (see below for more information). China might also not be able to come up with new ideas for cutting edge defence technology. In the early steps of modernizing its military, China could copy the US, Russian, and other advanced armies. Intelligentization, on the other hand, needs completely new combat technologies and operational ideas for how to use them.

The PLA's AI goals could be hampered by problems with people, the way the government is set up, or political power. Some of these problems are a lack of skilled workers to run AI systems and military organizations that are too rigid. The PLA's Strategic Support Force (SSF), which was formed in 2015 as a separate military force to focus on space, cyber, and electromagnetic warfare, seems to have the most power and resources for developing AI within the PLA. The SSF may have been formed in part to help the PLA work together through advanced networking and now AI. However, it may not want to give up control of its creations to the rest of the PLA, or other services may not want to depend on the SSF's services. Last but not least, the CCP puts power above all else. The saying "the party controls the gun" (first used by Mao Zedong, later reaffirmed by Xi) and the important role of political commissars in the PLA show this. Modern AI models are hard to predict, "explain," and make clear, even for researchers who are very good at what they do. Because it's not clear, commanders might not believe it because they think they can't control what it does. On the other hand, Chinese leaders might value machines more than people. Because of these conflicting desires, it is not yet clear how much China's military leaders and operational-level officers will use AI or stay away from it.

The Impact of Military AI on Strategic Risks in U.S.-China Relations

The United States and China are both moving quickly to add AI to their defence. A lot of experts have pointed out that this could make the already tense security race between Washington and Beijing even less stable. But it's not always clear how new AI powers in the military could make strategic risks higher. In order to fill that gap, this part describes five types of ways that military AI could be used in ways that could threaten stability and raise strategic risk between the US and China. Some of the uses of AI in the military that are described below are already out there, while others are still in the works or just ideas. Also, some strategic risks come from AI working the way it's supposed to. Others come from AI acting in ways that weren't meant to.

A. Individual Capability Improvements That Combine to Give China a Military Edge

The general military balance is probably the thing that will cause the most strategic risks between the U.S. and China when AI is used in the military. This is because it is hard to measure accurately and can't be blamed on AI alone. A lot of the most useful uses for military AI in the near future will be pretty normal ones. These uses could help the PLA make better use of its resources, which would lead to more military power per yuan or dollar spent. Some of these are helping to make upkeep, logistics, training, and decision-making processes better. These kinds of "back office" jobs don't get as much long-term attention as "tip of the spear" skills that show up on the front lines of battle. Modern armies, on the other hand, depend just as much on their supporting bureaucracies as they do on their soldiers and weapons.

Additionally, some new military AI systems will make the PLA better at fighting. At first, these changes are more likely to be evolutionary than dramatic. As just one example, think about the air domain. Unmanned systems that fly with people ones, like "loyal wingman" systems, might be better than what human pilots can do on their own. But totally autonomous and unmanned air systems—which can be more persistent, maneuverable, and have other benefits because they aren't limited by human bodies—will probably be needed for a complete shift in the way air combat is done.

In almost every part of the military, the same story is being told. As military AI gets better in all areas, the U.S.-China military balance could shift in favor of Beijing. This could make the chances of a war higher. China has become more assertive on its borders in line with the PLA's fast modernization drive since the 1990s, which has made the PLA the second-most powerful military in the world. With the U.S. military leading the way, along with a network of American security allies and multilateral organizations, East Asia has had a "long peace" without a major power war since at least 1979. That peace could be broken by China's growing military power and its use of force, especially if Beijing's fighting skills in the region become better than Washington's. In the words of the U.S. National Security Strategy, China is "the only competitor with both the will to change the international order and, more and more, the economic, diplomatic, military, and technological power to do so."

Of course, what the US and its allies do will also affect the regional military balance, which is not fixed but changes over time. Washington and its partners are also trying to use AI to improve their military power, just like Beijing. East Asia is in the middle of a terrible but unavoidable arms race between the military and technology. Military AI is a part of this race. And one way China could finally have more weapons than the US and its allies is to create and use technologies like military AI that would give Beijing a big edge.

B. AI's Effects on the Decision-Making and Information Domain

Three main ways that military AI tools could raise strategic risks are by shortening the time that policymakers have to make important decisions, by giving bad information to decision-making processes, and by encouraging people to try to sabotage states' discussions through large-scale information operations. First, adding AI to decision-making could speed things up on their own and make it easier for leaders to act quickly when they don't know what to do. It's possible that AI systems could be used to help national security processes that keep an eye on changing situations, come up with options, and make decisions about the danger or use of force.

For any one state by itself, speeding up the processing of information could buy people more time to make better, more well-informed choices. However, if many states shorten the time they have to make decisions, it could speed up crises and leave leaders with less time to make decisions generally. If computers can do some of these jobs faster than people, states might have to make quick decisions just to keep up with what their enemies are doing. This is especially true if both sides are afraid that the other will move and react more quickly. These kinds of time constraints could help start a disaster or make an existing one worse. There could be these kinds of pressures even if the tools do the analytical work "better" than a person would.

Second, AI that helps with decisions could give policymakers bad knowledge that makes them make bad choices. AI systems can go wrong in ways that are hard to see and guess. Policymakers could make important strategic choices based on false, skewed, or otherwise bad information and analysis if they don't pay close attention to and fully understand how AI systems work, including their flaws. Some researchers also think that nations with strict rules, like China, are more likely to make bad choices based on AI systems because their information systems are closed. In places where the U.S. and Chinese militaries interact, humans still have the final say on using lethal force, AI could still be used to help with discussions about foreign and security policy. However, AI could also be used to change information at the tactical level of military operations, which could lead to accidents that escalate the situation.

Lastly, military AI could change the way decisions are made and information is shared by revolutionizing large-scale operations that try to change the course of political situations in unpredictable ways. AI-generated text, audio, images, or video that is convincing and accurate on a large scale could make misinformation operations more effective. These could be used to break up an enemy's political unity, make it hard for them to make decisions, hurt their relationships with friends, or make third parties think negatively about them. A lot of Chinese planners already think that this kind of propaganda is an important way to break down enemy unity and initiative. And PRC party-state organs like the United Front Work Department and the Central Propaganda Department put a lot of work into internet campaigns that try to spread positive stories to important groups of people abroad. As for the PLA, it focuses on "cognitive domain operations," which "use people's will, belief, thinking, and psychology as direct combat targets and try to change the opponent's cognition to affect their decisions and actions."

To do this, people might use divisive message campaigns to play on political disagreements about U.S.-China ties or national security in general, or they might make up fake news to question an administration's decision to act in a crisis. According to research, Beijing has already started to use AI to improve the way it handles information about Taiwan's elections. The use of large language models (LLMs) like the well-known ChatGPT could make these activities cheaper and maybe even more convincing. Since generative AI has become more popular, many PLA commanders are worried that the US's expertise in the field could be used to spread false information about China that hurts its economy. But it's unlikely that anyone will be able to predict how a campaign will turn out. This is because the effects of even perfectly written text rely on how well the relevant societal divides are understood and how unstable public opinion is. If AI gives one side—most likely Beijing—a reason to get involved in these murky waters more often, it could start or make political problems worse.

C. Uncrewed Autonomous Systems

One of the most important military uses of AI could be to let unmanned systems, which are often called "drones," run themselves. The authors use the term "robotic systems" to refer to systems that can do their jobs mostly without any help from people, but they know that in real life, systems may have different levels of autonomy. More and more advanced military robots make it easier for things to get worse on purpose, by accident, or without meaning to, especially during times of stress. The US and China are both working on these kinds of systems. They come in both known forms, like planes and submarines, and less common ones, like "swarms" of small robots. A big part of functional autonomy is artificial intelligence, which can be machine learning or other types of computing like control theory.

There are four main ways that robotic systems can cause things to get worse on purpose. First, political and military leaders may be more likely to use force because they think they have a better chance of winning on the ground if autonomy gives people more freedom. Second, leaders on both sides might be more likely to use robots in combat operations because they are less likely to hurt people. In a strange way, the target country might also be more likely to use force in response. There may be times when leaders are less afraid of violence, which makes them more willing to take risks when operating and reacting to robotic systems in ways they wouldn't with crewed platforms. Recently, Chinese combat and surveillance drones flew around Taiwan four times, showing how this dynamic works.

Third, more computing power could also make current systems more autonomous in ways that could make them less stable during a crisis. For instance, military AI can help hypersonic weapons move better in the final stages of their flight to get around air and missile defences. To the other hand, machine learning could also make air and missile defences better at predicting attacks, which would allow the use of counter-hypersonic and other advanced missile defence systems. More generally, experts disagree on how much hypersonic weapons cause instability and give the countries that use them truly new powers. It is still too early to say for sure what the overall effects of AI-enabled autonomy will be on military technological ideas like cost-exchange ratios, first-strike benefits, and the costs of projecting power across different areas. But lawmakers will have to keep a close eye on the progress of military AI to see if it changes these factors in ways that could make things less stable.

Fourth, low-cost unmanned aircraft flying in groups could possibly open up new ways to use conventional weapons to attack an enemy's nuclear arsenal. This possible ability is part of a bigger trend that could throw off the strategic balance: Chinese experts are often worried about how effective U.S. nuclear counterattacks could be, even if they use advanced conventional weapons like swarms of drones. They think that this possibility would risk what they call the "asymmetric strategic stability" between the US and China by making Beijing less able to respond with a second attack. Plus, they say that Beijing's nuclear buildup is at least partly meant to make things fair in that area again. Next, similar dynamics could cause unintentional escalation, which is when someone does something on purpose but it has effects they didn't mean. Because robotic systems are still pretty new and people's ideas about them are changing, countries may have the wrong idea about whether an enemy sees a certain action as crossing a certain escalation barrier. If a country shoots down or seizes an enemy aircraft because it thinks its enemy sees it as normal international rivalry but the enemy sees it as a threat or even an act of war, the first country will have crossed an important strategic line without meaning to.

At first glance, the past seems to show that an event involving an unmanned system is not likely to get much worse. During the past few years, both Iran and Russia have shot down U.S. drones. The US did not respond with force in either case. In these cases, it looked like both states thought that an unmanned aircraft would not cause as much trouble as a crewed aircraft would. Both the US and China have been through a similar, if not as bad, situation: China took a U.S. Navy unmanned underwater vehicle (UUV) in the South China Sea in December 2016. That problem was solved quickly and without getting worse. China has also used drones as part of a bigger campaign to bother Taiwan's military and challenge Taipei's control over Taiwan and its surrounding islands' land, water, and airspace. Taiwan's military has shot down these kinds of civilian drones without immediately facing military retribution. But the above examples shouldn't make us feel safe because they miss important parts of realistic U.S.-China crisis situations. Neither the Iranian drone nor the UUV event between the US and China had weapons on board. The drone in question could have been used for attacks, and the event happened during a political crisis. However, both the U.S. and Russia have been very careful about getting into a direct fight, which is why both sides were cautious. In a possible future Taiwan scenario where high-level combat between the U.S. and China is real, moves against robotic systems, especially if they are armed, might not be met with such restraint.

Last but not least, autonomous systems may cause accidents to get worse in cases of mistake, malfunction, or the limited flexibility of autonomous systems. If machines are given the wrong instructions for a task or if they break down, they could go into an enemy's territory, run into enemy military or civilian forces in the air, sea, or space, or hurt people by accident. Depending on how the enemy responds, this could start a crisis or make it worse. Robotic systems might not be able to adapt to quickly changing, "out-of-sample" environments, even if they are designed to do so and are given the right parameters. Or, they might do what they're supposed to do, but the political situation or setting changes. When this happens, they might act in a way that is different from what a person would have done (or what they would have wanted the robots to do) in that situation. One more benefit of autonomous devices is that they tend to be cheaper per unit. Depending on how it's set up, that could mean more assets working alone in contested places, which means there are more chances for problems to happen.

D. Intelligence, Surveillance, and Reconnaissance

AI is already giving the military new tools to help them do their intelligence, surveillance, and reconnaissance (ISR) jobs, and it's possible that they'll be able to do even more in the future. AI in the military can be used with old technologies to make new things, do old things better or cheaper, or do new things. Using swarming for ISR drones or mixing AI with balloons or microsatellite constellations to keep an eye on things in "near space" are two examples. When rules about these kinds of surveillance devices are weak or don't exist at all, crises can happen. In the 1950s and 1960s, when high-altitude planes and satellite ISR first came out, this happened, even though the Eisenhower administration tried to work out an agreement with the Soviet Union about these capabilities. The United States brought up the idea of an international deal on aerial reconnaissance again in the last few days of the Cold War. This led to the signing of the Treaty on Open Skies in 1992.

Second, some improvements in military AI could lead to new powers that change the way military technology is built. AI systems could handle a lot of data from many sensors to keep an eye on mobile missile systems on land and even submarines at sea. This is especially true if they are combined with other new technologies, like quantum sensors. Those uses are still just ideas, but they might be possible in the next few years. These things would make things clearer and less stable if they happen. They could weaken the survivability—the ability of a military system to make it hard for enemy forces to find and destroy—of two legs of the nuclear triad by letting enemy forces watch and target those assets for counterattacks. Of course, some analysts don't agree with those forecasts.

Still, there is a real chance that military AI has the very unstable effect of suddenly making skills weak that were built and used because they were strong enough to survive. Fear of being hit by a quick first strike can lead to "use-it-or-lose-it" mentalities that raise the risk of a nuclear war. Chinese experts have actually noticed this trend, along with the fact that regular AI-powered drones could make it harder to use second strikes. The Center for International Security and Strategy at Tsinghua University's Chen Qi and Zhu Rongsheng say that China and Russia "fear that [the US'] powerful reconnaissance capabilities could mature into a threat to their more sophisticated retaliatory forces." They also say that "all AI needs to do is undermine the level of retaliatory capability" to get a response. Also, thinking or fearing that an enemy might be able to get a certain skill is sometimes enough to make someone feel weak or even start taking precautions, even if those capabilities don't exist yet or might not exist in a reasonable amount of time.

On the other hand, more openness might help keep things stable in some situations. AI could make radar tracking systems and other tools for keeping an eye on people better. Some experts say that military AI could improve stability and lower risks in a wide range of areas related to nuclear deterrence and arms control. Some of these are giving earlier warnings, making more accurate information to clear up misunderstandings or fix sensor problems, making military planning and wargaming better, and giving new arms control verification tools more power.

E. Command, Control, and Communications

Command, control, and communications (C3) could also be changed by improvements in military AI. Through its multidomain precision warfare strategy, China is trying to get ahead in C3. The United States also wants to get ahead with its Joint All-Domain Command and Control (JADC2) idea. Both sides want to make the C3 better so that it can quickly gather and combine data from different "sensors" to give leaders information about the battlefield and then be used as targets by "shooters." And they want to weaken, mess up, or kill the other side's C3 at the same time. It will be impossible to know ahead of time what will happen when those two systems meet in the real world—whether they will improve their own C3 or hurt their opponent's. This is because these totally integrated "system-of-systems" capabilities are still pretty new, there isn't enough information available, especially for China, and there are a lot of factors that are at play.

Still, AI promises to make things better in a number of areas linked to C3. Cyber and electromagnetic warfare (EW) strikes might be stronger if AI is used. As big data becomes more important as both an input to AI and an output from AI, both sides will have reasons to "poison" the other side's data by changing training or fine-tuning datasets to make the system work less well on purpose. That could cause AI-enabled C3 systems to behave in unpredictable ways or break down in known ways that attackers could use against them. It was found in one study that as few as 100 poison examples in a big data set can be used to poison dual-use systems, like large language models.

AI could also help China hit the satellites that are the core of C3 networks more effectively. There is no doubt that most of the current antisatellite (ASAT) systems do not use AI. As an alternative, they use regular weapons, EW, and cyberattacks. But news stories say that PRC experts are working on ideas for small "hunter" satellites that could use AI to control their movement and steering as they move in random ways to find satellites they want to destroy or disable. As both countries' C3 and counter-C3 capabilities improve, leaders may feel more pressure to "use or lose" weapons in times of crisis or war, which could cause things to get worse very quickly. Another specific worry is that military AI could have an impact on C3 systems that are used to make nuclear bombs. AI will be used more and more in nuclear early warning systems to combine and quickly analyze data from many sources. These kinds of systems might get the information wrong and either report that a missile is coming when it isn't or say there are no risks when in fact a missile is on its way. China's choice to put at least some of its nuclear forces in a "launch-on-warning" state could cut down on the time that can be used to check or reevaluate information about new threats.

Finally, worries about time constraints or threats to top government officials with command-and-control power could lead to changes in nuclear weapons, posture, or policy. People in both countries will want and be under pressure to pass on decisions about nuclear launches lower in the chain of command so that they can be made quickly in a crisis or even after a nuclear exchange. If you take things to their natural conclusion, China or any other nuclear state could decide to build an automated way to respond. A "dead hand" method from the Cold War is often used to describe this idea. Beijing and Washington don't seem to be working on building such a capability, and their stated policies don't allow it either. The structural forces will still be there, though, and they might get worse over time as military AI gets better.

Approaches to Addressing Strategic Risks Posed by Military AI

In order to protect its security relationship with China, the US will need to take a number of different steps to deal with the many threats that military AI presents. These sources of risk may combine in real life, and the strategies used in risk management will also try to lower a number of different sources of instability. This part talks about three main types of strategic risk reduction choices and, where relevant, the steps that Washington and Beijing have already taken in each one.

Strategic Competition through Disrupting China's Military AI and U.S. Capability Advancement

When AI gives one side a big enough military edge, that side might decide that starting a war is the only way to get what it wants at a price that is acceptable, this could lead to deliberate escalation. Because it wants to change the past, the PRC would be the first to act in almost all possible situations. So, one policy choice for Washington is to stop Beijing from using AI to completely shift the military balance of power in China's favor. To do this, the US can try to keep China from getting the new technologies it needs to help the PLA reach its "intelligentization" goals. On the other hand, Washington could work on making the US's AI skills advanced enough and good enough so that China never gets a big lead.

The leaders of the United States are already trying to do both at the same time. In October 2022, Washington passed strict rules that made it illegal to send advanced computer parts and manufacturing know-how to China. For this and other reasons, the US has also put sanctions and limits on exports on companies and people that work with the PLA, even when it comes to military AI problems. Washington limits some investments coming into the US, and it's likely that they will soon limit some investments going out of the US into China. All of these actions are meant to make it harder for China to create military AI by stopping commercial and industrial progress that the PLA could use. At the same time, the Department of Defence (DoD) is continuing to work on creating and using military AI that can make the military stronger overall.

So far, the U.S. has mostly focused on advanced semiconductors that process data for AI systems as a way to keep China from enjoying the benefits of military AI. Other basic building blocks of AI, such as data, human talent, and algorithms, are being dealt with using much more specific tools. But Washington might put limits on these other groups in the future. For example, there is a push to ban TikTok from operating in the US because some people are worried that American data could be used to help China make AI better. In the future, Washington could also take steps to stop China from getting data that is more useful for military AI. The U.S. government has already put some limits on exporting or sharing the source code of AI algorithms used for geospatial analysis. They are thinking about making similar rules for face recognition software because China has used that technology to violate human rights.

Policymakers might change their minds in the future and decide not to let general-purpose algorithms like big language models be published or exported. For instance, the Committee on Foreign Investment in the United States (CFIUS) would almost certainly turn down any Chinese company that tried to invest in OpenAI. Washington may also change how willing it is for people from the PRC to work on AI projects in the U.S. In 2020, Trump's administration made new rules that let the State Department refuse visas to Chinese graduate students with ties to the PLA. About 2% to 3% of Chinese graduate students in the US during the 2019-2020 school year were likely affected by the policy. However, it may have had an indirect effect on a bigger number of new students entering science, technology, engineering, and math (STEM) graduate programs. Even though the Biden administration has tried to make it easier for companies to hire STEM experts from other countries, it has also kept the power to turn down PRC applicants' visas. This authority doesn't go after AI directly, but in the future, the government might do more to stop Chinese students from coming to the US to study AI.

It's possible, though, that this would slow down U.S. AI study because there are a lot of Chinese students in U.S. graduate AI programs and the two countries work together on a lot of AI projects all the time. More top AI researchers come from China than anywhere else, even those who work in the US. This shows that human capital could be a strong advantage for China. In the past 20 years, Beijing has worked hard to bring top scientists to China. According to the Organization for Economic Co-operation and Development (OECD), more than 2,000 published scientists moved to China from the US in 2021, while scientists left the US in that year. In 2020, there was a sharp rise in the number of Chinese scientists leaving American institutions for ones in the PRC. This was reportedly because of a mix of anti-Asian racism in the U.S. and harassment of Chinese-origin scientists by the U.S. government under the guise of research security.

There are gaps in the data, and trends may have gone the other way because of changes in American politics, China's strict zero-COVID policies until late 2022, and Beijing's crackdown on the tech industry. Still, in the future, especially as China's own AI environment keeps getting better, the country could try to sway the flow of human capital toward itself by making it harder or impossible for its best AI minds to study or work in the US or other friendly countries. In general, trying to stop China's progress on military AI in too many ways could hurt the US's own AI innovation ecosystem, so lawmakers will have to find a tough middle ground.

Independent Responsible Governance

When military systems don't work right or act in a way that wasn't meant to, either because of human or machine error, it can cause problems or escalate situations without meaning to. In official statements, both Washington and Beijing have said that civilian deaths are a very bad result and that reducing them should be a main goal when designing military AI. As with any weapon, the best way to lower this risk is to put as much emphasis on the safety and dependability of systems as on how well they work or how many people they can kill, and to do strict test, evaluation, verification, and validation (TEVV) processes all the time. When it comes to military AI systems, these rules are especially important. For this reason, success on new or out-of-sample tasks can fail in a way that is hard to understand, and the system's behavior may change over time as it gathers more information.

In order to reduce doubt, both the US and China will need to agree on safe design principles and then say they are doing so in a way that can be believed. The United States has made a lot of unilateral statements about how it will create and use military AI. DoD's 2020 Ethical Principles for Artificial Intelligence say that AI used in the U.S. military should be "fair, responsible, able to be tracked, trustworthy, and able to be governed." Later documents, like the Responsible AI Guidelines in Practice, the Responsible AI Strategy and Implementation Pathway, and the January 2023 directive on Autonomy in Weapons Systems, have gone over and expanded on these core principles. They explain how AI should be used and integrated throughout the life cycle of defence programs.

Also, in February 2023, the State Department released a statement encouraging other countries to follow similar rules and be more open about their work on developing combat AI. The U.S. promised in the 2022 Nuclear Posture Review that all parts of nuclear weapons systems will always have "human-in-the-loop" control. This paper reaffirmed that promise. A group of lawmakers from both parties and both houses of Congress in the United States has also introduced a bill to make this strategy official.

Declaratory policy or even strong diplomacy can't always get rid of deep-seated suspicions or make military contacts in the field less uncertain. In working groups for this project, experts talked about how both Washington and Beijing are skeptical of any claims that the other side will be more self-controlled. Because there is still a lot of uncertainty, lawmakers might think about not letting AI be designed into (or out of) certain military systems. Some U.S. military officials have said that different systems, like the Navy's next-generation fighter aircraft and some military sealift ships, could be "optionally crewed" based on the mission. If it isn't clear that the rules of engagement for crewed and uncrewed systems are the same, China could accidentally target an aircraft with crew, thinking it is uncrewed, and hurt U.S. personnel, making the situation worse without meaning to. Washington will have to think about this kind of possible outcome when it decides whether to create and use certain confusing configurations, like airplanes that can fly without a crew. It might be possible to make indicators that show what's going on with an optionally crewed airplane. And in the end, aircraft with optional crews might provide practical benefits that are greater than the strategic risks. But U.S. leaders shouldn't just ignore the risks; they need to deal with them directly.

Two-way and Multifaceted Diplomacy

Bilateral and multilateral negotiation are two more ways to keep dangerous power imbalances, expensive arms races, and mistakes from happening. States can try to set limits on the creation or use of certain military technologies through negotiated arms control agreements or confidence-building measures (CBMs), and then make sure they are followed. It would be hard, maybe even impossible, to stop AI growth all together, and that's probably not what you want. AI is made up of a lot of different tools that can be used for different things. Pretrained algorithms, like Meta's LLaMA model, which got out on 4chan soon after it was announced, are digital goods that can't be copied or sold. Also, the field is changing very quickly. Even specific uses make it hard to set up the tracking and verification systems that are needed for arms control to work. Still, the US and China can and should talk about putting limits on the most dangerous uses of AI. For example, they could talk about how AI can and can't be used in nuclear command and control or military cyber operations.

There have never been formal arms control talks between the U.S. and China, but both participate in ongoing discussions in the Group of Governmental Experts (GGE) on limiting Lethal Autonomous Weapons Systems (LAWS). The GGE has met formally since 2014 as part of the U.N. Convention on Certain Conventional Weapons (CCW). Neither side has asked for or promised a ban on building these kinds of systems, but Beijing has hinted that it might support the idea before changing its mind. However, China's 2021 Position Paper on Regulating Military Applications of Artificial Intelligence said that countries should "develop and apply AI technology in the military field in a prudent and responsible manner," not try to get an absolute military advantage, and stop strategic mistakes from getting worse. It also said that "military applications of AI shall never be used as a tool to start a war or pursue hegemony." It asked military AI to usually follow international humanitarian law and limit the harm it could do to civilians. The paper also said that military AI should be "under human control" and that people should always be able to stop it from doing anything. These concepts have some things in common with the U.S. declaratory policies that were just talked about.

CBMs can be a useful diplomatic tool for setting basic standards, even if they don't lead to binding agreements. Washington and Beijing can talk about the effects of AI on national security through both one-way and two-way channels, as well as through international channels. They can share both broad and specific views. In an ideal world, the two sides would talk to each other militarily, so that each side could ask questions about the other's capabilities and how they are used, as well as share their views about rules of engagement, operational deconfliction, and other issues. But because the issue is touchy and the PRC often cancels military-to-military meetings when there are other differences between the two sides, neither side can count on the PLA and the U.S. military to keep talking.

In light of this, the countries could use Track 1.5 and Track 2 conversations along with the official routes. Since Chinese officials don't want to talk to American officials directly, European friends or other third parties could play a big role in bringing them together. In April of this year, NATO Secretary-General Jens Stoltenberg suggested that the Western alliance could start a conversation like this. However, it is still unclear whether China will see NATO as the right place to have this conversation. Because crises usually involve strange or surprising events, Washington and Beijing should have established ways to talk to each other during crises in addition to their regular AI talks during normal times. In theory, the second would help the first by providing personal ties and basic understandings.

Recommendations for Policymakers

The development of military AI is expected to make the competition between the US and China stronger and raise strategic risks. In light of these trends, U.S. leaders should:

Take bold action to constrain China's progress in AI for military and repressive purposes, but do so in a narrow way that avoids self-defeating steps.

The United States should keep putting strict limits on the tools and knowledge used to make semiconductors, as well as the finished goods like cutting-edge chips, that help China improve its military AI and its systems for repressing people at home. Washington should also look for creative ways to manage data, algorithms, and human capital—other basic building blocks of AI—when it is clear that they are being used for bad things. To do this, the US should only use technologies that have clear military (and dual-use) and repression uses, and it should keep changing its policies to make sure they work while avoiding too broad limits that hurt the country themselves. It's clear why we need to act: If China is successful in its military AI goals and gains a big lead in the highest levels of military technological power, it could make a danger that was already very serious even worse. And PRC brutality shocks the world's sense of right and wrong.

However, there are also good reasons to keep limits small: Some actions, especially those that stop the flow of talent, could hurt the U.S. AI ecosystem and, by extension, the country's ability to succeed technologically. A lot of restrictions won't work without the help of friends and allies, and a lot of them are wary of broad solutions. It's possible for U.S. businesses to miss out on good business prospects that are then filled by foreign competitors. Washington could cut off Beijing from possible sources of power, which would make things even more hostile if China thinks that the US is trying to stop not only its military progress but also its economic growth. In real life, it will often be very hard to find the right mix between these two main goals. Even the people who wrote this study have different ideas about which strategies are best. But balance is still important because there are both reasons to move and risks of going too far.

Build U.S. military AI capabilities to stay on the cutting edge.

To keep up with China's work on military AI, the US will have to move quickly—maybe even faster than it is now and with the same amount of TEVV—to match. That will need tough changes in a lot of areas. It's outside the scope of this chapter to go into detail about all of them, but changes to the purchasing system and, in some places, military service cultures that value old weapons systems are important to the DoD, the military services, and the U.S. Congress. As a key feature for new military systems, the DoD should also make resilience a top priority. This will increase deterrence and lower "use-or-lose" pressures during emergencies. To be successful in this area, the Department of Defence (DoD) alone won't be enough. New immigration and education policies are also needed to bring in, train, and keep the best scientists and engineers from around the world.

Develop, promulgate, and implement norms and best practices on responsible military AI.

Washington should take the lead in setting standards and best practices for the development and use of military AI around the world. The United States has already taken some big steps in this direction. But Washington can go even further by creating and sharing details about TEVV processes that make sure that military systems in action work in ways that are in line with the main ideas set out in those papers. In the near future, the United States should focus on two main things: figuring out how to better protect nuclear C3 infrastructure from cyberattacks (including AI-enabled ones) and keeping the promise made in the U.S. Nuclear Posture Review to "maintain a human 'in the loop' for all actions critical to informing and carrying out decisions by the President to initiate and terminate nuclear weapon employment." For any of these rules and best practices to be taken seriously, the U.S. needs to take real steps to put them into action and make sure that military AI is strong, reliable, and useful. This is especially important when dealing with a skeptical China. In other words, the U.S. must follow through on what it says about using combat AI responsibly.

Proactively engage with like-minded allies and partners and in multilateral institutions on military AI issues.

There is other stuff going on besides the competition between the US and China, like military AI and related security problems. The regional and world situation is very important in determining what will happen. Washington should make it a point to talk about these problems with its alliance and partner countries. Early talks about military AI in NATO, the AUKUS partnership, and bilateral alliances with Japan and South Korea should be widened, maybe even to include the G7 group. These forums are good places to talk about important tactical issues with people who share your views. For example, you can decide if agreements should focus on controlling certain results instead of specific technologies. They can also help make it clear where and how international rules already cover issues related to military AI. Washington should also keep proactively defending its stance in multilateral forums, such as the LAWS process we talked about earlier. These things will help China decide what to do about military AI. Beijing is more likely to agree with military AI principles and practices that are backed by a group of countries around the world than with those that are only pushed by the United States.

Negotiate risk reduction and confidence-building measures with China related to military AI.

Beijing has not been willing to have serious talks about lowering strategic risks that involve nuclear weapons. Chinese officials have said that their stance is based on the fact that their arsenals are different sizes, though China's nuclear upgrading is closing the gap. But Washington should look into the possibility of a route on military AI, since both sides are much more equal in how good they are at it. Early work should focus on making simple things happen, like making a list of military AI words and their English and Chinese translations. That would help make sure that both sides agree on how to define important ideas. This would make communication easier and lessen the chance of misunderstandings caused by language and cultural differences.

The two sides could also make a list of danger levels that are linked to different levels of capability. For example, using AI for upkeep and logistics is a low-risk thing to do, but using AI to make nuclear weapons work on their own would be a very high-risk thing to do. The two powers could talk more about how and where they are and aren't using AI for military reasons, as well as what the rules and expectations are for AI's role in using deadly force. Even if officials from the U.S. and China don't agree on these topics, talking about them can help them understand each other better and lower the chances of mistakes. A more ambitious goal could be to make agreements about incidents at sea, incidents in the air, and/or rules of engagement for autonomous systems that are not manned.

Continue to pursue universal U.S.-China risk reduction and crisis management mechanisms despite persistent challenges.

The job of building strong U.S.-China diplomatic channels for lowering strategic risks and handling crises that happen—what the Biden administration often calls "guardrails"—will become more important as both superpowers add AI to their military forces. Overall, U.S.-China strategic risk reduction and crisis management methods have not worked very well, though there may have been a few successes. Still, risk reduction and crisis management systems that only work sometimes are better than none at all, as long as Washington doesn't give up important policy goals just to keep meeting. Leader-level contacts, in particular, let you talk to someone directly, which can cut down on the misunderstandings and wrong ideas that happen when texts go through staff and middlemen. Lower-level meetings can't happen without Xi's backing for ongoing, tough diplomacy, especially in the Chinese system.

Make military AI a fundamental pillar of diplomacy with China related to nuclear weapons and strategic stability.

There are more nuclear risks between the US and China. This trend is caused by many things, one of which is that Beijing's nuclear stockpile is quickly growing in size and complexity. In this chapter, we saw that military AI is also becoming more important in balancing nuclear and other strategic weapons, which could be unstable. Biden and Xi are said to have agreed at their meeting in November 2021 that they would "start to carry forward discussions on strategic stability." There is no public proof that those talks ever started, which is a shame. Instead, Washington should ask the permanent five (P5) group of nuclear-armed states to start the process over again, and then include military AI in the talks. Chinese officials have already supported this idea, so they are more likely to get involved in a serious way. And earlier, the group made an important P5 statement on nuclear problems, though Russia's nuclear threats over Ukraine make Moscow's signature less trustworthy.

Take steps to reduce strategic risks not directly caused by military AI but potentially worsened by the inherent speed and unpredictability of military AI.

As military AI gets better, ties between the US and China are likely to become less stable and more uncertain. With this in mind, Washington should do what it can to lower geopolitical risks in other areas. It's smart for one country to make operational choices that show restraint, like the US delaying ICBM tests during times of high tension, especially when tests aren't needed right away to make sure a safe, secure, and effective nuclear deterrent. Another good example is the U.S.'s work to make rules that ban destructive, direct-ascent antisatellite weapon tests. In the future, the US and China might sign a deal like the ones they have with Russia to let each other know when missiles are launched.

Prioritize intelligence-gathering and analysis on, and net assessment of, China's military AI capabilities.

This chapter has shown that it is possible to do some basic research on how military AI will change the security relationship between the US and China and possibly make strategic risks worse. But we don't yet know what the full path and impact of military AI will be. Military AI could fail and not be as important as people think it will be, or it could completely change the way the military works in ways that are hard to imagine. The military AI itself will not be the only thing that changes; how it works with other things will also be important. Some of these are nuclear arsenals and the infrastructure that goes with them, conventional weapons, the relationship between the US and China, and progress in civilian AI technologies.

Therefore, it is very important to learn more about how military AI might or might not affect the arms race, the chance of a crisis getting worse, and general strategic stability. The U.S. director of national intelligence, secretary of state, and secretary of defence should ask their departments to improve or, if necessary, create joint offices and groups of experts to keep an eye on, study, and suggest policy changes that will help solve these problems. Each of these offices should have a formal connection to, or overlap with, the parts of each department (often called "China Houses") that are in charge of coordinating China policy across regional and functional problems.

Conclusion

The development of military AI could make the security situation between the US and China even more tense and unstable. To figure out how to handle the strategic risks that come with this, it will be important to keep a close eye on Beijing's civilian and especially military AI operations. For analysts and policymakers, it will also be important to learn more about how new military AI capabilities could open up new paths for crisis or war. Eventually, lowering strategic risks will need a mix of competition and selective interaction with China in this situation. U.S.-China relations are still trying to find a stable balance, and AI is getting better all the time. This means that lawmakers will have to deal with more problems caused by how these two trends affect each other.

Chapter 7
The Impact of Artificial Intelligence on Future Diplomatic Relations

Corneliu Bjola wrote in 2017 that the "first stage" of the digital transformation of communication was "an amazing success." The change to digital is called "nothing short of a revolution" because "90% of all UN Member States have set up a Twitter presence" and "Western embassies are performing successfully on some Chinese media platforms."

For Bjola and others, being able to connect with millions of people instantly and "at minimal cost" through digital networks is changing the very nature of diplomacy. It's becoming more global, moving from the mahogany corridors of power to the high-speed cyber highways of the future. "The rise of digital diplomacy has been nothing short of a revolution for a professional with an innate tendency to uphold tradition, defend institutional hierarchy, and fight change," he says.

People usually talk about the "first stage" of digital diplomacy in terms of social media and APIs. However, AI, along with Mixed Reality, Blockchain, Crypto, Nanotechnology, and the Internet of Things (IOT), will play a role in the second stage of diplomacy that is expected to happen later. "There isn't much chance of making a robo-diplomat in the near future," Bjola says, adding that AI technologies are already being used in diplomacy: "chatbots now help with visa applications, legal aid for refugees, and consular registrations."

This second stage of technology change is sometimes called the "Fourth Industrial Revolution." It is expected to bring about changes in the economy and government that will go beyond individual countries.

It's hard to imagine what these changes might mean for the way global communication is done. One important part of this second step of technological change is that military, civilian, and diplomatic use will move from the internet to real life. An story in Wired in 2017 about how AI could "cognitize objects" by "making them more intelligent and useful" was cited by Paul Scharre, Director of the Center for a New American Security. Scharre says that the internet is like a "layer on top of our existing reality." He quotes science fiction author William Gibson, who said, "Now cyberspace has everted." Inside out. Taken over the physical" There will be no longer any difference between "digital" and "traditional" communication because AI will speed up this trend.

To better plan and explain this process, we need to know more about the options of diplomacy as well as technology. It's one of the most important changes in diplomacy over the last thirty years that it has become more global, "multi-centric," and less controlled by independent states. Kelley thinks that the "age of diplomacy as an institution is giving way to an age of diplomacy as a behavior." This new geopolitical reality is made possible by the flow of trade and information around the world. Kelley says that "the very ontology on which official diplomacy has stood for more than three centuries" is changing because there are fewer "power asymmetries" between state and non-state players.

Kelley sees the first stage of digital disruption as a complex web of interconnected forces made possible by communications technology. These include more partnerships between the private and public sectors, the rise of "transactional networks" to "leverage legitimacy," more mobility and decentralization of institutions around the world, and the rise of human rights-focused NGOs, not-for-profits, and a global civil society. Diplomacy has different effects on different people. Kelley says that "new diplomats" will "continue to eclipse institutional diplomacy practiced by official diplomats in the 21st century."

Thinking about how AI will change diplomacy in the future, during the "second stage" of disruption, can help you understand how the first stage of digital disruption changed the way global diplomacy is done.

This chapter will argue that the new technologies that artificial intelligence has created will quickly speed up the first stage of diplomatic disruption. These technologies will also create opportunities, challenges, and moral questions that have never been seen before that will be central to how democracy, economics, and geopolitics are organized in the future. In this situation, we will need to rethink the meaning and potential of global diplomacy.

Defining 'Artificial Intelligence'

Artificial intelligence will be defined in the same way that Price, Walker, and Wiley did in "The Machine Beneath: Implications of Artificial Intelligence in Strategic Decision Making" (2018). In this paper, the topic of AI is broken down into three groups. The first is "artificial narrow intelligence" like the kind we have now, which can do things like recognize images and play chess better than humans. The second is "artificial general intelligence" (AGI), which is a "human-level intelligence" that can do many things (Ibid). Finally, there is "artificial superintelligence" (ASI), which is human intelligence that is much higher than human intelligence (Ibid).

There will also be a lot of talk about how AI can predict the future thanks to progress in machine learning. Machine learning is not the last theoretical category of human thought. Instead, it is the skill of sorting through teraflops of data and using algorithmic programming to make statistical conclusions and predictions. People named Agrawal, Gans, and Goldfard say that predictions are important because they help people make decisions. If you don't make a choice, a prediction is useless. In the past, one of the most important jobs of an institutional diplomat was to guess the behavior, plans, and intentions of both allies and possible enemies, both in terms of foreign policy and personal relationships. So, one thing that will be looked into is how much artificial intelligence will change the ways that predictions are made and decisions are made in global relations.

It's not always easy to figure out what "new diplomacy" means or how to define artificial intelligence. There is no longer any such thing as a "new diplomat" if everyone with a computer and a Twitter account is one. We criticize brick-and-mortar institutions for not being able to adapt to the network age. But can't it also be argued that we need new global institutions for cooperation? The meaning of artificial intelligence makes the idea more clear and takes into account the fact that AI is changing, just like diplomacy is. The kinds of jobs that AI might be able to do in the future are still being studied and debated in academia. It's important to note the tensions in the meaning. The AlphaGO AI application is still too fragile to solve even the most basic problems that aren't in its programming area, and this intelligence's "narrow" nature is still very upsetting. In short, AI applications that are already out there will be enough to change whole businesses before we even think about the idea of "superintelligence" with many goals.

New Developments in AI

There are a lot of different ways that AI-based technologies could be used, like driving an autonomous car in California or keeping an eye on an autonomous weapons system in the South China Sea. These uses will have a big impact on global peace and the economy. These changes will happen very quickly. It will be hard to get ready for them.

For starters, AI will grow at different rates in different industries, global companies, and between superpowers. When AI is used in war versus health, for example, the moral and legal issues are very different. The way an AI solution is built will have a big effect on its impact and outcome, whether it's in the private sector, the military, or as part of an open-data project run by citizens.

In order to give a good picture of what AI might mean for diplomats in the future in the time allotted, this chapter will concentrate on three important areas of foreign work: health, economics, and security. It is not possible to give an expert review of how artificial intelligence can be used in these areas. Instead, an overview of some of the ways that AI is changing and disrupting businesses that are important to the functioning of a global society will be given. There will be a part on conclusions that talks about five big trends that will affect the future of global diplomacy.

Part I: AI and Autonomous Weapons Systems

The most important job of negotiation is to keep states from going to war and to protect civilians. Throughout history, the "defence of the realm" has been seen as the first duty of government. New developments in AI are about to happen that will change the speed, the chain of command, the ties between security forces, and the rules for who is responsible for what in the twenty-first century. A general in the U.S. Air Force said this about the change: "The B-52 lived and died on the quality of its sheet metal." Today, how well our software works will determine the fate of our plane.

Machine Speed Warfare

Because war is changing, there may come a time when putting human forces in danger is not an option when unmanned underwater, surface, and air vehicles can do the same jobs already.

The speed at which these systems work and the level of oversight and control they need are two define policy problems that come up when autonomous weapons are used. Human Rights Watch uses the term "control paradigm" to describe three types of weapons systems: "Human-in-the-Loop," "Human-out-of-the-Loop," and "Human-of-the-Loop." These are fully automatic weapons systems that don't need any human supervision.

Japan wants to make robotic planes that can "help" jets that are manned, with a pilot giving them orders. A former head of the U.S. Department of Defence said that human troops could act as "quarterbacks" for Autonomous Weapons Systems teams because of the need for "human-machine collaboration." Human Rights Watch says that both of these talks meet their criteria. The right and moral choice of targeting is used as the main topic for the discussions on human control, hybrid human-machine control, and fully autonomous decisions. A 2018 report from the Center for Naval Analyses (CAN) said that "failure to recognize and mitigate factors besides the platform in the targeting process resulted in an increased risk to civilians from the use of drones, despite some desirable characteristics of these systems."

In fact, some parts of this discussion are no longer relevant because wars are moving faster and there is a race to be the best at AI and be the first to market. The Phalanx close-in weapons system (CIWSO) on US Navy War Ships can already be set to automatically detect and engage incoming missiles. This is because "the ship could be destroyed while waiting for a crew member to approve a defensive action against an incoming threat." During the Iraq War, people who worked on the Patriot Missile System were "trained to trust the system software" when they couldn't respond quickly enough. In both of these case studies, defensive methods are used instead of offensive ones.

This could change as "warfare speeds up to machine speed," making the battlefield more complex so that "human cognition may prove unable to keep up with the new operational tempo of intelligentized warfare." There are clear effects on the balance of armed power between countries, especially between the US and China.

AI, AWS and the Balance of Military Power

Predicting what will happen is one way that officials can handle things. Leaders of the military can practice how their units might do in a real fight by playing war games. Because making predictions isn't enough, diplomats build global organizations that can handle shocks, reach agreements, or make things change.

It's hard to guess how a mind that isn't human will act. It brings new problems for global organizations. For example, do theories of conventional and nuclear defence still work at machine speed? What happens when an AI makes a mistake? Who is at fault? .

People's Liberation Army (PLA) leaders were very interested in the development of an AI that could play Go, an old Chinese game that is very difficult. This was after the AI beat the world champion, Lee Sedol. AlphaGo was created by "DeepMind," which was backed by Google. Later, records of games AlphaGo had played against itself were made public. The AI had come up with strategies that were so strange that experts said they were "from another dimension." People say that similar algorithms, some of which handle up to 12 billion dollars on Wall Street right now, cause flash crashes by going into sell off loops against each other. People don't know what's going on until after the event horizon.

Today, China does more research in artificial intelligence than the U.S. The number of papers they print is higher, and they are second in the world in applying for AI patents. A Military-Civil Integration Intelligent Equipment Research Institute was set up in 2016 to help people get into PLA programs in areas like smart robots, AI, unmanned systems, and military brain science. In July 2017, a year later, China revealed a "New Generation Artificial Intelligence Plan" that laid out its plans to become the world leader in AI by 2030.

Military strategists are trying to imagine what would happen if autonomous AI systems in the U.S. and China accidentally started a "flash war" or if an AI system activated a preemptive strike protocol in a way that normal military strategy could not have predicted.

Diplomacy and Autonomous War

'Swarming' techniques, in which an enemy is swarmed by a group of coordinated autonomous drone or micro-drone attacks, or anti-submarine submersibles that can work even if communication and satellite systems are destroyed, could change the military balance of power between nations like the US and China. In the same way that new developments in weaponry changed the way wars were fought in 1914, AWS will make the world less safe if the international community doesn't stop their use. In short, "AI systems may make war less rough while making it foggerier."

To deal with the spread and uneven growth of AWS systems, new legal, technical, and battlefield rules will need to be made on a global level. In 2017, the UN Group of Governmental Experts (GCE) started talking about lethal autonomous weapons systems (LAWS). Most of the GCE members agreed that there needed to be a legally binding rule. Russia said in 2017 that it would not follow any "international ban, moratorium, or regulation on such weapons." China was one of 26 countries that said they would back a ban on fully autonomous weapons in 2018. The US didn't want to negotiate a legally or politically binding document on LAWS and said that such a deal would be unrealistic and come too soon.

If there aren't any world rules, devices for controlling arms could be looked into. Both the US and the USSR worked to reduce their nuclear arsenals while also improving their weapons technology and understanding, as Price, Walker, and Wiley point out. One idea could be to look at the Strategic Arms Limitations Talks or the Treaty on Open Skies that the leaders of the US and USSR agreed to during the Cold War as a model for how to check weapons.

In a strange way, the case for human negotiation may be stronger now than it was during the Cold War, when machines were used to fight. It becomes harder to break down and record every part of the programmatic decision-making process after an event as AI systems get better at putting together bigger and more different datasets. To put it simply, more powerful AIs might not have a "black box." Calls for "algorithmic transparency seem doomed to fail." Leys says that an audit report "only has so much utility" if an AWS problem means a conflict. Even if these kinds of audits were possible, they could reveal bugs in the code that close rivals could use against you. In this case, being able to look a foreign official in the eye might come in handy.

It's possible that the rules of war from the past need to be changed. When an AWS uses physical force against a third party, the normal right to a proportionate military reaction might have to be taken away. Instead, new ways of settling disagreements might have to be thought up, maybe at the level of the UN Security Council. To put it simply, an immediate reaction of violence may not be legal or morally okay in the case of AWS.

Second, the use of AWS in civilian areas will have to be limited, even though deadly force can be used in antisubmarine warfare, air-to-air fighting, and other areas where civilians are not present. Some things that could be talked about here are the ocean, space, and the defence of important global energy and infrastructure routes.

At the state level, countries like the US and China may try to set up rules that say the use of deadly or nuclear force can never be automatic and must always be controlled by people. It is possible to set up channels for emergency contact in case an algorithmic trip-wire or early warning system goes off.

Even though we have only scratched the surface of what AWS means for modern fighting, it is clear that it will have huge effects on global politics and play a key role in diplomacy.

AI and Economic Transition

Private-Public Partnership

A self-driving car has light radar, high-resolution cameras, and microphones to make sure it doesn't hit a person on the street. An AWS could use the same devices to keep an eye on the border with North Korea or kill militants in Pakistan. Global technology companies and the public sector are starting to work together in a new way that is good for the global economy. While this trend has been talked about in terms of defence, it is also starting to change other important areas, such as global healthcare, industry, and digital currency. Research and development in both the public and private sectors are starting to change what makes work valuable and important.

It is believed that the National Geospatial-Intelligence Agency (NGA) in the United States will either "disrupt" or "be disrupted." The NGA has also made available petabytes of geospatial data and imagery to help the creation of "AI," "augmentation," and "Automation." The NGA says it is okay to give partners access to this secret intellectual property because they plan to use it to train datasets "for the development of AI algorithms with the potential for government and commercial purposes."

There is two-way communication. The government may be adopting "lean startup" methods and the language of entrepreneurship common in the tech industry. At the same time, Silicon Valley is working closely with the government and starting to copy some of its actions. All of the big tech companies in the US have opened offices in Washington, DC. This is in addition to trying to get contracts with the Pentagon for cloud storage services.

In China, telecoms companies like Huawei and ZTE provide the core technologies for the country's social programs. At the same time, private healthcare companies like WeDoctor work with the local government to create and analyze AI datasets. According to the Intercept, the Ministry of Foreign Affairs is home to the United Arab Emirates' main private cyber-security company, which helps the government spy on people. A new group of civil servants in the UK is being trained by the Digital Civil Service to "design, build, and run digital services that transform the lives of millions of people."

It's kind of like the economy as a whole is changing slowly, but technology and government are becoming more alike. Mark Zuckerberg wants to give up to 2.7 billion Instagram, WhatsApp, and Facebook users their own currency. One writer recently said that Zuckerberg's goals are those of "not a company" but a "country." The writer also said that "bankers and regulators are starting to wonder if they even have the tools to set economic policy, like they used to". This new economy based on data and predictions is moving out of the network and into the real world more and more.

Internet of Things (IOT)

As microsensors "cognite" things, the buying habits of millions, and eventually billions, of people will become useful feedback loops for both businesses and governments. Smart gadgets that are online will connect to a shared network. This will provide information that could help governments make new plans for social services, tax benefits, and energy sharing resources. A lot of this data will be spread out across networks that don't connect to current state entities. This will create new types of economic activity and the need to come up with new ways to govern them.

CISCO says that by 2022, more than 12 billion mobile devices and Internet of Things (IoT) links will be able to connect to global mobile networks. As Zettabytes of information connect devices to each other, corporate databases will keep track of new types of economic activity. At the same time, sensors will let governments keep an eye on how much energy and water people use in real time, making off-grid or personal distributed systems that are less centralized and exist at the local or household level.

It's still not clear how IOT devices will be added on top of current and future technologies. Amazon bought Whole Foods grocery shops in the US for $13.7 billion in 2017. Soon after, they started testing a way to pay without cash. Analysts said it was only a matter of time before products bought at Whole Foods stores started to show up in ads and be mentioned as items that Amazon users should buy on other services. This case study shows how monopoly, competition, antitrust, and barriers to entry can affect mass consumption driven by the internet of things (IoT).

Health Care & AI

The rise of AI in healthcare is a good way to bring together and outline many of the issues that people are concerned about when it comes to automation, privacy, joblessness, and controlling machines by humans.

AI's ability to find value patterns in very big datasets much faster than humans can is changing medicine all over the world. The computational pathologist (C-Path) at Stanford University can find breast cancer signs that haven't been seen before by looking at the cellular features of hundreds of tumor images (Ibid). Companies like IBM and General Electric are also making tools like this. AI's are being trained by startups like "Zebra Medical Vision" to be able to spot heart disease in CT scans and other diseases like bone, liver, and lung disease. This technology is already commonly used in medical scans. AI helps people make decisions instead of taking their place completely. In these situations, machine modeling might be better than human diagnosis. One day, a machine might be able to do what it takes to train doctors around the world much more quickly and for much less money.

The effects of this are more complicated than they seem at first, especially when it comes to health. Many of the "tasks in the workflow" of a radiologist will not be replaced by AI, as Agrawal, Gans, and Goldfarb point out. For example, "choosing the exam, directing the technologists, reporting on results, and deciding on an action given the probabilities reported by the machine" have not been replaced. It might be necessary for someone other than a radiologist to read and explain the report to a person based on the patient's medical background. This could be a social worker or care physician. In this case, people will still have to do jobs, and new roles could be made.

In the defence industry, a predictive ALWS could possibly save thousands of lives. In the medical field, on the other hand, predictive AI will soon step in for trained professionals. This trend can also be seen in other important parts of the economy: "transcription jobs are being automated because the main skill needed is being able to guess which words to type after listening to a recording." When artificial intelligence was used to figure out the best way for car drivers to get around London, their jobs were in danger.

Because AI prediction works well with jobs that require making decisions, its effect on the economy can't be summed up in one sentence: it favors capital over labor. Mittelstadt has said that the Hippocratic Oath, the Declaration of Geneva, and the Declaration of Helsinki do not apply to "AI doctors." At the moment, there are no rules or licenses that allow the trusting connection between a patient and an AI system to be replicated.

If in the future an AI system were to physically perform on a person, how much would the public be able to look into its algorithmic programming? Who would be responsible if something went wrong, and would there need to be human oversight? Would the fact that a development team is at the other end of the world make people act less ethically and make it impossible to hold them accountable?

It will be most disruptive in areas of the economy where (i) a lot of trust is not needed, (ii) automation will cut costs and boost earnings without causing a lot of physical, legal, or moral harm, or (iii) a lot of trust is not needed. One example is the manufacturing industry, where the "robot threat" is often greater than the "robot dividend" for many industrial workers in China. Automation could lead to a 67–85 percent drop in the number of jobs available. Due to cost barriers to entry, these workers didn't have much of a chance to reskill, retool, or "learn to code." It is very hard for governments and lawmakers to figure out how to deal with the demographic and social effects of automation on the global economy in areas like manufacturing.

Conclusions: AI & Five Macro-Influences on Global Diplomacy

New developments in AI technologies have effects on global relations that can be roughly grouped into five main trends, though this is not a good way to do it.

'The second stage of digital communication' is the name of the first trend. In the "first stage," officials used digital tools to improve processes, talk to each other in new ways, and make data easier for people and groups to access. The second step in digital diplomacy will be defining it. Technologies like AI will change the rules of statecraft and the way countries work.

Second, there is more and more integration between the business and public sectors. In the US, improvements in cloud infrastructure or autonomy for civilians are coming together with the military and security establishment. The government in China has a lot of power over the private sector, which gives them access to huge amounts of data about things like medicine, industry, and online shopping. Diplomats and governments will work hard to control and get to this info.

A third trend is that people will become more aware of how weak global institutions are. It will be tried to fix, rebuild, and replace global organizations so that the world economy and security arrangements can be better managed. It will become clear that states cannot come together to make agreements on things like limiting the number of weapons or dealing digitally.

Fourth, the way officials act will change. In the first stage of digital diplomacy, the role of the official grew. In the second stage, it will shrink. Literacy in technology, knowledge of new ideas in the private sector, and global experience may become just as important as language skills and cultural awareness.

Lastly, AI will speed up the process of centralizing data around the world and create new ways for governments to keep an eye on things like economic data, culture trends, and public opinion. Online and offline services that cross borders will be offered by new types of companies or semi-government structures. The "datafication" of global government could be bad for democratic systems because policies are now backed up by claims that they are inevitable based on algorithms instead of what the people want.

We are putting forward these five trends hesitantly as an open call to talk. They are not perfect and need to be looked at in much more depth. Each trend is based on the main point of this chapter, which is that once AI becomes widespread, it will be very hard for global diplomats to think of, understand, and build the social and economic frameworks that will help the best outcomes happen and keep the worst ones from happening.

Chapter 8
AI Revolution in Military Operations

Introduction

The main thing that makes the international security situation interesting is the battle for global leadership between the US and China. Both countries want to be in charge, but they have different ideas about how to do it. The two nations have very different ideas about the global order, human rights, autocracy and democracy, and security hotspots like Taiwan and islands in the South and East China Seas. These disagreements affect global rules in a bigger way. China's strong economy and close ties to the U.S. private sector make the current struggle different from the problems the U.S. faced during the Cold War. China wants to work with the US on important global problems like climate change, but sees the US as in the way of its rise to global hegemony, and the US sees China as a growing threat to the rules-based order that was set up after World War II. This is becoming more and more clear in official language on both sides. The 2018 U.S. National Security and National Defence Strategies, for example, called China a hostile power and a rival to the U.S.

Competition in technology has become an important part of these economic and security changes. Both countries want to be the best at creating and selling cutting-edge technologies and goods that people all over the world want. China wants to be a world leader in technology, and its government wants to spread its vision by using organized planning and its close ties with big tech companies. The U.S. defence establishment is becoming more worried that China's military might use these companies' technological advances as part of its military-civil fusion (MCF) policy. This policy aims to use advances in both civilian and military technologies to benefit both sides.

AI may be the most important area of battle between the US and China in the tech world. The US and China are two of many countries that think AI could be revolutionary in both civilian and combat settings. AI is like electricity in that it can "animate" machines, and some people think it could cause long-lasting changes in society like a new Industrial Revolution. By 2021, 44 countries had released and were putting into action their own national AI strategies. However, the US and China stand out as the global leaders in a number of ways, such as spending, academic publishing, patents and applications granted, and the growth of AI research in the private, public, and academic sectors. They are also major players in the semiconductor business, where growth makes it possible for AI to keep getting better.

Most importantly for this part, both the US and China are thinking very hard about how AI could be used in the military, which they both see as a huge step forward. The military's ability to be changed by AI is exciting, but not certain. It is hard to guess how it will grow because it has had "winters" and then made quick progress in the past. Still, some U.S. and Chinese analysts, strategists, and technologists think it could completely change how people interact with machines. This could have a wide range of military impacts, from reducing the need for humans to fight on the battlefield to upsetting the calculations behind strategic nuclear deterrence. Computer vision, natural language processing, and recommender systems are some of the applications that could help reach strategy goals by providing new ways to handle operational problems in areas like autonomy, decision support, and command and control!

Both the U.S. and China's national AI policies recognize how important it is to stay on the cutting edge of progress. This is the 2018 Department of Defence The AI Strategy said that AI is "set to change the nature of the future battlefield and the speed of threats we must face." We will use AI to its fullest ability to improve every part of the Department. Putting AI first is at the heart of China's plans to modernize its military. China's Central Military Commission for Science and Technology Commission director, Lt. Gen. Liu Guozhi, said, "AI will speed up the process of military transformation, ultimately leading to a profound Revolution in Military Affairs... The combination of artificial intelligence and human intelligence can achieve the optimal, and human-machine hybrid intelligence will be the highest form of intelligence in the future." In its 2019 Defence White Paper, China talked about AI as an important part of the "Revolution in Military Affairs (RMA) with Chinese characteristics."

But does AI really mean a change in military affairs (RMA)? If so, what does it matter? The RMA idea, which is made up of four parts: technological change, the evolution of military systems, operational innovation, and organizational adaptation, is a good way to look at whether AI could change the way wars are fought, since AI is only useful for certain things right now. Technology may play a role in RMAs, but an RMA doesn't happen until certain technological uses lead to changes in tactics and organizations that help the military move forward. Former head of the Office of Net Assessment (ONA) Andrew W. Marshall came up

AI Revolution in Military Operations

with the idea for the RMA from a U.S. point of view. He said, "The main challenge in the RMA is an intellectual one, not a technological one." The RMA approach can help us avoid over-the-top guesses about AI's abilities and instead focus on how it impacts systems, operations, and businesses.

If AI is causing an RMA in either the U.S. or Chinese armies, new ideas and technologies could threaten the main way that either force operates. In the event that it isn't, knowing why and how it might happen in the future can help people spot signs of intellectual progress and growth, like new military AI apps and ways of doing things that might make an AI RMA more likely to happen. So, figuring out if AI could lead to an RMA could change how the US thinks about and plans its future military competition with China.

The research method used in this chapter looks at AI as a revolutionary military technology through the four elements of RMAs that Andrew Krepinevich named in his seminal 1992 paper. For the goals of the paper, it defines RMAs. Then, it looks at AI applications, how much they are changing U.S. and Chinese military systems, operations, and organizations, and what kinds of changes those changes are. It uses interviews, research, analysis, official papers, news stories, and examples from the past to come to the conclusion that AI is not currently leading to an RMA. As things stand, AI technologies can't be used in the military in many ways, which makes it hard for practical innovation and organizational change to happen.

A medium- to long-term AI RMA is more likely to happen, though, if technology improves and the US and China are better able to deal with the intellectual problems of operational innovation and organizational adaptation. Previous RMAs, especially the carrier aviation RMA that grew out of competition between the US and Japan between the wars and during World War II, can teach us about how competition between the US and China might change in ways that could lead to or cause an AI RMA. This chapter looks at these ideas and ends by talking about ways to understand a future AI RMA and places where more research is needed.

Characterizing and Recognizing Military Transformations

This part defines and analyzes RMAs and puts their unique features in the context of military innovations so that you can figure out if AI is currently driving a new RMA. It points out four important parts of RMAs that will be used for further evaluation and analysis, as well as tools and techniques for spotting revolutionary changes.

Defining Concepts

RMAs are made up of new organizational goals and frameworks for the military, as well as new ways of doing things on the battlefield that are sometimes driven by new technologies and sometimes not. Krepinevich, who worked at ONA with Marshall to understand the framework, said that RMAs usually have four parts: changes in technology, changes in military systems, changes in how things are done, and changes in how organizations work. An RMA is not new because of how quickly it happens, but because of how it changes the way wars are fought. Its main feature is that it is fundamentally different from the previous most common ways and patterns of military operations, which the RMA makes useless. It's possible for RMAs to take away one or more of the main skills of a dominating military or give a military actor new main skills in a certain area, or both. Hundley said that RMAs are often caused by a mix of technologies, that guns aren't always used, and that changes to technology, systems, operations, and organization often happen at the same time.

RMAs are usually linked to system improvements like tanks, aircraft ships, nuclear weapons, and reconnaissance-strike complexes. However, technology by itself is not enough to make an RMA. Marshall said, "Technological advances make a military revolution possible, but the revolution itself doesn't happen until new ways of doing things come up and, in many cases, new military organizations are formed." Also, military groups need to adopt new ideas and structures that help them reach new military goals and give them steady benefits over opponents who are still using an old style that worked well for them. A technology can't be part of an RMA if it doesn't help change the core skills of a dominant military or make new ones. Carafano did say, though, that it is hard to imagine a big change in the nature of war in the future without a major technology advance first.

RMAs can grow up over a long period of time. Most of the time, these are innovations that happened during times of peace, when people had more time and money to think about new ideas, test them, and come up with theories. But they might need competition to fully come true. Like, Marshall thought that the US hadn't come very far in the reconnaissance-strike RMA in 2009. Using the time between world wars as an example, he thought that the U.S. military had not yet reached 1930 in terms of implementing the RMA. This was because operations like Desert Storm and those in Iraq and Afghanistan against weaker conventional opponents and insurgents had not yet forced the military to combine improvements in military systems with changes in how they were used. Because the RMA didn't have a better traditional competitor, ideas and structures hadn't changed, so it was impossible to say when it would be fully mature. During times of peace, the technologies that make a new RMA possible may be met with skepticism, especially from experts, until they are shown to work in battle.

Cultural Impact

Different defence organizations have different levels of ability to develop, adopt, and carry out an RMA. It can be very different from one country or even within the same military in terms of how well they can integrate and use supporting technologies. This is often due to cultural factors. RMAs are the result of changes in technology, systems, operations, and structures. Because of this, culture can show how willing and able a military is to adopt new ideas. Because of this, countries that create similar technologies can use them in very different ways. There are some cultural traits that might make armies more likely to carry out RMAs. Unresolved military problems can inspire motivation and imagination. It's important for organizations and leaders to create environments that are open to new ideas and change. Focus can be gained by trying things out in a single technical or tactical area or a short list of them. Key factors include how willing and able an organization is to use trial results to change how ideas are developed, how people are trained, and how the force is organized.

For instance, the Soviet and American military establishments had different cultures that affected their ability to implement the new reconnaissance-strike RMA in the 1980s. The U.S. military knew they needed to come up with better technologies to counter Soviet conventional advantages without putting a lot of strain on ground or air forces after looking at how well Soviet integrated air defence systems worked in the Vietnam and Yom Kippur Wars, as well as new Soviet antitank weapons and other capabilities that made land and air environments more dangerous. Standoff precision strikes that combined the ability to find, recognize, and track targets with long-range guidance, navigation, and stealth showed promise as non-nuclear answers to this problem. The current reconnaissance-strike RMA was made possible by combining new technologies in these areas with new ways of doing things and organizing things to control movement through deep attack, such as AirLand Battle. This was most noticeable during the Gulf War. Adamsky said that the Americans were faster at solving the technological problem of the RMA by making precision weapons, but they were slower to solve the intellectual problem because new ideas and ways of doing things tended to come from below in the services instead of from above. On the other hand, the Soviet General Staff's culture of centralized military intellectualization at the operational level of war helped them correctly assess the threat of the U.S. military-technical revolution for Soviet numerical superiority and force echelonment. However, they were unable to realize the RMA's technological side because they did not have a culture of solving technological problems.

Emerging Military Transformations

Now that we know what RMAs are and how cultural factors can affect how militaries use them, this part talks about how hard it is to spot one in real life. In general, it is easier to see how the different parts of an RMA interact with each other after the fact. However, looking at similarities between past events and current trends may help you spot new RMAs. Studies of the past show examples of measures that can be seen, such as changes in the use of force, the size of an attack, and the time it takes to launch an attack.

Reporting, official statements, and new technological study are all things that can be seen today. Technologies that could make RMAs possible are likely to get news attention. Less powerful militaries may welcome innovations that threaten the status quo, while more powerful militaries may try to discredit innovations that question their dominance. A new RMA could also come from changes in military research and development patterns and new operating ideas, doctrine, or experiments. Concepts, doctrines, decision-making cultures, and views of war that are different from those of an enemy could reveal opportunities for new RMAs. Lastly, it is important to carefully consider a possible RMA's viability because many of them fail. Keep an open mind and be aware of the limitations of less likely scenarios. It's better to include a few choices that don't make sense than to be caught off guard.

If AI development in the US or China is what starts an RMA, then advances in AI technologies should lead to changes in military systems, causing new ways of doing things and new ways of organising them that are different from the way things are done now. This part talks about some definitions and ways to analyse data. The next section uses Krepinevich's four RMA elements to look at AI's effect on the military and decide if an AI-driven revolution in military affairs is starting.

Assessing AI using RMA Components

Technological Change

Over the past ten years, there has been a lot of fast and impressive progress in the technology behind some AI methods. AI techniques used in computer vision, natural language processing, and recommender systems have made machines better at some jobs than humans. This has made people in the US and China think of creative ways to use AI in the military. However, AI apps have major flaws right now that will probably keep them from being useful on the battlefield for a while. Also, steady fast progress isn't a given. The past of AI is full of winters of slow progress, and things like access to semiconductors could slow down U.S. and Chinese progress. This part talks about AI and its uses in a broad technological sense. It also talks about recent technological improvements, their pros and cons, and the main problems that need to be solved soon in order to make an AI RMA possible.

It can be hard to even agree on what artificial intelligence is because the technology and ideas behind it have changed so quickly over the years, and its subfields and uses are also changing all the time. In this chapter, "artificial intelligence" refers to a group of technologies that make it possible for computers to do things that normally require human intelligence. AI has historically included a variety of decision-making systems, such as expert systems. However, when the term is used to talk about futuristic capabilities, it refers to machine learning (ML) systems that use computers to finish tasks by running algorithms that are based on data. For advanced machine learning, algorithms, data, and processing power (hereafter, "compute") are the most important things.

Recent huge steps forward in AI have been driven by improvements in these three areas; as a result, they are useful and cost a lot. Cutting-edge programmes are usually made by people with advanced degrees. The best way for these algorithms to learn is to use high-quality datasets that are a good representation of the problem set at hand. This will make the algorithms more accurate and reliable while reducing bias. Better semiconductor production and chips designed for machine learning have helped AI make big strides by increasing compute: from 2012 to 2018, the compute used to train the best AI projects grew by a factor of 300,000.

Deep learning is used to train neural networks, which are responsible for many of the latest advances in AI. Neural nets are groups of programmes with input, hidden, and output node layers. They are based on how human neurons talk to each other. Different nodes in each layer are given weights and limits that help the model process data to reach a goal, like finding patterns or identifying images. People can train networks by giving them feedback on how they're doing, and they can fine tune models by changing the weights in a general model to fit the needs of a particular task. Deep neural nets (DNNs), which have more than three layers, have made big steps forward in computer vision and language processing. They can also do many narrow tasks much better than humans, like finding ideas in very large datasets. However, DNNs, like brains, are made up of thousands of interconnected nodes whose interactions are very complicated and hard to sum up in a useful way. This makes it harder to predict and explain what they will do, which makes them less reliable for sensitive jobs.

In 2016, the U.S. company DeepMind's AlphaGo system beat the world's best human player at the Chinese strategy game Go. This was the first time that ML advances like DNNs were widely known. AlphaGo came up with moves and strategies that human players couldn't predict or understand. This showed that machine learning is getting better at beating humans at some jobs. Many people called China's win in 2016 "Sputnik moment." This was especially true because of how important the game was to Chinese culture, and it led to strategic concern and a huge investment in AI research.

After more than five years, both the US and China think that AI has huge potential for use in both civilian and military settings. This is especially true in areas like computer vision, natural language processing, big data analytics, and recommender systems. Computer vision, the ability of systems to find, process, and recognise things in their surroundings, has made a lot of progress recently thanks to faster computers and shorter training times. Medical imaging, real-time object detection to find important details in complex environments, and social media picture trawling are all civil uses. Self-navigation, image-based data collection and analysis, identifying people through facial or gait recognition, and identifying targets are just a few of the military uses.

To do their jobs, natural language processing models understand how people talk. Models read existing texts to learn how words are used in context and then "learn" to answer open-ended questions, make predictions, translate, and do chatbot functions. This is made popular by search engines and virtual helpers like Apple's Siri and Amazon's Alexa. This technology could be used by the military to look through large groups of papers for specific information, translate foreign intelligence, or even make up textual lies.

AI also looks good for helping people make decisions. Decision-support algorithms can find insights that would be hard or impossible for people to find. They do this by using "big datasets," which are collections of structured and unstructured data from many different sources. In line with their name, recommender systems help people make decisions by using user tastes and gathered data. Spotify is known for using these kinds of algorithms to make playlists and offer new music to users based on what they've listened to before and data from the community. Armed forces believe that combining, analysing, and clearing up multisource sensor data from the battlefield could help them make decisions and improve the efficiency of difficult supplies or maintenance tasks.

These are just a few of the recent and promising advances in AI that can be used in the military. We'll talk about more of them later in this part. But people who are excited about these apps need to be aware of the big problems they have right now.

Problems with technology. DNNs can be fragile when they're not in their training settings. This means that even small changes to inputs that they are used to can cause them to give wrong results. Adversaries may use these problems against you. For instance, researchers were able to stop a cutting-edge DNN image analyzer from reading stop signs by putting black and white stickers on them. Other researchers found that a model could correctly identify a panda picture as a gibbon even when the image was randomly warped in a way that humans couldn't make out. People can only guess why a model gives a certain result because models don't see the world the same way we do and secret layers aren't see-through. This makes it hard to confirm how well a model will work with new data, even if you know how well it worked in the past. So, building trust and testing and evaluating systems for military use are big problems that might make DNNs less useful in the near future in combat settings that are very complicated and change quickly.

DNN datasets and training can also be hard to get and cost a lot of money. To collect and label data, humans have to do a lot of work. There may still be problems when moving from training data to real-world applications, even if the training data is generally representative. It might be hard to get to data that can be used. For example, when the U.S. Army tried to use big data for predictive maintenance, they found that old data was written by hand and couldn't be read by computers. Both in training and in the real world, enemies can taint data. Also, datasets that are created by people may contain their own biases without them meaning to, which raises serious ethics concerns about fairness, accuracy, and algorithmic justice.

On top of these problems, combining teams of people and machines is hard and could be dangerous. The problems that rivals bring to the battlefield are already hard enough for soldiers to solve without adding the complexity of new algorithms that work best in limited settings. Because AI systems make decisions more quickly than humans do, and because they can be hard to explain, there may be times when humans defer to system judgement. This is known as automation bias. This increases the risk of things getting worse if acts made possible by AI can't be stopped by enemies. A 2020 wargame by the RAND Corporation found that fast machine decision-making speeds led to faster escalation, weaker deterrence, and slower reactions to de-escalation signals. The study came to the conclusion that "widespread AI and autonomous systems could lead to accidental escalation and crisis instability."

U.S. and Chinese people can use AI. In addition to the problems with technology we already talked about, it's not always clear that the US and China will be able to access the latest AI developments in the long run. This could make it less likely for either country to get an AI RMA passed. To keep technology moving forward, countries will need to find ways to get access to talent, materials, and money to support military AI development. Each country faces this task with its own set of strengths and weaknesses.

The United States' progress in AI is mostly due to a thriving private tech industry and academic study, not to centralised government efforts. When U.S. tech hubs get big enough, they bring in global companies and talented people. They also build innovation ecosystems where companies don't have to give government technology as quickly as they would have to in China. While the U.S. government has worked with some tech companies, especially those started by the Department of Defence (DoD), those relationships have been slow to start and sometimes tense. However, the DoD can't change the research goals of private companies or get to their data in the same way that China's authoritarian government can. It has tried new ways to get technology by working more closely with companies in Silicon Valley as well as its usual innovation hubs like the Defence Advanced Research Project Agency (DARPA). However, the DoD is still having trouble getting companies to follow strict defence procurement rules and keeping up with technological advances. There isn't a single set of rules or goals for AI schooling and training in the United States, which is similar to how AI innovation is spread out across the country. Different educational programmes can be more innovative with decentralisation, but it might be hard to evaluate and scale up different efforts. The US has had trouble developing STEM talent at home, but it has been better at getting and keeping foreign talent at its colleges and universities, including Chinese students.

China, on the other hand, wants to centralise the buying of AI for the military through a plan called "military-civil fusion," which uses new technologies for both military and civilian purposes. Xi Jinping said in 2017 that the MCF's goal was to make sure that "efforts to make our country prosperous and efforts to make our military strong go hand in hand." People in China used MCF as part of their New Generation Artificial Intelligence Development Plan to create new AI for "command and decision-making, military deduction, defence equipment, and other applications." The government thinks that being able to make its own AI is important for modernising the military and protecting that technology from being stolen by other countries. The Central Military Commission and People's Liberation Army (PLA) branches have even held public AI challenges to solve joint military issues. This is to take advantage of new ideas both inside and outside the military. MCF has also been linked to AI business alliances backed by the government that work like successful programmes in the U.S., Europe, and Japan. But MCF and China's reputation for stealing intellectual property (IP), forcing tech transfers by the government, and breaking international rules can turn off some foreign businesses, and some governments will punish companies with ties to the PLA.

Still, the Chinese tech industry has begun to resemble other advanced tech environments. Some of the biggest AI companies in the world are based in China, where they work on cutting-edge projects. The country is also building a stronger patent system and public-private investment funds. Its education in science, technology, engineering, and math (STEM) is growing much faster than the U.S.'s, which suggests that it could have a strong, competitive talent pool in the future. By 2025, China is expected to have graduated almost twice as many STEM PhDs as the U.S. Tracking plans like the Thousand Talents Plan actively seek out and hire top academics from China and other countries. Still, China has a hard time getting foreign workers and relies mostly on people in China.

Access to semiconductors could affect both the US and China's efforts to make AI that is very advanced. When it comes to making and controlling intellectual property (IP), design tools, advanced semiconductor manufacturing equipment (SME), and leading logic chips, the US and its partners in cutting-edge semiconductor supply chains are ahead of China. But most of the world's most advanced AI chips are made in Taiwan and South Korea. This means that supply problems in East Asia could affect U.S. access. Also, China is expected to make more chips than any other country by 2030, but it is still ten years behind the United States when it comes to making cutting-edge AI chips and mostly buys the most advanced chips. The US and its allies might be able to stop advanced chip and small and medium-sized business exports to companies with ties to the PLA. So, China's ability to get advanced electronics for military use in the future may depend on how well it manages its supply chain and helps small businesses grow.

With all of that said, an AI RMA would probably need much stronger and more stable technology to support it. Also, both the US and China will need to stay on the cutting edge of technology to make sure they have access to better technology as it develops. Each approach, decentralised and centralised, has pros and cons. For example, the US can attract companies and talent and protect cutting-edge intellectual property (IP), while the Chinese government can plan and organise resources and data. These problems and limitations with technology affect both countries' abilities to meet the other three RMA requirements, which will be talked about in the parts that follow.

Military Systems Evolution

To help with an RMA, technology needs to be well integrated into defence systems, which are part of system networks. The US and China have taken test runs at integrating their AI systems. This shows how both countries plan to use AI in their defence, though the specifics aren't always clear. Systems that are further along in development are probably classified. This means that public comments from officials don't give many details, and experiments like DARPA's that are open to the public may not turn into programmes of record.

So, instead of listing all the known programmes, this part gives a few examples of AI-enabled systems to show how they work. It is important to note how hard it is to put AI skills into groups because the technology can be used in so many different situations. Several of the systems listed here use AI in different ways, such as computer vision and autonomous guidance.

On its own and robots. This is something that both the US and China are looking into: AI-powered automated systems that can do many things. People like the idea of military autonomy because it can lower the risk of casualties, do dangerous or repetitive tasks, analyse and make decisions faster than humans, and eventually increase the strength of the military. Self-driving cars with AI could help people on missions, patrol areas in groups, and watch multiple targets from afar. Autonomous lethal systems with AI that can act based on targeting analysis are still very controversial. However, as far as the public knows, fully autonomous lethal weapons systems have not been used, but states have not ruled out the possibility that they will be in the future. Some people think that lethal liberty will have to be added eventually.

While the U.S. was funding AI research from Fiscal Years 2018–20, most of the money went to projects that dealt with autonomy: "All U.S. military services are working to incorporate AI into semiautonomous and autonomous vehicles, including fighter aircraft, drones, ground vehicles, and naval vessels." As part of the Army's Next Generation Combat Vehicle programme, machine learning is used to help vehicles navigate and move around without GPS. The Air Force Loyal Wingman Programme looks into putting a manned F-35 or F-22 fighter on the same trip as an unmanned F-16 fighter so that the unmanned fighter can help the manned fighter with things like carrying weapons and blocking electronic threats. Sea Hunter is a surface ship that can navigate itself and is designed to hunt submarines and find mines for the Navy for months at a time.

Scientists and military planners in China more often call self-driving weapons "AI weapons" or "intelligentized weapons," which seems to emphasise the role intelligence will play in choosing targets and attacking them.

According to open-source research, China's security and defence establishment thinks that AI could improve intelligent weapons, robotic vehicles, and intelligence, surveillance, and reconnaissance (ISR) software in ways that could help them carry out operations against the US. The PLA and its branches have done a lot of research and writing on how AI can be used to watch and target multiple targets and make autonomous systems that can operate in the air, on the ground, or at sea. During exercises in the South China Sea, the PLA Navy tried the HN-1 unmanned undersea glider. For a long time, China's defence industry has been trying to improve the intelligence of cruise and ballistic missile targeting. The JARI is an unmanned surface vehicle that can work on its own with the help of AI to help human ships with fire support or to work with other ships in a swarm. Navy has talked about similar ideas.

Decision Support. Decision support conveys different AI applications of models like recommender systems and computer vision that could help warfighters reason more quickly about battlefield or intelligence information. These applications could theoretically facilitate better and more rapid command and control (C2) and analysis stemming from ISR. Eventually, AI-enabled C2 assistants could even recommend courses of action to commanders. The U.S. Joint All Domain Command and Control (JADC2) system, in development, intends to use AI to aggregate and prioritize data from across the services' systems and sensors into a common, deduplicated joint operating picture. Project Maven uses computer vision to identify hostile behavior from drone footage, allowing human analysts to focus on decision making rather than sorting through data. Recent PLA contracts for AI-enabled ISR systems include the GL-AI Speech Recognition System 001, which uses natural language processing to translate foreign texts into Chinese, as well as the GeoSide 1400, an unmanned subsurface craft that conducts seabed target detection.

- **Maintenance, Logistics, and Sustainment.** The United States and China both see AI as capable of helping fulfill maintenance, logistics, and sustainment needs in multiple ways. One is by using performance data to predict system maintenance. The U.S. Army's Logistics Support Activity contracted IBM's Watson to identify signs of engine trouble in its Stryker vehicles based on data from seventeen sensors, as well as to analyze incoming logistics requests from the field to make money-saving shipping decisions. The Air Force has explored similar programs to anticipate aircraft maintenance. The Army envisions combining predictive algorithms that anticipate force sustainment needs and use autonomous vehicles to deliver supplies to contested areas. PLA branches and affiliates recently contracted for multiple AI-based predictive maintenance products, including software that diagnoses soldering faults and mechanical noise recognition equipment.

- **Modeling and Simulation.** AI applications also support modeling and simulation (M&S), whose broad umbrella covers training, analysis to support new capability procurement, tactical analysis, and systems testing. AI appears to hold potential for data-heavy M&S applications. Both China and the United States have used AI-enabled aerial simulators to test human pilots against AI emulations of adversary aircraft. The DoD recently awarded a $500 million contract to an AI software company to provide services for AI-enabled M&S. U.S. officials have also noted that China "is investing in all the enabling technologies needed for advanced modeling and simulation."
- **Information Operations and Cyber.** Beyond these battlefield, maintenance, and command support decisions, AI could augment information and offensive and defensive cyber operations (though gains in the latter area appear likely to be incremental for the near future). Generative image and text AI applications could create convincing disinformation by producing high-quality fakes of pictures or intelligence. China has explored information operations and disinformation creation using ML techniques, as well as spearfishing cyberattacks. The PLA also recently contracted for firms to provide it with software that uses AI to conduct threat sensing.

In conclusion, there are many defence uses for AI systems in many areas. Even though the technology doesn't seem fully developed enough to lead to big changes in how the U.S. or Chinese armies do their jobs, more advanced uses like autonomous systems could (or may already be) incorporated into how they do their jobs now. The next part will talk about whether and how AI systems might impact operational innovation in a world where the US and China are competing.

Operational Innovation

To take advantage of changes in technology and military systems and make the conditions for an RMA, operational innovation is needed. For AI to be driving operational innovation, there would need to be proof that its uses are fundamentally changing how the US or China plan and run their operations. People have said that AI will change everything, and it's even mentioned in some joint operational papers from both countries. However, neither military seems to be changing how they do things based on AI yet. Open sources say that armies are looking into using AI to improve systems and ways of fighting in the current reconnaissance-strike RMA instead of making huge changes.14 Overall, it looks like these factors will keep making the battle between the hiders and seekers more important, as Krepinevich talked about in 1992, though the ways they do it will have changed. It looks like neither the US nor China thinks AI will change the rules of the game just yet.

Current and future U.S. approaches to operational concepts at the joint and service levels are based on open-source documents and analysis. These methods focus on a few key areas. These include (a) being able to use long-range precision fires to get effects made possible by remote sensing, (b) being able to carry out joint operations and manoeuvres across large areas of land and warfighting domains that make things hard for enemies, (c) having the upper hand in information by using technology to take advantage of U.S. strengths in C2 and ISR for battle management, and (d) being able to project joint forces into foreign theatres. People who are talking about new service-level operational concepts that could be used to fight China stress how important it is for them to have distributed operations, autonomous powers, and cross-domain integration that make them different from older concepts. As we talked about in the last part, these ideas include AI used in the military as an autonomous force multiplier, to help create shared operating pictures, and to make it easier to quickly gather and analyse new data and intelligence to help make decisions. However, it doesn't look like these AI applications will quickly change how things are done.

Additionally, the Future of Defence Task Force Report from the House Armed Services Committee says that "the Pentagon's emerging operational concepts have the potential to provide the U.S. military a decisive advantage, but they are not yet fully viable...the Department of Defence must more aggressively test new operational concepts against emerging technologies." It wasn't until recently that the US updated ideas from the current RMA for a near-peer threat. This comes after decades of fighting terrorism and insurgencies. Because of this, newer operational concepts take parts of older ones and add an understanding of new technologies and rivals. The RMA, which was first used in Desert Storm, combined information processing, stealth, long-range precision fire, and dominating manoeuvrability. These traits still apply to new joint and service ideas, even though technology has improved. AI isn't yet making changes because the technology isn't quite there yet and it doesn't work very well in war settings. Based on how the U.S. does things now, AI seems to be one of several technologies that are making the reconnaissance-strike model better rather than making a whole new one.

China develops operating concepts from the top down, while the US does the same thing from the bottom up. It comes from the way powerful people in politics and the military think about war, which is heavily affected by science and technology. But, like the US, China sees AI as having a place in its future plans. Its 2017 New Generation Artificial Intelligence Development Plan set goals to "strengthen the use of AI in military applications that include command decision-making, military deductions, and defence equipment." Chinese military analysts and thinkers who write about future operations have used language that is in line with these goals. This is China's plan for how to compete with the US. They want to weaken the US's tactical strengths by blocking U.S. maritime areas, raising costs, and attacking the political system.

The way China operates now is through "informatized warfare," and this may be how they do things for the next ten years. Chinese defence experts say that information control is a must for dominance in what they see as the three most important domains: information, maritime, and air. These ideas are at the heart of China's 2015 Defence White Paper, which summarises its 2014 concept of Winning Informatized Local Wars. This concept aims to destroy the enemy's entire operational system across all domains by controlling information and launching precise attacks on key points. This model attacks what the other side sees as their weaknesses across areas and tries to take control of the war by going after their information networks, such as C2 nodes. It imagines joint operations on the battlefield that use China's very advanced arsenal of precision-guided weapons, such as antiship cruise missiles and ballistic missiles, along with multiple area denial capabilities that could use AI to take over the mental space. Autonomy, weapons, and decision support made possible by AI could help even out differences with the US and speed up operations, which the PLA sees as essential to controlling information. However, it is not clear how informatized warfare sees AI as a tool that will completely change the way operations are usually done. Instead, it seems to be an attempt to balance out U.S. qualitative advantages and block access to the area by using AI to improve current skills in precision weapons, manoeuvring, and information operations. Since computerised warfare is likely to stay the way things are done for another ten years, Chinese operational thought doesn't point to an AI RMA any time soon.

In 2019, however, it was found that Chinese military leaders are planning for a longer-term shift to "intelligentization" or "intelligentized" combat. From "systems confrontation" to "algorithm confrontation," this model changes the focus. The side that can make the best use of AI-supported actions and decisions will stay ahead. The PLA thinks that smarter joint operations will help them get ahead of the U.S. instead of just catching up. They plan to do this by finding weak spots in U.S. systems that used to be better and using their own better systems to take the lead. The fact that people aren't on the battlefield may be something that makes these activities stand out. Some PLA thinkers believe that the combination of humans and machines could get close to a battlefield singularity, with humans in charge of fully autonomous systems that make quick choices without any help from humans. At the same time that intelligent combat is being developed, better C2 architectures and modelling will be made. This will help the US military get even better than it is now.

Chinese military experts have said that AI will bring about a new RMA, and intelligent warfare seems to be at the heart of their claims. The future holds intelligentization, and its success will rest on China's ability to modernise and make progress in information warfare at the same time. It will also depend on how well the military can combine new operational ideas with joint tools and ideas that are already in place. Even though intelligentization goals need to be met by 2027, it will probably be hard to use AI and other new technologies in operations, especially for a force that hasn't been in battle in a while. It is also hard to imagine politicians or military leaders giving up power to AI-powered systems, especially since there are efforts to tighten political control over military decisions. But even if intelligentization doesn't happen by the ambitious date that Chinese strategic thinkers have set, it shows that they are thinking about the changes that AI-enabled technologies could make to the fight. Krepinevich's four RMA parts don't have to be done in order (as this chapter talks about in the next section): A lot of work can be done on an RMA's intellectual problems before technology grows faster. Even though they don't have the means or systems to make it happen, the PLA leadership seems to be open to the idea of intelligentization as the next step in the evolution of war. It will be important to find out how and to what degree China's future plans for military AI are different from the US's (this could be explained in upcoming Defence White Papers), if they get better, and what that means for competition between the US and China.

Organizational Adaptation

Krepinevich looked at a possible RMA from the point of view of organisation. He said, "For those states that want to develop the capability to wage war effectively in a new era of conflict, it is important that they begin to organise themselves to promote the innovations—in terms of technologies, systems, and operational concepts—that will be needed for a successful transition." Dealing with the intellectual challenge that an RMA brings up often needs fresh ideas about how to organise the force to make the most of the opportunities that come with new systems and operations. One example is how the Germans used mechanised manoeuvre and stressed how important operational speed was, which separated tanks from troops and created the panzer divisions that carried out the Blitzkrieg.

In this way, it's clear that both U.S. and Chinese government and military leaders are open to the idea that AI could change future warfare. They don't seem to need to be persuaded of AI's future importance. Still, AI hasn't changed the way tactical organisations are set up. This is probably because the technology isn't ready for use in battle yet. Few or no publicly available pieces of evidence support the idea that either the US or China has used AI-powered systems for military purposes in ways that change the structures of their own armies. If AI were to lead to an RMA, we might see new ways of winning wars that make the most of the benefits of new systems and ways of doing things. China's PLA Strategic Security Force was recently built to protect new technologies, but it wasn't made with AI in mind. In the end, the fact that there aren't any new operating organisations supports the idea that an AI RMA isn't coming soon.

Both the US and China have changed their bureaucratic processes to better get and use AI in their defence systems, but they haven't changed how their operations are organised. By changing how their bureaucracies work, both countries seem to understand how important it is to fund research and keep up with the latest developments in AI. When Krepinevich wrote about organisational adaptation, he wasn't talking about this kind of change. However, it is worth quickly mentioning that some of these changes in the way things are run in the government show how the U.S. and China see AI as a strategically important technology. The next part talks about how bureaucracies can adapt.

Exploring the Potential of AI as a Military Revolution

AI is a general term that can be used for a lot of different things. Generalisations about its uses don't cover all of its possibilities. Some applications will develop faster than others, which will make militaries accept them more quickly. It may look like change is more evolutionary than revolutionary, and AI's historically nonlinear growth path makes it hard to guess when things will change. Still, this part makes the case that there isn't an AI RMA yet and probably won't be for at least ten years.

To sum up: In the past ten years, machine learning methods like deep learning have come a long way. However, AI technology is still too young for most military uses and can fail in many ways. Computer vision, picture recognition, and speech recognition models are weak when they are not being trained. They are not reliable and can fail or be manipulated by an enemy. There are ethical concerns and questions about the reliability of military performance when datasets could be tainted or introduce unhelpful bias into AI-enabled systems. It is also hard to understand models with hidden layers, which makes people less likely to believe systems that use them.

So, it looks like U.S. and Chinese defence systems that use AI are limited in what they can do because of the way technology is now. These armies are making some progress while they figure out how to best improve AI capabilities that have already been proven. For example, they are looking into how to make unmanned vehicles fully autonomous in terms of navigation and sensing. More conceptually ambitious and well-known features, like the U.S. JADC2 network, may have a hard time being implemented reliably. AI may have a bigger impact right away in non-combat areas like logistics management and predictive maintenance, where it consistently does a better job of analysing huge datasets than people. Even then, defence organisations may find it hard to gather machine-readable datasets that are both large and of good enough quality, as well as to deal with the unexpected problems that come up with new models.

Even though both the US and China have said that AI is revolutionary, it doesn't seem to have led to any major tactical or organisational changes or innovations. According to sources that are not secret, AI technologies have not significantly changed how the US and China plan to attack each other. These tools will make some things possible that weren't possible before, but they aren't yet changing how things are done. Both sides believe that AI-enhanced autonomy will help with tactical effects in spread operations, do tasks that lower the risks for human soldiers, and make their own C2 and ISR systems stronger while weakening their opponents'. These applications don't change how things work. The fact that military organisations don't seem to be changing adds to the evidence that there isn't an AI RMA. When it comes to the intellectual core of the problem, neither the U.S. nor the Chinese armies have made much progress. Unless something unexpected happens, big changes in operations, organisations, and then doctrine don't look like they will happen for a long time.

So, what should we know about the military implications of an AI RMA if one is neither happening nor is it about to happen? To put it another way, why should anyone care that there isn't an RMA if AI isn't going to soon change a lot of systems, processes, and organisations?

AI might cause short-term changes in the way things evolve. For instance, AI could greatly improve current skills and the current reconnaissance-strike RMA without changing how things are done or the most important parts of today's security environment. This finding is supported by public discussion of JADC2 in the US, which focuses on the system's ability to better connect "sensors to shooters." This saying has been used since the first operational use of reconnaissance-strike in the Gulf War. AI could help the US deal with problems that come up when it tries to dominate China in areas like space, cyberspace, stealth, and projecting power. As operations move faster, decision support systems that use AI could help leaders make better choices more quickly. Threat-warning systems that use AI could help find and stop new threats like area denial tactics that are meant to counter U.S. benefits. AI could be one of the technological breakthroughs that brings the reconnaissance-strike RMA systems from 1918 more in line with what would happen in a war in 1940.

But there are risks that come with only thinking about this model of evolutionary change and ignoring more upsetting options. Thinking too little about how AI will help reconnaissance-strike capabilities develop in the future opens the door for rivals to be faster at incorporating fast technological changes into new and creative operational ideas.

Because of this, it is also important to think about how long-term advances in AI technology and new ways of operating and organising forces could be truly revolutionary. It may seem far away now, but an AI RMA is possible. By recognising AI's ability to change the game and understanding its limits through the lens of RMA, we can find: (1) technical progress towards a future RMA; (2) missing pieces that could make it possible; and (3) conditions that could help make missing pieces come true. Looking at RMAs through the lens of history can help you understand these situations. The parts that follow talk about these points.

Tech Development and Uncovered RMA Aspects

First, while it's hard to tell how AI will develop, policymakers and military leaders may be able to tell by seeing signs of technological progress that an RMA is becoming more possible. Most big steps forward in AI come from outside of government institutions. This means that open-source monitoring of private sector and academic research could help find revolutionary gains in AI and work with other ways of gathering intelligence to find technology that changes the game. China already uses an open-source tracking system that has been around for a long time to keep up with changes in science and technology around the world. Some examples of technological signs could be the improved development of computing technologies like quantum computing, which could lead to improvements in AI and algorithmic training. As Moore's Law slows down and breakthroughs that need a lot of computing power become more expensive, AI could move forward with new learning methods that use less computing power. As explainability and interpretability improve, warfighters may be able to believe capabilities that were previously hard to understand. This could help them use AI-powered systems more carefully, instead of mistrusting them or blindly accepting what the systems say.

The steps that states are taking could show that AI development is moving forward quickly. AI assurance cases and reliable test, evaluation, verification, and validation (TEVV) models and standards would show that people understand complex systems and need to be able to test their performance on a large scale. New doctrines that include AI and that would guide future training and force growth could also be a sign of big progress. For instance, looking at the new Chinese strategy will help us figure out how important the PLA thinks it is for its future force to use AI. If these early- and late-stage markers are crossed, it means that AI technology is getting better than its current flaws, which increases the chance that it will change the way the military works.

Second, admitting that there isn't an AI RMA yet helps you figure out which of Krepinevich's four parts are missing and would be needed to make a future RMA happen. Taking into account the limitations of current technology, the US and China have not made much progress on the creative parts of an AI RMA, such as coming up with new ways to do things and adapting their organisations. To quote Marshall, the main problem with an RMA is not a technological one but an intellectual one. So, for either the US or China to start an AI RMA in the future, they will need to have a better understanding of the armed problems each country faces. AI is expected to stay mainly an enabling technology until it reaches that point.

Third, looking at past RMAs can help us understand why the US or China might pay more attention to the intellectual side of a future AI RMA. The carrier aviation RMA that grew out of U.S. and Japanese competition in the Pacific between the wars may have lessons that can be applied to the competition between the U.S. and China in artificial intelligence. There are many similarities between these times' military problems, such as similar geographical settings, fast rates of innovation in both the military and the private sector, and problems with putting new operational and organisational changes into place. The comparison isn't perfect, but it may be interesting to people in the U.S. for another reason: the carrier aviation RMA was one of the few times when the United States, which had a clear military edge, implemented an RMA without losing that advantage.

Conditions for Fulfilling RMA Elements

The U.S. and Imperial Japanese Navies chose to use aircraft carriers based on how they thought the future of war would be fought and how valuable they thought carrier-borne naval aviation forces would be compared to battleship-borne artillery, which was thought to be the most important part of the fleet. During the years between the wars, both sides struggled to understand the intellectual effects of new carrier aircraft technologies. These battles helped them make the RMA possible. Within a generation, carriers with planes delivering weapons by air took over from gunships as the most important type of ship at sea after more than 500 years of control. This was made possible by rapid improvements in naval aviation technology. In the 1920s and 1930s, both carrier and aircraft technologies were developing at the same time. To do correct experiments and theories, people needed to keep up with new technologies. In the late 1930s, private sector and government innovation sped up technological progress, which was built on top of creative military intellectualization. This led to major changes in operations and organisation. It is important to note that our knowledge of carrier aviation tactics, operations, and doctrine grew during times of peace. However, carriers didn't fully replace battleships as the standard until the war, when luck and chance played a big role.

Here are short accounts of what happened in the U.S. and Japan, along with some useful lessons for a possible AI RMA. This part tells a story about a process of creation that isn't linear and is bound to be messy. So, the descriptions of the different ideas below usually go in order of when they happened, but this shouldn't be taken literally because many important events happened at the same time.

- The importance of analytical focus and experimentation. Identifying their likely adversary and theater of combat gave the United States and Japan a concrete military problem to innovate against. The Americans and Japanese came to view carrier aviation as significant and worthy of future investment during World War I after seeing it pioneered by the British, who taught both navies flight operations and carrier design near the war's end and in the early interwar period. The Americans and Japanese viewed one another as likely adversaries in a Pacific conflict as early as the first decade of the twentieth century. Compared to multipolar Europe, a clear opponent in a contest for sea control focused U.S. and Japanese strategy and capability development.157 While their early naval aviation doctrine followed British thought, emphasizing carrier aviation in support of battleship-led fleets, the confluence of American-Japanese competition, treaty-based fleet construction limits through the late 1930s, and geography led the U.S. and Japanese navies to seek and adopt innovations that eventually made sea control largely dependent on control of the air.

When it comes to the AI competition between the U.S. and China, focusing on one enemy can help define the military problem set and make sure that strategy, planning, and experiments are based on facts and a specific working environment. One big difference between AI and the carrier analogy is that AI will be used for a lot of different operational tasks, from C2 to resupply to self-driving systems, while air and sea control will only be used for one or two. But the idea still stands that working on a single military problem might help figure out which AI uses are more revolutionary than others in a certain setting.

Thinking about the goals of innovation from the point of view of the competition may also help lower the risks of mirror imaging. For example, because of where they were stationed and the limited range of shore-based aircraft in the early years of the war, the U.S. Navy could only use sea-based aircraft to fight the Japanese and protect its moving fleet as the Americans looked for land to take. U.S. aircraft carriers had to do a lot of different jobs. The Japanese, on the other hand, were close to islands in the South Pacific, so they planned to use a mix of carrier aircraft, land-based aircraft, and other naval combatants to intercept and weaken U.S. forces before a decisive battle dominated by Japanese battleships (although this strategy had changed by 1941).159 The United States and Japan came up with new ideas in different ways because they had different ideas about the strategic situation. In the U.S.-China competition, where a lot of cutting-edge AI progress is made in public view, comparing the other team's problem set to your own in the same operational setting may help you figure out their relative strengths and weaknesses and how they might use new military AI applications in different ways.

The Imperial Japanese and U.S. Navies based their experiments on real-life situations. They used new technology, simulations, exercises, and real-world data to look into new carrier aviation jobs, capabilities, and structures. Navy Fleet Problems and simulations at the U.S. Naval War College used imagination, real-world data, and self-critical analysis to look into new roles for carrier aviation in a war against Japan. The models put Navy carrier aviation force structures to the test beyond what they could actually do. They also called into question the idea that carrier aircraft were best for spying, not fighting. In the 1920s, simulations showed that the number of aircraft kept in the air was a key indicator of how well a carrier worked. Aviators tried to meet this need by speeding up takeoffs and landings with new launch and land processes, deck parking, and crash barriers. These made the U.S. carriers look different. In the 1920s and 1930s, fleet problems that used simulations' ideas let operators test the usefulness of new strategies and ideas in big manoeuvres that happened in real life. This gave carrier commanders situational experience and helped them learn important things about naval aviation. In 1929, Fleet Problem IX, which was probably the most important in the series, showed how carriers could be used as independent strike platforms. This was a forerunner of the future invention of the carrier task force. It was very important to do critical thinking after each task as a way to learn. It showed where operations could be better, helped with technical and tactical assessments, and showed the U.S. Navy and other interested parties how useful carrier aviation could be.

Japan also used carriers and naval planes in its fleet manoeuvres between the wars, and its Naval Staff College and operational navy units worked together to make these moves successful. The Imperial Japanese Navy used Sengi combat training to focus on different possible tactics, operations, and force mixes. This let them try out different roles for naval aircraft and carriers, and the fleet as a whole learned from their results. With the help of data and experience from the Sino-Japanese War and a lot of trial and error, new ways of doing things and new ways of organising things were created, such as the first joint land- and carrier-based strike units. They also made the Japanese focus on longer-range planes that could harass coming U.S. forces at the farthest range of their surface ships' guns. This pushed the line of when Japanese interception-attrition tactics could start to happen farther east. By the 1930s, Japanese aviators knew that planes could beat battleship-led fleets and maybe even balance out the U.S. advantages in resources, military power, and economic growth.

To get people in the US and China to think of new ways to use AI, accurate simulations and experiments could be very helpful. The carrier aviation RMA case shows that being realistic in wargames and exercises is important for correctly imagining the future operating environment. This, along with careful analysis and critical insights after the fact, can help get people on board with new operational and organisational ideas. Accurate, realistic simulations can help militaries imagine how they might use AI-enhanced capabilities that go beyond what they already have. On the other hand, real-world drills can connect theory to operations and show operational challenges that, in the end, make mental models of future combat stronger. It's possible that both the U.S. and Chinese militaries are already testing AI applications for military use, but it's important to stress that experimentation must be done carefully if it's to help with RMA parts like operational innovation and organisational adaptation. In January 1941, Admiral Yamamoto Isoruku, who was in charge of the Combined Japanese Fleet, changed the plan from a decisive fleet battle to an offensive defence strategy. This was because of some questionable results from tests. Even though Yamamoto supported carriers, the sudden change may not have given the Imperial Japanese Navy enough time to plan for new operations, like the disastrous carrier defeat at Midway. William Moffett, the first director of the U.S. Navy's Bureau of Aeronautics (BuAer), told the Secretary of the Navy in 1931 that a carrier's "offensive value is too great to permit it to be ordinarily devoted to scouting," and that its role "should be the same as that of a battleship." He could back up his claim with rigorous simulation results. Even though U.S. carriers didn't become a major tactical weapon or change the way battleships were thought of until the war, by 1939, Navy doctrine based on the Fleet Problems saw carriers operating in many of the roles they would later play on their own during the war. The U.S. Navy was better ready to carry out the carrier aircraft RMA after doing realistic tests.

Influence of Bureaucratic Structures and Cultural Norms on Mental Model Flexibility

In the years between the wars, the US and Japan both set up new bureaucratic systems that centralised resources for new operational ideas about carrier aviation. This made it easier to try new things and make changes. In 1921, the U.S. Congress created the Bureau of Aeronautics. This organisation protected the Navy from outside pressure to turn naval aviation into a separate air force. During the years between the wars, BuAer steered towards change despite the Navy and political winds that were blowing at the time. They gave aviators more freedom and space to come up with new ideas and further their own interests than their British and Japanese peers. The bureau was a link between the Fleet Problems and the exercises at the Naval War College. By including aviation problems in mid-level professional education at the Naval War College, it brought naval aviators into the chain of command and taught senior officers to value airpower. BuAer got money for private research into aircraft designs that could change the game and built a wider range of relationships in the business. It looked far and wide to find aeroplanes that met its own strict technical needs. This led to important new ideas like radial engines and aeronautical streamlining.

In 1928, the Imperial Japanese Navy set up its own separate Aviation Bureau. This made it possible for the military to improve its skills by combining study and funding for airpower development. Like BuAer, the air Bureau had a close connection with the Naval Staff College, which studied how carriers worked and worked with real-life air units. In the 1930s, it held competitions for aircraft designs to try to balance out the U.S.'s quantitative benefits with qualitative superiority. It also gave manufacturers like Mitsubishi information about combat and exercises.

Even though both the US and Japan made changes to their bureaucracies that helped them create carriers faster than other navies, the US and Japan were able to adopt new carrier ideas more quickly because they were better at spreading ideas through the military and navigating both civilian and military politics. By the 1930s, naval aviators in both countries knew that carriers could be used for offence, but their service departments were slower to adapt to new ideas because of politics, vested interests, and other things. The way that U.S.

and Japanese naval aviators flew over these seas affected their ability to carry out the RMA. In the end, the U.S. Navy realised how useful carriers could be and made a lot more of them than the Japanese did. Without good organisational relations, technological progress alone wasn't enough to move the RMA forward.

Japan had better planes than the US at the start of World War II, but its inability to implement the carrier aviation RMA was hampered by its rigid organisational structure and adherence to the decisive fleet battle strategy right before the war. The Imperial Japanese Navy didn't have to deal with as many pressures from other navies or civilians outside of the navy as the U.S. Navy did. This meant that the Japanese navy didn't have many reasons to question its beliefs about how important carriers and battleships were. It was hard to get enough young officers trained as pilots and navy aviators put in charge of carriers. There were some bad leaders in aviation command because of this, which hurt carriers' growth and tactical efficiency and left few people arguing for a main role for carrier aviation. Also, there were problems within the navy that made it hard for technical and doctrinal carrier innovations to spread throughout the force. For example, there were problems between operational fleet staff and a Navy General Staff that wanted the decisive fleet fight. Even after the attacks on the U.S. battleship fleet from carriers at Pearl Harbour were successful, most high-ranking officers and fleet leaders still preferred battleships to carriers.

BuAer, on the other hand, especially when Moffett was in charge, smartly dealt with civilian political and military forces inside and outside the U.S. Navy to keep naval aviation separate from any independent U.S. air force. Moffett used a law from 1925 to create a strong corps of pilots as officers and to train senior officers who were not pilots in aviation. This finally made high-level support for carrier aviation official in the force. For example, Admiral Ernest King retrained as a naval pilot after commanding surface ships and submarines. He became Chief Naval Officer in 1942 and put buying carriers ahead of buying battleships. Moffett used data from exercises in the 1920s to support his claims to Navy leaders that carriers were mobile airfields that could support a wide range of actions, not just accompany battleships. Navy leaders didn't quickly think that the carrier would replace the battleship, but they did accept analytical evidence about the value of carrier aviation and added new ideas to the rules. This gave carriers new roles and force formations, which were strengthened by their successes in the war. Between 1942 and 1943, after Midway, Japan built seven new carriers. In contrast, the US built ninety, with almost thirty of them being fleet carriers.

One of the most important things for U.S. and Chinese competition right now may be how to get around political and organisational problems in order to use military innovation. This is because AI has caused a lot of changes in how bureaucracies work in both countries. In order to add AI to their military, both the US and China are creating new bureaucratic organisations. How well these organisations work will depend on how well they can deal with cultural attitudes towards adopting new technologies, organisational and inter-organizational interests, and political factors.

The DoD and the services have set up a number of new AI-related joint and service-level bureaucracies. The Department of Defence (DoD) has a new office called the Chief Data and Artificial Intelligence Office (CDAO). Its job is to make sure that AI technology and skills are used across the whole department and workforce. It will bring together the work of the Joint Artificial Intelligence Centre (JAIC), the DoD Chief Data Officer, and the Defence Digital Service. It will be in the Office of the Secretary of Defence. The JAIC's jobs were to "strengthen current military advantages" and "accelerate the delivery of AI-enabled capabilities." The CDAO will now take on those jobs, along with joint scaling proven AI programmes. The services are also coming up with new or improved ways to run the government. The Army's new Chief Data Officer, who was formed within the last ten years, was given new duties that include focusing on AI. Other groups, like the Army's AI Task Force and the Air Force's AI Accelerator, use their connections with colleges to study AI applications and insights that aren't related to strategy or operations.

China has also made changes to its military and government that are linked to AI and other technologies. Military-civil fusion was officially accepted as a strategy for getting new technologies as part of China's defence reforms in 2015–16. It has led to changes in the country's defence industry that are meant to make it easier for the military to get cutting-edge technologies that can be used for both military and civilian purposes.194 China has also built new technological research institutions with dual uses and made changes to current ones that are related. The Unmanned Systems study Centre and the Artificial Intelligence Research Centre were set up by the Ministry of National Defence as AI-focused study groups to work with the National University of Defence Technology on dual-use AI technology research.195 In 2019, China's Academy of Military Science added study into science and technology to its main focus on developing doctrines.196 To make up for a lack of study talent, civilians with advanced degrees in technology were added to its staff with military experience in 2020.197 Lastly, the government has set up more than 35 MCF funds for research investments since 2015. As of 2021, these funds are expected to have raised more than 447.16 billion yuan ($68.5 billion).

In public comments, both the U.S. and Chinese militaries have said that they think AI is important for military progress. But whether the U.S. and Japanese navies succeeded or failed in the carrier aviation RMA depended on how well top officers accepted new technologies and ideas. Adopting AI will be put to the test on a much larger, force-wide level. The US and China may face some of the same big problems when it comes to adopting AI technology, but there are also some subtle differences.

It's not clear how much policymakers and top military leaders in both countries know about AI. Even though there is evidence that elites see AI as a revolutionary tool, there aren't many AI training programmes for U.S. policymakers and decision-makers. The way the U.S. military works may make it hard to use AI: it's hard to work enlisted soldiers and officers who are good at and knowledgeable about AI into regular operations, and officers who are promoted or rotated through positions that don't value AI literacy may not be rewarded for their skills. A study from 2021 said that DoD employees with AI experience who are able to make policy changes that are needed do so "despite, not because of, their organisations' incentives." Jointly focused civilian coordination offices like the CDAO might be able to help change department goals, policy, and strategic thinking about how to combine AI, data, and security, but they might have trouble getting things done because the services don't have enough money or people. It will also be hard to find good people to work in civilian and military AI jobs because the business sector is so competitive. These problems are on top of the problems we talked about earlier with getting DoD technology.

There isn't a lot of public research or comments on how well Chinese civilian and military leaders understand AI, and it's hard to say for sure if the PLA will be able to implement AI across the whole force. Numerous public pieces in the PLA Daily and other places have called for more AI training for C2 and pointed out the lack of highly skilled tech workers in AI fields. The Chinese military career system is characterised by silos, which may make it hard for officers who aren't trained or knowledgeable in AI to adapt. Since 2016, joint assignment chances have only grown, which may make it harder for officers to think about AI's potential together. Because of how important it is in Chinese politics, the PLA may feel pressured to make AI progress—or at least say it has—by politically important dates, like the 2027 intelligentization strategy milestone. This could make it hard to tell how well it is actually doing at incorporating science and technology into policy. The PLA may not have had much recent combat experience, which could make it harder for them to adopt AI military skills on a large scale. On the other hand, this could make leaders less attached to old ideas. According to Chinese assessments, the military will be able to use AI in operations and match or even beat U.S. skills. In the end, it's not clear whether U.S. or Chinese bureaucratic or service-level rules are better suited to revolutionising AI apps.

What part luck and circumstances play. Finally, luck and events play a part in making RMAs happen. Not every event can be predicted or explained. BuAer was lucky to have strong leaders like Moffett who encouraged experimentation and research and looked out for new ideas that were just starting out. There are historians who think that the loss of American battleships at Pearl Harbour made carriers the U.S. Navy's best strike unit by accident, not because they wanted to be. It was at Midway that U.S. carrier warfare really came of age. U.S. doctrine that wanted to establish air control as quickly as possible, scout bombers, and fast aircraft recovery times helped take advantage of Japanese weaknesses, but luck covered up a big lack of operational polish.

Things that happen and luck could affect a developing AI RMA in many ways for both the US and China. One country's private sector could come up with a game-changing technological application, that country's leaders could be great at supporting and adopting new ideas, or that country's military could need to use a new AI application they wouldn't have had otherwise. Culture, training, and social norms all play a role in these three examples, and luck realising an AI RMA could come from preparation meeting chance.

Finally, an RMA might be created by looking more closely at how AI can be used to solve certain military issues that the US and China are having. For instance, studying, modelling, simulating, and experimenting could reveal a lot about how AI-enabled features could be used by both sides in emergency situations, such as a war over Taiwan. For example, the US and China might develop their military AI in different ways depending on whether they want to project power or fight local wars. They might also use different AI technologies to counter what they see as the other side's advantages in maritime or area denial operations. To avoid cultural blind spots, reduce the risks of mirror imaging, and get a more accurate picture of China's capabilities, the U.S. needs to look at Chinese intellectual styles and organisational dynamics in the context of a particular military problem.

Final Thoughts and Areas for Future Investigation

There is no AI RMA going on right now. When you accept this as true, you can look at the RMA parts of AI that are missing from the way the military thinks about it now, like operational innovation and organisational change. You can also look at why these parts are missing and what conditions could make them possible.

If the battle between the US and China in AI is going to lead to an RMA, history shows that a lot of focused testing on real-world military problems needs to be done first. Making new technologies won't be enough to start a shift; military leaders will also need to be open to new ideas and innovations from everyone in the ranks. It's possible that new technologies will be created faster than the force will accept them. Also, parts of the government will have to make sure that they always have access to the newest AI semiconductors, talent, algorithms, and computer power.

In the strategic competition between the US and China, one side may have big benefits depending on how well they understand AI's value for operations and how it could change the security environment. Politicians, soldiers, and tech experts in the US and China see the world in different ways, which will affect how new technologies are made and used. More research should be done on how different views on different military issues and situations could impact the growth of AI. RMAs are shaped by specific cultural settings. From the U.S. point of view, it will continue to be important to closely follow what the Chinese think about AI growth and how things will work in the future in a variety of situations. This will help figure out where China might use AI-enabled tools to take advantage of what it sees as its competitive benefits against the U.S., and it will also help U.S. strategists, policymakers, concept developers, and others avoid mirror imaging.

Futures research could help build a framework for what a new RMA might look like. Finding the least, average, and most upsetting possible futures for AI capability growth could help figure out how far we've come towards an RMA. It's possible that AI applications will change some areas faster than others. This could affect whether and how new RMAs are affected by AI. This kind of research should pay close attention to the private and academic sectors, which are where most technology progress is likely to happen. It should also look into the different plausible effects of AI on the military.

There might not be just one AI RMA, but several hyphenated ones, like an AI-cyber, AI-autonomy, or even AI-nuclear RMA. This is because narrow AI uses seem to hold the most promise for military use. Taking an enemy's physical powers offline before a battle starts could become more important when AI and cyber applications are used together. Virtual wars over who controls and protects datasets that train AI algorithms could have an effect on the safety and effectiveness of armed AI. Generative AI models might spread or create false information, which could hurt people's trust in the government, especially in democracies, and could even make it harder to make accurate working pictures for soldiers. The way we currently use AI to give machines autonomy could slowly change to include new jobs for fighting and non-fighting that can be done by machines with less human supervision.

In addition to possible futures that seem linked to or nearby to what we can do now, assessments should also look at how AI could completely change the way wars are fought. For instance, if the use of AI-enabled autonomy changed more quickly and with fewer bumps in the road, there might be a sudden, big drop in the number of soldiers on the ground. Increasing operational speed, whether from AI or other technologies like hypersonic weapons, could make armies question whether decisions made by people are really the best way to make things happen. As long as technology keeps getting better, some armies might rather give faster, AI-powered machines with less human oversight a lot of tactical decision-making duties. Different types of fully autonomous systems could work together, creating new autonomous units and ways of doing things with little or no human input. As we already said, these changes should have a thorough analysis of what they mean for traditional deterrence and crisis de-escalation.

As it stands, some people think AI could completely change nuclear defence, which would be an even bigger change. Human reasoning, perception, and signalling are all part of current nuclear deterrence. This means that any use of AI that questions the current paradigm could be game-changing and have far-reaching effects. It is possible that AI could be used both effectively and defensively in a nuclear situation. Competitors like China and Russia could use AI to improve early warning systems for nuclear attacks, and self-driving cars with AI could be used as attack platforms. A lot of people have thought that AI could help find an enemy's nuclear missiles or help people make decisions in a nuclear emergency. Importantly, how people see these systems as threats to first- and second-strike powers creates risks as AI develops, maybe even regardless of how well the systems work. It could be hard to use nuclear weapons to keep people safe "not because it works too well, but because it works just well enough to feed uncertainty." It goes without saying that this subject and what it means for nuclear arms control, modernization, and overall international security will stay very important to research.

More generally, more study could be done to find out how AI's wider societal and economic effects may, in the short and long term, strengthen or weaken U.S. national security. Scharre said, "AI can improve military capabilities, but the more important long-term benefits may come from non-military AI applications across society," such as better health care, higher economic growth and productivity, and the improvement of other tools of national power. In terms of the big changes it makes to society and the economy by replacing human thinking work, some experts say AI could be as important as the Industrial Revolution. In the future, researchers could look at times in history when social and economic changes were very big and how those changes affected foreign security.

Finally, the connection between people, technology, and war as AI develops is a very significant issue that needs more thought and study than what is covered in this chapter. Philosophical questions about whether AI and autonomy are useful for war purposes have already been talked about a lot of times. Varying countries may be hesitant to give AI too much power to make decisions. Policymakers, strategists, and warfighters need to carefully consider the pros and cons of incorporating AI more into human-led fighting. The heated discussion at the UN about lethal automated weapons systems between states and nongovernmental organisations shows the wide range of factors that states might consider when deciding to use these systems. It might be good to look at the ethical issues raised by military systems that use AI in comparison to other platforms and technologies that have caused controversy in the past. Taking care of these kinds of worries will be very important for using AI's revolutionary potential in a careful and responsible way.

Bibliography

Abdel Moneim, A. . Information Security and National Security. Al-Siyassa Al-Dawleya, 53, 202-207.

Agrawal, Ajay, Joshua S. Gans, and Avi Goldfarb. "Artificial Intelligence: The Ambiguous Labor Market Impact of Automating Prediction." The Journal of Economic Perspectives 33, no. 2 (2019): 31-50. https://www.jstor.org/stable/26621238.

Ai.google. Available at: https://ai.google/principles/ (Accessed: 15 September 2022)

AI and the Military: Forever Altering Strategic Stability. . Retrieved from https://www.tech4gs.org/

Al-Doweek, A. A. . Cyber Deterrence Strategy. Al-Siyassa Al-Dawleya, 53, 196-201.

Algorithmic Warfare or Algorithmic Warfare and Focal Point Analysis | Small Wars Journal (2022). Available at: https://smallwarsjournal.com/jrnl/art/algorithmic-warfare-or-algorithmic-warfare-and-focal-point-analysis (Accessed: 20 September 2022)

ALKA DIRECTED ENERGY WEAPON SYSTEM - Roketsan (2022).

Allen, G., & Chan, T. . Artificial Intelligence and National Security. Retrieved from https://www.belfercenter.org/publication/artificial-intelligence-and-national-security

Allen, General (USMC Ret) John R. and Husain, Amir, 'On Hyperwar', USNIProceedings Magazine, Vol. 143, No. 7, July 2017, pp. 30-37.

Allen, Greg and Chan, Taniel, Artificial Intelligence and National Security, Belfer Center for Science and International Affairs, Cambridge, July 2017.

Allison, G. . English Translation of the Official Strategy of the Israel ... Retrieved from https://www.belfercenter.org/sites/default/files/legacy/files/IDF doctrine translation - web final2.pdf

Altmann & Frank Sauer Autonomous Weapon Systems and Strategic Stability, Survival, 59:5, 117-142, DOI:10.1080/00396338.2017.1375263

Andrei Ilnitsky and Aleksandr Losev 'Iskusstvennyy Intellekt - Eto i Riski i Vozmozhnosti' ['Artificial Intelligence - Here Are the Risks and Opportunities'] Krasnaya Zvezda [Red Star] 24 June 2019 accessed 15 September 2022

Appleyard, Adam. (2014) "The sheer stupidity of artificial intelligence" [Online]. The Spectator. Available from: https://www.spectator.co.uk/2014/07/the-sheer-stupidity-of-artificial-intelligence/ [Accessed 7th May 2019]

Artificial Intelligence Enabled Cyber Defence. . Retrieved from https://www.eda.europa.eu/webzine/issue14/cover-story/artificial-intelligence--enabled-cyber-defence

Autonomous Robots and the Future of Just war Theory 1 (2013) pp. 338-351.

Autonomous Weapons and Human Control. . Retrieved from https://www.cnas.org/publications/reports/autonomous-weapons-and-human-control

Available at: <https://www.jstor.org/stable/26864279> [Accessed 6 September 2022]

Available at: https://warsawinstitute.org/russian-interference-u-s-presidential-elections-2016-2020-attempt-implement-revolution-like-information-warfare-scheme/ (Accessed: 20 September 2022)

Available at: https://web.archive.org/web/20200205165711/https://www.roketsan.com.tr/en/p roduct/alka-directed-energy-weapon-system/ (Accessed: 18 September 2022)

Available at: https://www.taylorfrancis.com/chapters/edit/10.4324/9780203107164-37/autonomous-robots-future-war-theory-1-keith-abney (Accessed: 17 September 2022)

Balance of Power - Texas National Security Review Texas National Security Review. Available at: https://tnsr.org/2018/05/artificial-intelligenceinternational-competition-and-the-balance-of-power/ (Accessed: 16 September 2022)

Bates, S. J. . Artificial intelligence: A revolution waiting to fiappen. Thesis / Dissertation ETD. Retrieved 2018, from https://apps.dtic.mil/dtic/tr/fulltext/u2/1041675.pdf

BEREJIKIAN, J. D. . A Cognitive Theory of Deterrence*. Retrieved from http://web.mit.edu/sabrevln/Public/GameTheory/Journal of Peace Research/A Cognitive Theory of Deterrence.pdf

Bibliography

Blanchard A. Taddeo M. Autonomous weapon systems and jus ad bellum. AI & Soc (2022). https://doi.org/10.1007/s00146-022-01425-y

Bostrom, Nick. (2014). "Superintelligence." Oxford: Oxford University Press. Chapter 1.

Boulanin, V. . AI & Global Governance: AI and Nuclear Weapons - Promise and Perils of AI for Nuclear Stability - Centre for Policy Research at United Nations University. Retrieved from https://cpr.unu.edu/ai-global-governance-ai-and-nuclear-weapons- promise-and-perils-of-ai-for-nuclear-stability.html

Bouskill, K., Chonde, S., & IV, W. W. . Speed and Security: Promises, Perils, and Paradoxes of Accelerating Everything. Retrieved from https://www.rand.org/pubs/perspectives/PE274.html

Brundage, et al. . The Malicious Use of Artificial Intelligence. Retrieved from https://maliciousaireport.com/

Bunz, Mercedes. "The Need for a Dialogue with Technology." In The DatafiedSociety: Studying Culture through Data, edited by Schafer Mirko Tobias and Van Es Karin, 24954. Amsterdam: Amsterdam University Press, 2017. http://www.j stor.org/stable/j .ctt1v2xsqn.24.

Burk, Dan L. "Algorithmic Fair Use." The University of Chicago Law Review 86, no. 2 (2019): 283-308. https://www.jstor.org/stable/26590556.

Burri, T. . International Law and Artificial Intelligence. Retrieved from https://www.researchgate.net/publication/320938178_International_La w_and_Artificial_Intelligence

Buzan, B. . The national security problem in international relations. International Affairs,60, 289-290. doi:10.2307/2619056

Carayannis E.G. Draper J. Optimising peace through a Universal Global Peace Treaty to constrain the risk of war from a militarised artificial superintelligence. AI & Soc (2022). https://doi.org/10.1007/s00146-021-01382-y

Cavelty, M. D., Fischer, S., & Balzacq, T. . "Killer Robots" and

Centre for Emerging Technology and Security 'The Information Battlefield: Disinformation declassification and deepfakes' CETaS Expert Analysis June 2022

China may match or beat America in AI. . Retrieved from https://www.economist.com/business/2017/07/15/china-may- match-or-beat-america-in-ai

Chui, Michael, Manyika, James and Miremadi, Mehdi, 'What AI can and can't do (yet) for your business', McKinsey Quarterly, January 2018, pp. 2-11.

Civil Service Digital Faststream Website, UK. Available from: https://www.faststream.gov.uk/digital-data-technology/ [Accessed 8th June 2019]

Cole-Turner, Ronald, ed. Transhumanism and Transcendence: Christian Hope in an Age of Technological Enhancement. WASHINGTON, D.C.: Georgetown University Press, 2011. http://www.jstor.org/stable/j.ctt2tt2w3.

Concluding Report: Recommendations to the GGE. . Retrieved from https://www.ipraw.org/recommendations/

Corneliu Bjola. (2017): "Digital Diplomacy 2.0: From Social to Computerised Reality," Medium. Available from: https://becominghuman.ai/digital-diplomacy-2-0-from-social-to-computerised-reality-388d8a83b809 [Accessed 27th April 2019]

Couldry, Nick. "The Myth of Big Data." In The Datafied Society: Studying Culture through Data, edited by Schafer Mirko Tobias and Van Es Karin, 235-40. Amsterdam: Amsterdam University Press, 2017. http://www._jstor.org/stable/j.ctt1v2xsqn.21.

Craig, A. . Understanding the Proliferation of Cyber Capabilities. Retrieved from https://www.cfr.org/blog/understanding-proliferation-cyber-capabilities

Crosston, M. D. . World gone cyber MAD: How "Mutually assured debilitation" is the best hope for cyber deterrence. Strategic Studies Quarterly, 5, 100-116.

Davis, Erik "Techgnosis: Myth, Magic and Mysticism in the Age of Information,"" in Duffin, Brendan. Fortnight, no. 381 (1999): 31. http://www.istor.org/stable/25559785.

Davis, P. K. . Toward Theory for Dissuasion by Denial: Using Simple Cognitive Models of the Adversary to inform strategy. Retrieved from https://www.rand.org/content/dam/rand/pubs/working_papers/WR1000/WR1027/RAND_WR1027.pdf

Davison N. (2022) A legal perspective: Autonomous weapon systems under international humanitarian law | United Nations iLibrary Un-ilibrary.org. Available at: https://www.un-ilibrary.org/content/books/9789213628942c005 (Accessed: 19 September 2022)

Defence Artificial Intelligence Strategy (2022). Available at: https://www.gov.uk/

government/publications/defence-artificial-intelligence- strategy/defence-artificial-intelligence-strategy (Accessed: 11 September 2022)

De Spiegeleire, S., Maas, M., & Swejis, T. . ARTIFICIAL INTELLIGENCE AND THE FUTURE OF Defence. Retrieved from https://www.hcss.nl/sites/default/files/files/reports/Artificial Intelligence and the Future of Defence.pdf

Deterrence and Surprise. [online] National Defence University Press. Available at: <https://ndupress.ndu.edu/Media/News/News-Article-View/Article/1979401/artificial-intelligence-on-the-battlefield-implications-for-deterrence-and-surp/> [Accessed 10 September 2022]

Deutschewelleenglish director. How AI Is Driving a Future of Autonomous Warfare | DW Analysis. YouTube YouTube 25 June 2021 https://www.youtube.com/watch?v=NpwHszy7bMk. Accessed 20 Sept. 2022

Dilulio, J. J. . Deterrence Theory. Retrieved from https://marisluste.files.wordpress.com/2010/11/deterrence-theory.pdf

Eckersley, et al. The Malicious Use of Artificial Intelligence: Forecasting, Prevention, and Mitigation. Retrieved from https://www.eff.org/deeplinks/2018/02/malicious-use-artificial- intelligence-forecasting-prevention-and-mitigation

Ekelhof, Merel A. C. "Lifting the Fog of Targeting: "Autonomous Weapons" and Human Control through the Lens of Military Targeting." Naval War College Review 71, no. 3 (2018): 61-95. https://www.jstor.org/stable/26607067.

Emiliano Trere. (2016). "The Dark Side of Digital Politics: Understanding the Algorithmic Manufacturing of Consent and the Hindering of Online Dissidence." http://bulletin.ids.ac.uk/idsbo/article/view/41/PDF

Ethics and Governance of AI. . Retrieved from https://cyber.harvard.edu/topics/ethics-and-governance-ai

Etzioni, A., et al . Pros and Cons of Autonomous Weapons Systems. Retrieved from https://www.armyupress.army.mil/Journals/Military-Review/English-Edition-Archives/May-June-2017/Pros-and-Cons-of-Autonomous-Weapons-Systems

Fairbanks, C. H. . MAD and US Strategy. In In Getting MAD: Nuclear Mutually Assured Destruction, Is Origin and Practice. Strategic Studies Institute. doi:http://ssi.armywarcollege.edu/pdffiles/pub585.pdf

Folgieri, Raffaella. "Technology, Artificial Intelligence and Keynes' Utopia: A Realized Prediction?" In Utopian Discourses Across Cultures: Scenarios in Effective Communication to Citizens and Corporations, edited by Bait Miriam, Brambilla Marina, and Crestani Valentina, 73-86. Frankfurt Am Main: Peter Lang AG, 2016. http://www.i stor.org/stable/i .ctv2t4bv7.8.

Forrest E. Morgan Karl P. Mueller et al. "Dangerous Thresholds: Managing Escalation in the 21st Century (Santa Monica CA: Rand Cooperation 2008) p. 8.

Foster M. 2019. Artificial Intelligence and Stability in Nuclear Crises. [online] Usafa.edu. Available at: <https://www.usafa.edu/app/uploads/Space_Defence_Vol12_No01.pdf> [Accessed 16 September 2022]

Fournier, G. . The liability issues related to the use of Lethal Autonomous Weapons Systems . UN Special, , 1213.

Fuhrmann, M. . The Logic of Latent Nuclear Deterrence. Retrieved from http://www.iserp.columbia.edu/sites/default/files/Deterrence without Bombs 2018-0129.pdf

Gain N. (2020) NAVAIR progressing towards LRASM integration on P-8A MPA - Naval News Naval News. Available at: https://www.navalnews.com/naval-news/2020/05/navair-progressing-towards- lrasm-integration-on-p-8a-mpa/ (Accessed: 6 September 2022)

Garcia, D. . Lethal Artificial Intelligence and Change: The Future of International Peace and Security | International Studies Review | Oxford Academic. Retrieved from https://academic.oup.com/isr/article/20/2/334/5018660

Geist, E., & Lohn, A. J. . How Artificial Intelligence Might Affect the Risk of Nuclear War?. Retrieved from https://www.rand.org/blog/articles/2018/04/how-artificial-intelligence- could-increase-the-risk.htm l

Geist, E. M. . It's already too late to stop the AI arms race-We must manage it instead. Retrieved from https://www.tandfonline.com/doi/abs/10.1080/009 63402.2016.1216672

George, A . Coercive Diplomacy. In The Use of Force . Rowman and Littlefield.

Geraci, Robert M. "Apocalyptic AI: Religion and the Promise of Artificial Intelligence." Journal of the American Academy of Religion 76, no. 1 (2008): 138- 66.http://www.istor.org/stable/40006028.

Glaser, C. L. . The security dilemma revisited. World Politics, 50, 171-201. doi:10.1017/S0043887100014763

Goosen, R. et al. . Artificial Intelligence Is a Threat to Cybersecurity. It's Also a Solution. Retrieved from https://www.bcg.com/publications/2018/artificial-intelligence-threat- cybersecurity-solution.aspx

Green, Ronald M. "Challenging Transhumanism's Values." Hastings Center Report 43, no. 4 (July 2013): 45-47. doi:10.1002/hast.195

Groll, E. . How AI Could Destabilize Nuclear Deterrence. Retrieved from https://foreignpolicy.com/2018/04/24/how- ai-could-destabilize-nuclear-deterrence/

Guay, J., & Rudnick, L. . What the Digital Geneva Convention means for the future of humanitarian action. Retrieved from https://www.unhcr.org/innovation/digital-geneva-convention-mean- future-humanitarian-action/

Hanley, John T. "Changing Dod'S Analysis Paradigm: The Science of War Gaming and Combat/Campaign Simulation." Naval War College Review 70, no. 1 (2017): 64103. http://www.istor.org/stable/26398006.

Harding T. 2022. Russia's KUB-BLA kamikaze drone intercepted in Ukraine. [online] The National News. Available at: <https://www.thenationalnews.com/world/uk-news/2022/03/14/russias-kub-bla- kamikaze-drone-intercepted-in-ukraine/> [Accessed 15 September 2022] Horowitz M. (2018) Artificial Intelligence International Competition and the

Hawkins, Amy, 'The Ailing Farmers Keeping China's AI Industry Healthy,' Wired Magazine, June 2019.

Hawley, Dr. John K., Patriot Wars: Automation and the Patriot Air and Missile Defence System, Center for a New American Security, Washington, January 2017.

Heatherly, Christopher J., and Ian Melendez. "Every Soldier a Cyber Warrior: The Case for Cyber Education in the United States Army." The Cyber Defence Review 4, no. 1 (2019): 63-74. https://www.istor.org/stable/26623067.

Hennessey, S. . Deterring Cyberattacks. Retrieved from https://www.foreignaffairs.com/reviews/review- essay/2017-10-16/deterring-cyberattacks

Horowitz, M., & Scharre, P. . Meaningful Human Control in Weapon Systems: A Primer. Retrieved from https://s3.amazonaws.com/files.

cnas.org/documents/Ethical_Autonomy_Working_Paper_031315. pdf?mtime=20160906082316

Horowitz, M. C., & Allen, G. C. . Artificial Intelligence and International Security. Retrieved from https://www.cnas.org/publications/reports/artificial-intelligence-and- international-security

How the Russian government used disinformation and cyber warfare in 2016 election - an ethical hacker explains (2018). Available at: https://theconversation.com/how-the-russian-government-used-disinformation-and-cyber-warfare-in-2016-election-an-ethical-hacker-explains-99989 (Accessed: 20 September 2022)

https://defence.nridigital.com/global_defence_technology_jun18/intelligent_des ign_inside_frances_15bn_ai_strategy (Accessed: 19 September 2022)

https://www.academia.edu/28785811/_Killer_Robots_and_Preventive_Arms_Control_in_The_Routledge_Handbook_of_Security_Studies_2n d_Edition_Routledge_Hardback_2016_pp._457-468

Husain A. 2021. AI is Shaping the Future of War. [online] Ndupress.ndu.edu. Available at: <https://ndupress.ndu.edu/Portals/68/Documents/prism/prism_9- 3/prism_9-3_50- 61_Husain.pdf?ver=7oFXHXGfGbbR9YDLrnX3Fw%3D%3D> [Accessed 18 September 2022

Ilachinski, Andrew, AI, Robots, and Swarms: Issues, Questions, and Recommended Studies, CNA: Analysis and Solutions, Arlington, January 2017.

Intelligent design: inside France's €1.5bn AI strategy - Global Defence

Jervis, R.. The Use of Force . Rowman and Littlefield.

Johnson J. (2022) "Inadvertent escalation in the age of intelligence machines: A new model for nuclear risk in the digital age" European Journal of International Security. Cambridge University Press 7(3) pp. 337-359. doi: 10.1017/eis.2021.23

Johnson J. (2022) "Inadvertent escalation in the age of intelligence machines: A new model for nuclear risk in the digital age" European Journal of International Security. Cambridge University Press 7(3) pp. 337-359. doi: 10.1017/eis.2021.23

Johnson J. (2022) "Inadvertent escalation in the age of intelligence machines: A new model for nuclear risk in the digital age" European Journal of

International Security. Cambridge University Press 7(3) pp. 337-359. doi: 10.1017/eis.2021.23.)

Johnston, T., Smith, T. D., & Irwin, J. L. . Additive Manufacturing in 2040: Powerful Enabler, Disruptive Threat. Retrieved from https://www.rand.org/pubs/perspectives/PE283.html

Joint Concept Note 1/18 HumanMachine Teaming (London: United Kingdom Ministry of Defence May 2018) iii available at https://assets.publishing.service.gov.uk/government/uploads/system/uploads/att achment_data/file/709359/20180517-concepts_uk_human_machine_teaming_j cn_1_18.pdf

Jon R. Lindsay Stuxnet and the Limits of Cyber Warfare, Security Studies, 22:3, 365-404, DOI: 10.1080/09636412.2013.816122

Julian E. Barnes and Josh Chin (2018). The New Arms Race in AI. Wall Street Journal. Available from: https://www.wsj.com/articles/the-new-arms-race-in-ai- 1520009261?mod=e2tw [Accessed May 7th 2019]

Kallberg, Jan, W. Blake Rhoades, Marcus J. Masello, and Rosemary A. Burk. "Defending the Democratic Open Society in the Cyber Age - Open Data as Democratic Enabler and Attack Vector." The Cyber Defence Review 2, no. 3 (2017): 12938. http://www.jstor.org/stable/26267390.

Kania, Elsa. (2017): China's Quest for an AI Revolution in Warfare." The Strategy Bridge , June 8, 2017. URL: https://thestrategybridge.org/the-bridge/2017/6/8/-chinas- quest-for-an-ai-revolution-in-warfare

Kania, Elsa B., Battlefield Singularity: Artificial Intelligence, Military Revolution, and China's Future Military Power, Center for a New American Security, Washington, November 2017.

Kelley, "The New Diplomacy: Evolution of a Revolution", in Diplomacy & Statecraft, 7th June 2010. Online. Available from: 10.1080/09592296.2010.482474 [Accessed May 5th 2019]

Kelly, Dr. John E., Computing, cognition and the future of knowing: How humans and machines are forging a new age of understanding, IBM Global Services, October 2015.

Kent, R. . Are We Ready for the Future of Warfare? Retrieved from https://blogs.scientificamerican.com/observations/are-we-ready-for-the-future-of-warfare/

Kietzmann J. et al. (2020) "Deepfakes: Trick or treat?" Business Horizons 63(2) pp. 135-146. doi: 10.1016/j.bushor.2019.11.006

King, T. C., & Aggarwal, N. . Artificial Intelligence Crime: An Interdisciplinary ...Retrieved from https://papers.ssrn.com/sol3/Delivery.cfm/SSRN_ID3183238_code279 2915.pdf?abstractid=3183238&mirid=1

Klare, M. . Arms Control Today. Retrieved from https://www.armscontrol.org/act/2019-03/features/autonomous- weapons-systems-laws-war

Kott, A., Alberts, D. S., & Wang, C. . Will Cybersecurity Dictate the Outcome of Future Wars ... Retrieved from https://www.researchgate.net/publication/288857290_Will_Cybersecuri ty_Dictate_the_Outcome_of_Future_Wars

Kreipinevich, A. F. . Cavalry to computer; the pattern of military revolutions. Retrieved from http://users.clas.ufl.edu/zselden/Course Readings/Krepinevitch.pdf

Kreps, S. E., & Kaag, J. . The Use of Unmanned Aerial Vehicles in Contemporary Conflict: A Legal and Ethical Analysis. SSRM Electronic Journal. doi:10.2139/ssrn.2023202

Layton, P. . Algorithmic Warfare: Applying Artificial Intelligence to Warfighting. Retrieved from http://www.academia.edu/36620913/Algorithmic Warfare Applying Art ificial Intelligence to Warfighting

Layton P. (2018) "Algorithmic Warfare: Applying Artificial Intelligence to Warfighting" Air Power Development Centre p. Available at: https://www.academia.edu/36620913/Algorithmic_Warfare_Applying_Artificia l_Intelligence_to_Warfighting (Accessed: 20 September 2022)

Lebow, R. N., & Stein, J. G. . Deterrence and the cold war. Political Science Quarterly, 110, 157-181. doi:10.2307/2152358

Left of Launch - Missile Defence Advocacy Alliance (2022). Available at: https://missiledefenceadvocacy.org/alert/3132/ (Accessed: 5 September 2022)

Legal reviews of weapons means and methods of warfare involving artificial intelligence: 16 elements to consider - Humanitarian Law & Policy Blog (2019). Available at: https://blogs.icrc.org/law-and-policy/2019/03/21/legal-reviews- weapons-means-methods-warfare-artificial-intelligence-16-elements-consider/ (Accessed: 17 September 2022)

Lethal Autonomous Weapons Systems: Recent Developments (2019). Available at: https://www.lawfareblog.com/lethal-autonomous-weapons- systems-recent-developments (Accessed: 19 September 2022)

Lewis, Dustin A., Blum, Gabriella and Modirzadeh, Naz K., War-Algorithm Accountability, Harvard Law School Program on International Law and Armed Conflict, Research Briefing, August 2016.

Lewis, J. . The Case for Regulating Fully Autonomous Weapons. Retrieved from https://www.yalelawjournal.org/comment/the-case-for- regulating-fully-autonomous-weapons

Leys, Nathan. "Autonomous Weapon Systems and International Crises." Strategic Studies Quarterly 12, no. 1 (2018): 48-73. http://www.jstor.org/stable/26333877.

Lieber, K. A. . Grasping the Keir A. Lieber Technological Peace. Retrieved from http://web.stanford.edu/class/polisci211z/2.3/Lieber IS 2000.pdf

Liff A. Cyberwar: A New 'Absolute Weapon'? The Proliferation of Cyberwarfare Capabilities and Interstate War, Journal of Strategic Studies, 35:3, 401-428, DOI: 10.1080/01402390.2012.663252

Locatelli, A. . THE OFFENSE/Defence BALANCE IN CYBERSPACE. Retrieved from https://www.ispionline.it/sites/default/files/pubblicazioni/analysis_203_2013.pdf

Lonsdale, D. J. . Warfighting for Cyber Deterrence: A Strategic and Moral ... Retrieved from https://link.springer.com/content/pdf/10.1007/s13347-017-0252-8.pdf

Lucioano Floridi. (2017). "Should we be afraid of AI?" Aeon. Available from: https://aeon.co/essays/true-ai-is-both-logically-possible-and-utterly-implausible [Accessed May 7th 2019]

M.T. Kloda Stany Zjednoczone Ameryki: przegląd projektow prawa stanowego USA dotyczących badan nad wykorzystaniem technologii blockchain w elekcjach panstwowych „Przegląd Sejmowy" 2020 No. 4 (59) pp. 252-253

Maas : How viable is international arms control for military artificial intelligence? Three lessons from nuclear weapons, Contemporary Security Policy, DOI: 10.1080/13523260.2019.1576464

MacDonald N. and Howell G. 2019. Killing Me Softly: Competition in Artificial Intelligence and Unmanned Aerial Vehicles.. [online] JSTOR.

Machi V. 2022. France approves final phase of Artemis big-data processing platform. [online] Defence News. Available at: <https://www.defencenews.com/global/europe/2022/07/11/france-approves- final-phase-of-artemis-big-data-processing-platform/> [Accessed 19 September 2022]

Manor, I. (2017, October). "The Contradictory Trends of Digital Diaspora Diplomacy. Working Paper #2. Exploring Digital Diplomacy." Available from: https://digdipblog.files.wordpress.com/2017/08/the-contradictory-trends-of-digital- diaspora-diplomacy.pdf [Accessed May 7th 2019]

McLaughlin, 'How the UAE is Recruiting Hackers To Create The Perfect Surveillance State,' The Intercept, 2016. Available From: https://theintercept.com/2016/10/24/darkmatter-united-arab-emirates-spies-for-hire/ [Accessed 8th June 2019]

Mearsheimer, John J. "Conventional Deterrence: An Interview with John J. Mearsheimer." Strategic Studies Quarterly 12, no. 4 (2018): 3-8. https://www.jstor.org/stable/26533611.

Menn, J. . New AI Programs Can Learn How to Beat Best Cyber Defences. Retrieved from https://www.insurancejournal.com/news/national/2018/08/10/497443.ht m

Meserole, C. . Artificial Intelligence and the Security Dilemma - Lawfare. Retrieved from https://www.lawfareblog.com/artificial- intelligence-and-security-dilemma

Missiles And Bombs Actually Cost The Drive. Available at: https://www.thedrive.com/the-war-zone/32277/here-is-what-each-of-the- pentagons-air-launched-missiles-and-bombs-actually-cost (Accessed: 6 September 2022)

Mittelstadt, Brent (2019), "AI Ethics - Too Principled to Fail?" SSRN. Available from: https://papers.ssrn.com/sol3/papers.cfm?abstract_id=3391293

Mohan, C. R. . The tragedy of nuclear deterrence. Social Scientist, 14, 3-19. doi:10.2307/351717

Monaco, Christina. "The Mandate to Innovate." PRISM 7, no. 4 (2018): 1829. https://www.jstor.org/stable/26542704.

Bibliography

Nusca, A. . Japan developing rockets with artificial intelligence. Retrieved from https://www.zdnet.com/article/japan- developing-rockets-with-artificial-intelligence/

Open Letter on Autonomous Weapons. . Retrieved from https://futureoflife.org/open-letter-autonomous-weapons/?cn-reloaded=1

Oracle, Crypto (2018), "The Fourth Industrial Revolution: The Rise Of The Autonomous Economy," AltCoin Magazine. Available from: https://medium.com/altcoin-magazine/the-fourth-industrial-revolution-the-rise-of-the-autonomous-economy-cfe0886ad8b3 [Accessed 12th June 2019]

Osoba, O., & IV, W. . The Risks of AI to Security and the Future of Work. Retrieved from https://www.rand.org/pubs/perspectives/P E237.htm l

Pabmann, Johannes, and Asher Boersma. "Unknowing Algorithms: On Transparency of Unopenable Black Boxes." In The Datafied Society: Studying Culture through Data, edited by Schafer Mirko Tobias and Van Es Karin, 139-46. Amsterdam: Amsterdam University Press, 2017. http://www.j stor.org/stable/j .ctt1v2xsqn.14.

Pavel Sharikov (2018) Artificial intelligence cyberattack and nuclear weapons—A dangerous combination Bulletin of the Atomic Scientists 74:6 368373 DOI: 10.1080/00963402.2018.1533185

Payne, K. et al. . A New Nuclear Review for a New Age -nipp.org. Retrieved from http://www.nipp.org/wp-content/uploads/2017/06/A-New-Nuclear-Review-final.pdf

Petrella S. Miller C. and Cooper B. (2021) "Russia's Artificial Intelligence Strategy: The Role of State-Owned Firms" Orbis 65(1) pp. 75-100. doi: 10.1016/j.orbis.2020.11.004

Petro, Greg (2017), "Amazon's Acquisition Of Whole Foods Is About Two Things: Data And Product," Forbes. Available from: https://www.forbes.com/sites/gregpetro/2017/08/02/amazons-acquisition-of-whole-foods- is-about-two-things-data-and-product/#64c9faf0a808 [Accessed 22nd May 2019]

Pike J. 2022. Intercontinental Ballistic Missiles. [online] Federation of American Scientists. Available at: <https://nuke.fas.org/intro/missile/icbm.htm> [Accessed 16 September 2022]

Pistono F. & Yampolskiy R. V. (2016). Unethical Research: How to Create a Malevolent Artificial Intelligence. arXiv. https://doi.org/10.48550/arXiv.1605.02817

Polyakova, A. . Weapons of the weak: Russia and AI-driven asymmetricwarfare. Retrieved from https://www.brookings.edu/research/weapons-of-the-weak-russia-and- ai-driven-asymmetric-warfare/

Preventive Arms Control, in: The Routledge Handbook of Security Studies, 2nd Edition , pp. 457-468. Retrieved from

Price, Matthew, Stephen Walker, and Will Wiley. "The Machine Beneath: Implications of Artificial Intelligence in Strategic Decision Making." PRISM 7, no. 4 (2018): 92105. https://www.jstor.org/stable/26542709.

QUACKENBUSH, S. L. . Deterrence theory: Where do we stand? Review of International Studies, 37, 41-762. doi:10.1017/S0260210510000896

Ray B. Forgey J. and Mathias B. (2020) Harnessing Artificial Intelligence and Autonomous Systems Across the Seven Joint Functions DTIC. Available at: https://apps.dtic.mil/sti/citations/AD1104964 (Accessed: 13 September 2022)

Rod Thornton & Marina Miron (2020) Towards the 'Third Revolution in Military Affairs' The RUSI Journal 165:3 12-21 DOI: 10.1080/03071847.2020.176551

Russell, S. J., & Norvig, P. . Artificial Intelligence: A Modern Approach. Retrieved from https://www.cin.ufpe.br/~tfl2/artificial- intelligence-modern-approach.9780131038059.25368.pdf

Russian Interference in the U.S. Presidential Elections in 2016 and 2020 as an Attempt to Implement a Revolution-like Information Warfare Scheme (2021).

SABAH D. (2021) Turkey's Baykar to mass produce Akinci UCAV soon Daily Sabah. Available at: https://www.dailysabah.com/business/defence/turkeys-baykar-to-mass-produce- akinci-ucav-soon (Accessed: 8 September 2022)

Safeguards agreements. . Retrieved from https://www.iaea.org/topics/safeguards-agreements

Sandre, Andreas (2018) "Blockchain for Foreign Policy and Development," Medium. Available from: https://medium.com/digital-diplomacy/blockchain-for-foreign-policy-and-development-aid-86c092412c6 [Accessed May 7th 2019]

Bibliography

Scharre, P. . Robots and Artificial Intelligence Could Change War. Retrieved from http://time.com/4948633/robots- artificial-intelligence-war/

Scharre, Paul, and SSQ. "Highlighting Artificial Intelligence: An Interview with Paul Scharre Director, Technology and National Security Program Center for a New American Security Conducted 26 September 2017." Strategic Studies Quarterly 11, no. 4 (2017): 15-22. http://www.jstor.org/stable/26271632.

Scharre, Paul, Robotics on the Battlefield Part II: The Coming Swarm, Center for a New American Security, Washington, October 2014.

Schelling, T. C. . Arms and influence. New Haven: Yale University Press.

Schneier, B. . Schneier on Security: Artificial Intelligence and the Attack/Defence Balance. Retrieved from https://www.schneier.com/blog/archives/2018/03/artificial_inte.html

Segal, Adam. "Bridging the Cyberspace Gap: Washington and Silicon Valley." PRISM 7, no. 2 (2017): 66-77. https://www.jstor.org/stable/26470519.

Sharkey, N. E. . The evitability of autonomous robot warfare. Retrieved from https://www.icrc.org/en/inte,rnational- review/article/evitability-autonomous-robot-warfare

Shead, S. . Canada And France Create New 'International Panel On AI'. Retrieved from https://www.forbes.com/sites/samshead/2018/12/07/canada-and-france-create-new-international-panel-on-ai/#d2c5c3d2ef22

Shifting the narrative: not weapons but technologies of warfare - Humanitarian Law & Policy Blog (2022). Available at: https://blogs.icrc.org/law- and-policy/2022/01/20/weapons-technologies-warfare/ (Accessed: 17 September 2022)

Simpson, Thomas W and Muller, Vincent C., 'Just War and Robots' Killings', The Philosophical Quarterly, Vol. 66, No. 263, 2016, pp 302-322.

Smith, B. . The need for a Digital Geneva Convention. Retrieved from https://blogs.microsoft.com/on-the-issues/2017/02/14/need-digital-geneva-convention/

Steven I. Davis (2022) Artificial intelligence at the operational level of war Defence & Security Analysis 38:1 74-90 DOI: 10.1080/14751798.2022.2031692

Stevens, Rock, and Jeffrey Biller. "Offensive Digital Countermeasures: Exploring the Implications for Governments."The Cyber Defence Review 3, no. 3 (2018): 93 114. https://www.jstor.org/stable/26555000.

Taddeo, M. . Deterrence by Norms to Stop Interstate Cyber Attacks. Retrieved from https://link.springer.com/content/pdf/10.1007/s11023-017-9446-1.pdf

Tang, S. . The security dilemma: A conceptual analysis. Security Studies, 18, 587-623. doi:10.1080/09636410903133050

Technology | Issue 88 | June 2018 (2022). Available at:

The New Dogs of War : The Future of Weaponized Artificial Intelligence. Retrieved from http://threatcasting.com/wp-content/uploads/2017/09/ThreatcastingWest2017.pdf

The Weaponization of AI and How It Exacerbates the Security Dilemma Between States [Personal interview]. . Ambassador Aly Erfan is a Professor of Practice and Program Direction at the Department of Global Affairs and public Policy at the American University in Cairo

The Weaponization of AI and How It Exacerbates the Security Dilemma Between States [Personal interview]. . Ambassador Karim Haggag is a Professor of practice at the American University in Cairo

The Weaponization of AI and How It Exacerbates the Security Dilemma Between States [Personal interview]. . Dr/General Mahmoud Khalaf is an Advisor at Nasser Military Academy.

The Weaponization of AI and How It Exacerbates the Security Dilemma Between States [Personal interview]. . Mona Soliman is a Ph.D candidate at the Faculty of Economic and Political Science at Cairo University and an Associate Researcher at International Politics Journal

The Weaponization of AI and How It Exacerbates the Security Dilemma Between States [Personal interview]. . Prof. Dalal Mahmoud Al-Sayed is a Professor of Political Science at the Faculty of Economic and Political at Cairo University and Nasser Military Academy

The Weaponization of AI and How It Exacerbates the Security Dilemma Between States [Phone interview]. . Dr. Waleed Rashad is an assistant professor at the National Center for Social and Criminological Research.

Bibliography

Trevithick J. (2020) Here Is What Each Of The Pentagon's Air-Launched

Tweedie, M. . 3 Types of AI: Narrow, General, and Super AI. Retrieved from https://codebots.com/ai-powered-bots/the-3-types-of-ai- is-the-third-even-possible

Tweedie, M. . 6 Technologies Behind AI. Retrieved from https://codebots.com/ai-powered-bots/6-technologies-behind-ai

Unal, B., & Lewis, P. . Cybersecurity of Nuclear Weapons Systems: Threats, Vulnerabilities and Consequences. Retrieved from https://www.chathamhouse.org/publication/cybersecurity-nuclear- weapons-systems-threats-vulnerabilities-and-consequences

Uricchio, William. "Data, Culture and the Ambivalence of Algorithms." In The Datafied Society: Studying Culture through Data, edited by Schafer Mirko Tobias and Van Es Karin, 125-38. Amsterdam: Amsterdam University Press, 2017. http://www.jstor.org/stable/j.ctt1v2xsqn.13.

US Navy funds LRASM integration onto P-8A Poseidon MPA (2021). Available at: https://defbrief.com/2021/04/22/us-navy-funds-lrasm-integration- onto-p-8a-poseidon-mpa/ (Accessed: 6 September 2022)

Waltz, K. Nuclear Myths and Political Realities. In The Use of Force. Rowman and Littlefield

Wasser, B., Connable, B., Atler, A., & Sladden, J. . Comprehensive Deterrence Forum. Retrieved from https://www.rand.org/pubs/conf_proceedings/CF345.html

Webmaster O. (2022) IC - US | India Defence Technology and Trade Initiative Acq.osd.mil. Available at: https://www.acq.osd.mil/ic/dtti.html (Accessed: 7 September 2022)

Why we urgently need a Digital Geneva Convention. . Retrieved from https://www.weforum.org/agenda/2017/12/why-we-urgently-need- a-digital-geneva-convention/

Williams, P., & McDonald, M. . Security studies: An introduction. London: Routledge, Taylor & Francis Group.

Winter, Jenifer Sunrise. "Introduction to the Special Issue: Digital Inequalities and Discrimination in the Big Data Era." Journal of Information Policy 8 (2018): 1-4. doi:10.5325/jinfopoli.8.2018.0001.

Wirkuttis, N., & Klein, H. . Artificial Intelligence in Cyber Security. Retrieved from http://www.inss.org.il/publication/artificial-intelligence- cybersecurity/

Wood, Molly, 'Facebook's Libra Cryptocurrency Betrays The Company's True Ambitions,' Wired Magazine, June 2019

Woolf A. 2022. Russia's Nuclear Weapons: Doctrine Forces and Modernization. [online] Congressional Research Service Reports. Available at: <https://crsreports.congress.gov/product/pdf7R/R45861> [Accessed 16 September 2022]

Woolley & Howard (2016) "Political Communication, Computational Propaganda, and Autonomous Agents" International Journal of Communication, 10, 4882-4890. http://ijoc.org/index.php/ijoc/article/view/6298

Work, Robert O. and Brimley, Shawn, 20YY: Preparing for War in the Robotic Age, Center for a New American Security, Washington, January 2014.

World Economic Forum. (2017). The Global Risks Report 2017 12th Edition. pp. 4253. Available from: http://www3.weforum.org/docs/GRR17_Report web.pdf [May 7th 2019]

Yen Koh T. n.d. Intelligent Machines vs. Human Intelligence. [online] Ebsco.com. Available at: <https://www.ebsco.com/apps/landing-page/assets/POVRC_Intelligent_Machines_vs_Human_Intelligence.pdf> [Accessed 19 September 2022]

Yu, HUANG. "Robot Threat or Robot Dividend?: A Struggle between Two Lines." In Dog Days: Made in China Yearbook 2018, edited by Franceschini Ivan, Loubere Nicholas, Lin Kevin, Nesossi Elisa, Pia Andrea E., and Sorace Christian, 54-59. Acton ACT, Australia: ANU Press, 2019. http://www.jstor.org/stable/j.ctvfrxqcz.13.

Zeynep Tufekci (2018). "YouTube, the Great Radicalizer." New York Times Available from: https://www.nytimes.com/2018/03/10/opinion/sunday/youtube-politics-radical.html [Accessed May 7th 2019]

'Cisco: Global Mobile Networks Will Support More Than 12 Billion Mobile Devices and IoT Connections by 2022; Mobile Traffic Approaching The Zettabyte Milestone.' Available from: https://newsroom.cisco.com/press-release-content?type=webcontent&articleId=1967403 [Accessed 8th June 2019]

Index

A

Abovementioned scenarios 38
Accidentally escalation 22
Accidental shoot downs 104
Accurate cost calculations 33
Additive Manufacturing 36, 231
Adequate legal framework 149
Admiral Yamamoto Isoruku 214
Advanced conventional weapons 117, 128, 165
Advanced cyber powers 43, 49
Advanced European militaries 145
Advanced missile defence 165
Advanced persistent threat 112
Advanced Research Projects 10, 136
Advanced technology 42
Advanced weapon 47, 81
Advanced weapon systems 81
Adversarial defence systems 43
Adversary aircraft 204
Adversary battle networks 86
Aerial reconnaissance 167
Affect future wars 20
Affect national polices 19
Affect offensive powers 147
AI-based technologies 181
AI-based warfare 29
AI-driven asymmetricwarfare 236
AI-driven offensive capabilities 131
AI-driven revolution 196
AI-enabled aerial simulators 204
AI-enabled features 160, 219
AI-enabled ISR systems 203
AI-enabled machines 52
AI-enabled nuclear strikes 57
AI-enabled systems 160, 202, 209
AI-enabled tools 220
AI-enhanced autonomy 209
AI-enhanced capabilities 118, 214
AI-Enhanced Combat Systems 64
AI-enhanced cyber capabilities 113
AI-enhanced weapons 116
AI-focused study groups 217
AI-like MAD structure 53
AI-nuclear RMA 220
AI-powered automated systems 202
AI-powered systems 143, 207, 208, 211
Air defence sites 95
Air defence systems 47, 195
AI-Related Offensive Technologies v
AirLand Battle 195
Akinci UCAV 236
Al-enabled capabilities 217
Al-enabled technologies 207
Al-enabled tools 145
Algorithmic battle 71
Algorithmic conflict 90
Algorithmic recommender systems 158
Algorithmic Warfare v, 22, 72, 74, 143, 223, 232
Algorithms control 78
ALKA DIRECTED ENERGY 223
Alpha DogFight 136
Al-powered cyber guns 104
Altering Strategic Stability 223
Ambassador Aly Erfan 41, 47, 238
Ambiguous Labor Market 223
American battleships 219
American military establishments 195
American military thinkers 84
American rule 150
American Security 129, 179, 229, 231, 237, 240
Anomaly identification 69
Anti-aircraft defence 31
Anticipate aircraft maintenance 203
Anticipated risk materialises 103
Anticipate force sustainment 204

Anti-missile defence 82
Anti-missile systems 25
Anti-personnel land mines 98
Anti-satellite weapons 111
Antisatellite weapon tests 178
Antiship cruise missiles 206
Anti-surface capabilities 102
Applying Artificial Intelligence v, 63, 232
Applying machine-learning algorithms 88
Armed Conflict 29, 98, 100, 233
Armed conflicts 26, 100
Armed Services Committee 205
Armed weapons 150
Arms control agreements 34, 172
Arms control verification 167
Arnold Wolfers 26
Artifical Intelligence 109
Artificial Augmented Intelligence 128
Artificial general intelligence 42
Artificial Intelligence Crime 232
Artificial Intelligence Development 6, 12, 13, 126, 156, 200, 206
Artificial Intelligence Industry 13
Artificial Intelligence Plan 184
Artificial Intelligence Research 8, 217
Artificial Intelligence Strategy 127, 226, 235
Artificial intelligence systems 101
Artificial Narrow Intelligence 42
Artificial superintelligence 42, 138, 147, 181, 225
Artificial Super Intelligence 42
ASIs solution 148
Asymmetric deterrence 40
Asymmetric powers 40, 54
Asymmetric strategic stability 165
Atomic energy Agency 61
Attack nuclear arsenals 46
Attack oil installations 145
Authoritarian regimes 100, 101
Automated Patriot missile 104
Automated track engagement 78
Automated weapons 99, 222
Automatic stock trading 74

Automating chores 149
Automating data analysis 22
Automating Prediction 223
Automation bias 114
Autonomous drones 145
Autonomous financial trading 111
Autonomous force multiplier 205
Autonomous Systems Strategy 7
Autonomous weapon 59, 104, 110, 136, 145, 150
Autonomous weapon discrimination 104
Autonomous weapons 3, 21, 22, 25, 26, 29, 50, 54, 57, 116, 118, 140, 141, 181, 182, 184
Autonomous weapon systems 59, 110, 145
AWS systems 184

B

Ballistic missile targeting 203
Ban intelligent machine 83
Basic offense-defence theory 42
Battlefield effects faster 79
Battlefield knowledge 16
Battlefield targets 78
Battle network grid 85
Battle network improvements 85
Biggest private companies 15
Bilateral Agreements 57
Binding legal ground 149
Binding speculative rules 57
Bob Fischer 82
Bob Work 55
Boeing P-8 Poseidon 133
Border Patrol 145
Bottom-up method 29
Bound international body 147
Bureaucratic Structures 215

C

Carrier aviation tactics 212
Carthaginian civilization 101
Causing political pain 36

CCP Politburo 156
CCP puts power 161
Central Committee oversees 13
Centralizing data 189
Central Military Commision 13, 14
Central Military Commission 192, 201
Central Propaganda Department 163
Change sensor technology 151
Chaotic system 26
Chesapeake Bay 10
Chinese Academy 13
Chinese armies 193, 204, 209
Chinese Communist Party 13, 91, 153, 155
Chinese defence experts 116, 206
Chinese economic policymaking 157
Chinese government 11, 12, 15, 16, 94, 201, 208
Chinese managers 156
Chinese militaries interact 163
Chinese military leaders 66, 206
Chinese Military Strategy 94
Chinese Ministry 13
Chinese national strategy 2
Chinese scholars 159
Chinese strategists 93
Chinese strategy game 198
Chinese tech industry 201
Chuck Hagel 7
Civilian deaths 22, 25, 171
Civilian flight 22
Civilian purposes 20, 25, 200, 217
Civilian reasons 28
Civilian targets 31
Classic ultimatums 33
Clever machine assistants 93
Clever machine swarms 90, 103
Closed scripted settings 71
Cloud computing 70
Cloud infrastructure 70, 189
Cognitive domain operations 164
Cognitive heuristics 110
Cognitive machines 64
Cognitive robots 65
Cognitive theory/prospect theory 33

Cold War 24, 30, 31, 34, 50, 56, 63, 83, 111, 115, 142, 144, 167, 169, 184, 185, 191
Collateral damage 36, 58, 100
Colonel General Nogovitsyn 132
Combat Industrial Committee 95
Combat zones 110
Complementary strategies 12
Complex data strategies 70
Complicated problems 70
Comprehensive Deterrence Forum 239
Computer attacks 44
Computer power built 89
Computer vision systems 14
Conceptual Model 37
Concrete military problem 212
Conducting AI-Driven Warfare 80
Conflicting desires 161
Consistently execute tasks 103
Constructive ambiguity 42
Constructive debate 109
Consumer drones 88
Consumer-grade quadcopter drones 88
Contemplating algorithmic conflicts 100
Contested nuclear multipolar 109
Control verification tools 167
Conventional attack 40
Conventional deterrence 86
Conventional force power 84
Conventional weapon 51
Conventional weapons 43, 46, 52, 54, 117, 118, 128, 149, 165, 178
Conventional Weapons Group 147
Convolutional neural networks 73
Cooperative actions 90
Corrupt data 28
Counter-C3 capabilities 168
Covert monitoring 28
Creative military intellectualization 212
Credible threats 33
Crewed aircraft 165
Criminological Research 41, 46, 238
Crisis management methods 80
Critical infrastructure 48

Cuban Missile Crisis 33, 35, 113
Cultural awareness 189
Cumulus cloud 70
Cutting-edge chips 174
Cutting-edge dual-use technology 116
Cutting-edge programmes 197
Cyber/AI realm 49
Cyber attack 45
Cyber battlefields 149
Cyber capabilities 22, 31, 37, 38, 45, 48, 52, 53, 113, 136
Cyber defence 20, 21, 22, 36, 43, 45, 48, 49, 51, 53
Cyber defence stronger 20, 22, 43
Cyber defence system 51
Cyber-defence tools 112
Cyber-defensive capabilities 37
Cyber deterrence 20, 43, 44, 48, 49, 52, 53, 226
Cyber deterrence stronger 20
Cyber-enabled software 28
Cyber force separate 52
Cyber MAD 37, 226
Cyber military weapons 40
Cyber policies 41
Cyber security 43, 47, 48, 69
Cybersecurity systems work 42
Cyber skills 22, 28
Cyber spread 43
Cyber technologies 22
Cyber technology 20
Cyber threats 37, 43
Cyber troops fighting 80
Cyber warfare 21, 23, 42, 230
Cyberwarfare Capabilities 233

D

Dangerous Chinese enclaves 93
Decentralized local experimentation 157
Decision-making power 55
Decision-support algorithms 198
Deep-Learning algorithms 146
Deep learning machines 85

Deep Learning technology 137
Deep Reinforcement Learning 135
Deep societal spying 95
Defence Artificial Intelligence 127, 226
Defence equipment 14, 200, 206
Defence Innovation Unit 112
Defence intelligent machine 82
Defence Science Board 84
Defence Technology 150, 217
Defence White Papers 207
Defence Advocacy Alliance 232
Defence Donald Rumsfeld 21
Defence Science Board 41
Defensive nuclear policy 49
Defensive technological skills 150
Delaying ICBM tests 177
Delegating control 110
Democratic Open Society 231
Desert Storm 194, 205
Developing AI-enabled thresholds 62
Developing STEM talent 200
Developing weapons technologies 149
Development Strategic Plan 8
Digital Civil Service 186
Digital Diaspora Diplomacy 234
Digital Geneva Convention 23, 229, 237, 239
Direct-ascent antisatellite weapon 178
Dishonest actions 103
Dishonest enemies 103, 104
Disproportionately high fighting 82
Dispute Settlement Mechanism 62
Dissertation ETD 224
Distributed intelligent machine 87
Doctrinal carrier innovations 216
Domain adaptability 73, 74, 76
Driving operational innovation 204
Drone swarms 116, 134
Dual-use intelligent machine 92

E

Early-warning systems 113
Eclipsing human control 55

Economic Co-operation 171
Economic Perspectives 223
Economic power competition 11
Economic warfare 54
Effectively utilise missiles 102
Eisenhower administration 167
Electromagnetic warfare 161, 168
Electronic countermeasures 70
Electronic warfare 74, 85, 93, 104, 126, 133, 137, 160
Electronic warfare settings 93
Emergency situations 219
Emerging Industries 12, 13
Emerging intelligence 90
Emerging Military Transformations 196
Emerging technologies 60, 61, 62, 205
Endangers international peace 60
Enemy AI-powered cyberattack 130
Escalation barrier 165
Ethical Considerations 98
European Commision 5
Exhibits similarities 103
Exploring Digital Diplomacy 234
Exponential rise 105

F

F-22 fighter 202
Face recognition software 94, 170
Facing military retribution 166
Facto firebreak 117
Fair bids 82
Fascinating projects 23
Fast data processing 23
Fierce competition 54
Financial trading algorithms 111
Fire-and-forget weapon systems 79
First drone ship 11
First-strike capability 31
Fix sensor problems 167
Flight redirection 23
Force Research Laboratory 135
Force structures built 81
Free market economy 55

Fricking robot 85
Fully automated refuelling 10
Fully autonomous applications 49, 55
Fully-autonomous applications 59
Fully autonomous weapons 22, 29, 50, 140, 184
Future cyberattacks faster 112
Future digital battlefield 115
Future Diplomatic Relations 179
Future force structures 86
Future military competition 193
Future Military Power 231
Future strategic-level competition 92
Future Taiwan scenario 166

G

Game-changing technology 88
General adversarial networks 44
General Intelligence Treaty 148
General Khalaf 53
General machine intelligence 72
General Paul Selva 140
General-purpose technology 2, 160
Generation Artificial Intelligence 6, 12, 13, 126, 156, 184, 200, 206
Generative Adversarial Networks 66
Geneva Conventions 38, 147
Geoffrey Blainey 80
Georgetown University Press 226
Global mobile networks 187
Global Peace Treaty 147, 225
Government officials 15, 169
Growing military power 162
Guided weapons systems 86

H

Hard-to-replace individuals 87
Help neutralize weapons 52
Help spread resources 90
Help submarine captains 93
Hierarchical command structure 94
High-altitude Long-Endurance 133

Highly automated Patriot 104
High-performance machine learning 106
High processing power 65
High-speed battlefield actions 79
High-speed communications 79
High-speed hostile missile 79
High-speed rockets 22
High-tech threats 86
Homeland Security 1, 8
Homemade bombs 4
Hostile guided weapons 86
Hostile power 191
House Armed Services 205
Human-AI Collaboration 75
Human-AI Interactions 78
Human decision-making 88, 148
Human intelligence 23, 30, 42, 56, 72, 114, 148, 181, 192, 197
Human intervention 78, 123
Humanitarian law 123, 147, 148, 173, 226
Human-led fighting 222
Human-Machine Interaction 3
Human-machine interfaces 80, 83, 106
Human-machine teaming 23, 58, 85
Human-machine teams 77, 78
Human-out-of-the-loop operations 78
Human-out-of-the-loop systems 96
Human Rights Watch 182
Human strategic guidance 76
Hybrid human-machine control 183
Hypersonic weapons 165, 221

I

Ian Melendez 229
Image-recognition techniques 3
Imperial Japanese Navies 212
Imperial Japanese Navy 214, 215, 216
Implementation Pathway 171
Improvement Strategies 86
Incoming threat 183
Independent variables 41
India Defence Technology 239
Industrial Revolution 2, 179, 191, 222, 235

Information-based warfare 14
Information Protection Law 158
Information Technology 13
Information warfare 8, 22, 51, 54, 92, 93, 125, 126, 132, 133, 143, 207
Inhabited fighter jets 11
Integrated battle networks 86
Integrated Threat Warning/Assessment 44
Intelligence autonomous systems 73, 102
Intelligence Development Plan 6, 12, 13, 126, 156, 200, 206
Intelligence machines 73, 230
Intelligence machine tools 72
Intelligent computer 103
Intelligent computers act 72
Intelligent decision-making 88
Intelligentization strategy milestone 219
Intelligent loitering weapons 126
Intelligent machine developers 71
Intelligent machine era 96
Intelligent machine heavy 82
Intelligent machine learning 74, 92
Intelligent machine method 86, 87
Intelligent machine population 94
Intelligent machines prompt 101
Intelligent machine systems 82
Intelligent machine technologies 83, 92, 103
Intelligent machine technology 81, 83, 92, 93, 94, 99, 102, 107
Intelligent machine tools 92
Intelligent machine vehicles 85
Intelligent robots possess 101
Intelligent violence 29
Intelligent warfighting machines 99
Interconnected nodes 198
Intercontinental ballistic missiles 144
Internal surveillance 14
International authority 60
International community 21, 57, 58, 59, 184
International Criminal Law 29, 59
International humanitarian 123, 147, 148, 173, 226

International Humanitarian Law 26, 55
International law 29, 50, 55, 59, 148, 149, 150
International law document 148
International laws 29, 146
International lawyers 19, 29
International legal instruments 58, 61
International peace system 46
International policies 20
International relations 20, 22, 31, 35, 36, 48, 121, 225
International relations experts 35
International security 24, 153, 154, 191, 221
Internet governance 60
Interpreting Artificial Intelligence 2
Intrinsically indiscriminate weapons 100
Investment partnerships 150
Iranian drone 166
Isolated terrestrial regions 102
Israel Aerospace Industries 145
Israeli Harpy 4, 31
Israeli Harpy drone 4
ISR drones 166
ISR systems stronger 209

J

JADC2 network 209
Japan developing rockets 235
Japanese interception-attrition tactics 214
Japanese naval aviators 216
Japanese Navies chose 212
Jeffrey Bekejikian 33
Jetson TX2 chip 89
Joint All-Domain Command 168
Joint Artificial Intelligence 10, 127, 217

K

Kasparov played chess 76
Killer Robots movement 100
Kinetic cyberattacks 43

L

Labor Market Impact 223
Land battlefield 96
Language processing models 198
Language recognition software 14
Large-scale AI-enabled systems 160
Large-scale information operations 163
Latent force 36
Launch automatic attacks 148
Launch high-speed attacks 85
Law enforcement 16
Lead smart robots 68
Learning algorithms 65, 66, 88, 89, 95, 98, 110
Learning machine technology 89
Legal framework creation 146
Legally-binding multilateral agreement 58
Legally binding tools 56
Legal Ramifications 98
Lethal automated weapons 222
Lethal autonomous weapons 57, 184
Lethal weapons systems 15, 202
Liberation Army 12, 14, 91, 126, 153, 155, 183, 201
Libra Cryptocurrency Betrays 240
Lieber Technological Peace 233
Limit asymmetric math 52
Limited economic opportunities 91
Line-of-sight datalinks 89
Live fighting networks 107
LLaMA model 172
Lockheed Martin Skunk 135
Logical reasoning inherent 102
Logistics Support Activity 203
Loitering bomb 145
Loitering munitions 134
Loitering munitions type 126
Long-standing moral rules 98
Lowering strategic risks 176, 177, 178
Loyal wingman 162
Loyal Wingman programme 11
LRASM integration 228, 239

M

Machine-Based Decision Processes 113
Machine-based deterrence 51
Machine command advisers 93
Machine cyber troops 80
Machine intelligence 23, 72, 74, 75, 89, 90
Machine intelligence organises 90
Machine Learning 8, 111, 121, 138, 140, 152
Machine learning methods 2, 69, 70, 106, 208
Machine legal consultant 101
Machine population monitoring 94
Machine-powered evolution 86
Machines interact 50
Machine-waged war 87
Made-up situations 49
Major nuclear powers 149
Major strategic opportunity 12
Making fast progress 25, 160
Making mistakes 25
Malevolent Artificial Intelligence 236
Malfunctioning machine 103
Manned F-35 202
Manned/unmanned force organisation 81
Mao Zedong 161
Maritime surveillance 127
Market computer programmes 65
Mass destruction 24, 34, 46
Mathematical sense 76
MCF funds 218
Mechanized wars 55
Medical apps 28, 33
Medium-sized business exports 201
Mi-28N attack helicopters 126
Michael Kratsios 9
Middling uncertainty 93
Militarised artificial superintelligence 147, 225
Militarised setting 149
Military affairs 125, 192, 196
Military applications 21, 34, 134, 173, 206
Military change 24
Military-civil fusion 13, 191, 200
Military-Civil Fusion system 157
Military-Civil Integration Intelligent 184
Military clouds 70
Military considerations 51
Military cyber operations 173
Military cyberwarfare operations 132
Military disparity 46
Military dominance 11
Military edge 21, 153, 169, 211
Military escalation risk 117
Military experts 22, 207
Military force structures 72
Military innovations 2, 193
Military leaders 14
Military movements 24
Military national command 95
Military necessity 58, 100, 101, 103
Military Operations 1, 3, 191
Military organisations 4, 209
Military procurement office 127
Military revolutions 24, 232
Military robots alone 5
Military sealift ships 172
Military strength 47, 116
Military tactical operations 21
Military technological edge 7
Military technology 20, 83, 115, 118, 167, 193
Miscellaneous members representing 60
Missile Defence Advocacy 232
Missile defence systems 165
Mitigation Mechanism 62
Mitsubishi information 215
Mixed manned/unmanned force 81
Mobile missile systems 167
Moderate stance posits 101
Modern intelligent machines 72
Modern intelligent tools 70
Modern testing methods 71
Monopoly behavior 158
Moral Responsibility 59
Multidomain precision warfare 159, 168
Multilateral Agreement 58

Multilateral agreements 60
Multilateral institutions 154, 175
Multilateral negotiation 172
Multilateral regime 57
Multi-role platforms 81
Mutual Assured Destruction 50
Mutually Assured Deletion/Delibitation 36
Mutually Assured Destruction v, 20, 34, 35, 38, 50, 227
Mutual vulnerability 36, 47, 53
Mythical Centaur 75

N

Nagorno-Karabakh war 129
Narrow artificial intelligence 42, 101
Narrow intelligence machine 72
Narrow intelligence tools 73
Nasser Academy 45
National Artificial Intelligence 8
National Data Administration 156, 158
National Defence Strategy 8
National Defence Strategies 191
National Geospatial-Intelligence Agency 186
National Natural Science 13
National Security Programme 129
National Security Strategy 8, 162
NATO operation 144
NATO Secretary-General Jens 173
NATO troops 145
NAVAIR progressing 228
Naval aviation technology 212
Naval Phalanx Close-In-Weapon 79
Naval Staff College 214, 215
Navy Fleet Problems 213
Navy funds LRASM 239
Navy War Ships 183
Negotiated arms control 172
Negotiate risk reduction 154, 176
Network-centric combat 91, 107
Neurala software 89
Neural network machines 67, 106
Never-ending business competition 55

Next-generation fighter aircraft 172
NFU pledge 117
Noise recognition equipment 204
Non-governmental organisations 8
Nongovernmental organisations 222
Non-kinetic weapons 85
Non-nuclear states 35, 45, 53
Non-state actors 7, 19, 46, 51, 54, 55, 86, 116
Normal international rivalry 165
Normal military conflict 117
Notable strike-capable UAVs 133
NPT-like agreement 34
Nuclear arms control 45, 62, 221
Nuclear arsenals safe 111
Nuclear ballistic missile 132
Nuclear bombs 32, 128, 168
Nuclear defence 22, 35, 48, 50, 183
Nuclear instability 109, 115
Nuclear latency 32
Nuclear MAD 20, 36, 53, 54
Nuclear multipolarity 115
Nuclear parity 35
Nuclear policy 46, 48, 49
Nuclear posture 45
Nuclear Posture Review 172, 175
Nuclear restraint 57
Nuclear stockpile 177
Nuclear strategic stability 44
Nuclear strategy 48
Nuclear superiority 35, 36
Nuclear technology 56
Nuclear uncertainty 42
Nuclear vulnerabilities 45
Nuclear war 20, 31, 36, 45, 116, 117, 118, 142, 153, 155, 167
Nuclear Warfare v
Nuclear weapons 7, 8, 19, 20, 24, 25, 30, 31, 32, 33, 34, 35, 36, 38, 40, 44, 45, 47, 48, 49, 51, 53, 57, 58, 109, 112, 114, 115, 116, 117, 118, 125, 132, 137, 142, 144, 154, 169, 172, 176, 177, 194, 221, 233, 235
Nuclear weapons system 49, 112
Nuclear weapons systems 44, 45, 132, 172

O

Obama administration 8, 81, 127
Oceanic Multipurpose System 142
Offense-defence balance theory 27
Offense-defence dominance 38
Offense-defence variables 27
Offensive technologies 62, 129, 130, 133, 147
Offset strategy 15
One-ASI solution 148
OODA loop 84, 88, 90
OODA loop domination 90
Open-source agencies 86
Operational-fielded skills 10
Organizational structure 60
Overcome enemy defences 89

P

Parallel warfare 86
Patriot Missile System 183
Patriot systems 110
Patriot Wars 229
Pattern recognition systems 112
Paul Schare 152
Pearl Harbor 56
Perceive battlefield patterns 85
Perpetrate mass killings 100
Phalanx close-in weapons 183
Phalanx Close-In-Weapon System 79
Philosopher Nick Bostrom 113
PLA adopts 92
PLA leadership 207
PLA Navy 93, 94, 203
Planned system 53, 54
PLA reach 169
PLA strategic thinkers 92
PLA work 161
Poison dual-use systems 168
Populated terrestrial settings 102
Possesses nuclear capabilities 37, 38
Power Equilibrium 38
Powerful reconnaissance capabilities 167
Practice restraint 56

PRC applicants 170
PRC experts 168
PRC government 158
PRC party-state organs 163
Precision-guided missiles 3
Precision-guided weapons 15, 86, 206
Precision warfare strategy 168
Predictive ALWS 188
Predictive analysis 69, 137
Preemptive attacks 27
Preemptive cyber deterrence 43, 48
Preemptive deterrence 52
President Vladimir Putin 95, 125
President Zelensky 146
Pretrained algorithms 172
Preventing future intelligence 23
Preventive attacks 27
Preventive prohibition 58
Preventive strikes 32
Prioritize intelligence-gathering 154, 178
Private cyber-security company 186
Probabilistic machines 76
Programmable computers 66, 102
Programmable machines 67
Progress affects security 34
Proliferation begets 57
Promoting Development 13
Proportionality necessitates 101
Proposed regime 56
Protecting noncombatants 60
Protect nuclear command 44
Prototype vehicles 11
Public international law 29

Q

Quality-quantity problem 5
Quantitative proliferation 58
Quantum computing 21, 65, 159, 210

R

Radar parametric data 74
Radar station 31
Radar tracking systems 167

Reach predetermined human 113
Real-life battlefield experience 14
Real security problem 26
Real-time speech 86
Real-world proof 46
Recognizing Military Transformations 193
Reconnaissance-strike complexes 194
Reconnaissance-strike model 205
Reconnaissance-strike RMA 194, 195, 205, 209, 210
Reconnaissance-strike RMA systems 210
Reducing false negatives 113
Regional military balance 162
Regular controlled machines 106
Regulating Military Applications 173
Reinforcement learning 24, 66, 77, 131
Relational systems 67
Remotely controlled vehicles 96
Research Projects Agency 10, 137
Responsible ensuring nuclear 60
Retaliatory forces 167
Revolutionizing large-scale operations 163
Robert Jervis 26
Robert Work 81, 84
Robot fighters 72
Robotic air vehicles 21
Robotic Industry 13
Robotic surface vehicles 15
Robotic systems 81, 96, 164, 165, 166
Robots movement asserts 100
Robot threat 188
Routine activity 57
Russian Information Warfare 96
Russian Methods 95
Russian Military Encyclopaedia 125
Russian President Vladimir 125

S

Sabotage states 163
Safe nuclear weapons 49
Satellite ISR first 167
Scale drone delivery 88
Schafer Mirko Tobias 225, 226, 235, 239

Sea Hunter 11, 202
Second nuclear attack 44, 110
Second Offset strategy 15
Second-strike capability 31, 52
Second-tier states 55
Security Council 60, 61, 185
Security dilemmas 37
Security experts 28
Security problem 19, 20, 21, 23, 24, 25, 26, 27, 28, 29, 30, 32, 34, 35, 36, 40, 43, 46, 47, 48, 54, 225
Self-driving cars 65, 88, 221
Self-driving systems 4, 126, 150, 213
Self-driving trucks 85
Self-driving weapons 25, 26, 29, 131, 145, 150, 203
Self-healing network 90
Semi-autonomous drones 21
Semi-autonomous system 3
Semi-autonomous weapons 21, 29
Sensitive nuclear sites 45
Sensors spread 67
Separate Aviation Bureau 215
Separate military force 161
Settle high-stakes disputes 80
Shocking claim stops 44
Short-term virtual intelligence 90
Silicon Valley 186, 200, 237
Single battlefield entity 89
Situational awareness 58, 74, 130, 134, 135, 137
Skeptical China 175
Skills-based behaviors 48
Skynet system 94, 109
Smart computers 68, 105
Smart killing tools 103
Smart machine algorithms 91, 92
Smart machine characters 87
Smart machine cyber 80
Smart machines change 71
Smart machines fighting 80, 82
Smart machine switch 73
Smart machine technologies 88, 94, 95, 96, 104

Smart machine technology 90, 92, 93, 107
Smart machine viruses 104
Smart robots astray 68
Smart tools help 81, 107
Social media giants 97
Societal spying systems 95
South China Sea 166, 181, 203
Soviet era 96, 129
Soviet leaders 111
Soviet numerical superiority 195
Soviet Union 91, 143, 144, 167
Speculative rules 57
Spoofing adversaries 43
Spread false information 28, 142, 164
Spreading fake news 36, 96
Spread smart machines 86
Sputnik Event 29
Standoff precision strikes 195
Stanford University 187
State Department refuse 170
State Internet Information 13
State organisations 2, 7
State responsibility 47, 56, 59
State-sponsored cyberattacks 62
States unilaterally deter 57
Stealth operations 45
STEM experts 170
Strategic alliances 150
Strategic Arms Limitations 184
Strategic climate 47, 49
Strategic stability 25, 44, 54, 55, 115, 119, 154, 165, 177, 178
Strategic Support Force 161
Stryker vehicles 203
Study nuclear powers 22
Successful eradication 101
Sufficient information 58
Supervised machine learning 69
Support self-driving weapons 26
Supreme Council 60
Swarm concept 89
Swarm drones 5, 10, 14
Symmetrical conflicts 52
Symmetric relations 46

T

Tactical level commanders 92
Tactical-level commanders 101
Task-optimized human-machine interfaces 80, 106
Task-oriented force packages 88
Technical Assistance 61
Technical progress affects 34
Technological advancement 57
Technological research institutions 217
Technology Commission 13, 192
Technology named Kevin 2
Technology Policy set 8
Terrorist groups 4, 17, 51, 86
Test robot Tay 68
TEVV processes 175
Texas National Security 224
Third Offset Strategy 7, 21, 127
Threaten nuclear weapons 48
Threatens international peace 61
Threat Warning/Assessment system 44
Threat-warning systems 210
Track engagement decision 78
Traditional battlefield 145
Traditional military attack 22
Train intelligent machines 69
Train smart machines 69
Transfer learning methods 73
Trouble developing STEM 200
Trump administrations 7, 8, 9
Trust machine-generated data 114
Turning nuclear command 44
Twin-rotor plane 126

U

UAV sub-category 134
Unavoidable arms race 162
Unblockable route 71
Uncommon military technologies 51
Uncontrolled algorithms 23
Uncovered RMA 210
Uncrewed Autonomous Systems 164

Index

Undeniable trend 25
Underwater drones 10, 50
Unintentional escalation 117, 118, 165
United Kingdom Ministry 231
United Nations Convention 62, 147, 148
Universal Global Peace 147, 225
Unmanned aerial vehicle 16
Unmanned aerial vehicles 126, 128
Unmanned surface vehicle 203
Unmanned troops 82
Unmanned underwater 166, 182
Unmanned vehicles 14, 25, 27, 209
Unopenable Black Boxes 235
Unstable effect 167
Unstructured data files 68
Usually programmable machines 88
UUV event 166

V

Vandenberg Air Force 113
Violate human rights 141, 170
Violent conflict 35
Violent machine destruction 80

W

War-Algorithm Accountability 233
War calculations 47, 52

Warfighting scenarios 102
Warfighting speeds 87
War situations 24
Washington passed strict 169
Weaken nuclear 45, 48
Weaken nuclear deterrence 45, 48
Weak global institutions 189
Weaponized Artificial Intelligence 238
Weapon suppliers 28
Weapon system work 47
Wearable electronics 85
Weather conditions 69
Western alliance 173
White House Summit 9
Wide-area imaging sensor 74
Wide-ranging effect 64
Willing armed groups 4
Wireless networks 73
Worried government leaders 23
Worries scholars 21
Writing arms control 34

X

X-47B test drone 10

Z

Zebra Medical Vision 187

www.ingramcontent.com/pod-product-compliance
Lightning Source LLC
LaVergne TN
LVHW020425070526
838199LV00003B/287